Space and Time Perspective in Northern St. Johns Archeology, Florida

Southeastern Classics in Archaeology, Anthropology, and History

Southeastern Classics in Archaeology, Anthropology, and History

Edited by Jerald T. Milanich

Archeology of the Florida Gulf Coast, by Gordon R. Willey
Early History of the Creek Indians and Their Neighbors, by John R. Swanton
Space and Time Perspective in Northern St. Johns Archeology, Florida, by John M. Goggin

Space and Time Perspective in
Northern St. Johns Archeology, Florida

John M. Goggin

Preface to the 1998 edition by James J. Miller
Foreword by Jerald T. Milanich, series editor

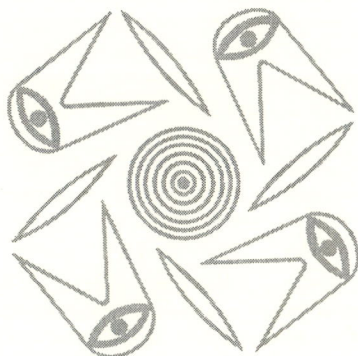

University Press of Florida

Gainesville · Tallahassee · Tampa · Boca Raton · Pensacola · Orlando · Miami · Jacksonville

03 02 01 00 99 98   6 5 4 3 2 1

Library of Congress Cataloging-in-Publication Data

Goggin, John M. (John Mann), 1916–1963.
Space and time perspective in Northern St. Johns archeology, Florida /
John M. Goggin; foreword by Jerald T. Milanich.
p. cm. — (Southeastern classics in archaeology, anthropology, and history.)
Originally published: New Haven: Yale University Press, 1952.
Includes bibliographical references.
ISBN 0-8130-1634-7 (paper: alk. paper)
1. Indians of North America—Florida—Saint Johns River Region—Antiquities.
2. Archaeology and history—Florida—Saint Johns River Region.
3. Saint Johns River Region (Fla.)—Antiquities. I. Title. II. Series.
E78.F6G64 1998
975.9'101—dc21   98-35755

University Press of Florida
15 Northwest 15th Street
Gainesville, FL 32611
http://nersp.nerdc.ufl.edu/~upf

CONTENTS

ILLUSTRATIONS

PLATES

TEXT FIGURES

TABLES

FOREWORD

What makes a classic? Why are some books and articles as useful today as when they were first written? For archaeologists, anthropologists, and historians interested in the native American cultures of the southeastern United States and the events of the colonial period, classics are references that contain ideas and knowledge essential to research. Some classics helped to shape a field of study, others developed the fundamental taxonomies used today, and still others offer basic building blocks of information that can be used to fuel theoretical models. Many classics exhibit all these characteristics. All are publications that active researchers cannot live without.

In my own personal research library I have a number of southeastern classics and I consult them frequently. They are the books my students covet and which I guard zealously, for scholarly as well as financial reasons. Classics—if one can still find them at all—can cost a pretty penny!

The knowledge published in classics continues to endure. Unfortunately, many of the books themselves have been less fortunate. Originally published in paperback with non-acid-free pages and bindings, in limited printings, or in hard-to-find journals, some of them have become rare indeed.

The Southeastern Classics Series will put back into print books and articles deemed by scholars to be timeless treasures, resources we all use, but which are difficult to find or, in some cases, have literally disappeared. One such book is *Space and Time Perspective in Northern St. Johns Archaeology, Florida*.

I am very pleased that our series can bring this classic back to life and that my colleague James Miller, chief of the Florida Division of Historical Resources Bureau of Archaeological Resources (and himself the author of a recent book on the St. Johns region), has provided an erudite introduction placing Goggin's St. Johns book in the context of its times. Nearly fifty years after it was first published, *Space and Time Perspective* continues to yield a considerable impact on archaeology.

Jerald T. Milanich
Series Editor

[*Publisher's note:* The arabic page numbering in this edition begins on the first page of the introduction with page 15. When the book was originally published, there were only fourteen pages of front matter; new material has been added to this reprint edition, necessitating the renumbering of the front matter pages with roman numerals.]

PREFACE TO THE 1998 EDITION

In the late 1940s and early 1950s John Mann Goggin was one of a small group of collaborators who brought the archaeology of Florida into the modern era. His *Space and Time Perspective in Northern St. Johns Archeology, Florida* was one of the several principal works that established the culture history of the state from first human occupation to the eighteenth century. To understand the importance of this monograph, written nearly half a century ago, it is necessary to review some of the history of Florida archaeology itself.

It is hard to imagine a time when Florida, one of the largest and fastest-growing states, was regarded as remote. Yet, up to the time of World War II, Florida was sparsely populated and well out of the mainstream. For the outdoor sportsman as for the archaeologist, Florida was a foreign destination, little known and somewhat inaccessible. Philadelphia, New York, Washington, D.C., New Haven, and Chicago were home to the important adventurers, botanists, biologists, historians, and archaeologists who left their mark in the literature of exploring and documenting the Florida landscape. Florida has only within the past half-century had the intellectual centers capable of educating its own scholars. The Philadelphia Academy of Natural Sciences, the New York Botanical Garden, the Smithsonian Institution, Yale University, the University of Chicago—these were the long-established and well-supported scientific and academic institutions whose scholars were attracted to the Florida peninsula. Here there were intellectual challenges unaddressed as yet, new species to be described, mounds to be explored, and entire prehistoric cultures to be pieced together from results of surveys and excavations.

During the several decades following the Civil War, the antiquities of the St. Johns region attracted the attention of three important figures: Jeffries Wyman of the Peabody Museum at Harvard University, Andrew E. Douglas, trustee of the American Museum of Natural History in New York City and amateur archaeologist, and J. Francis LeBaron, a professional engineer who spent much of his career in the Jacksonville area. Their surveys and minor excavations constitute the first understanding of the identity, location, and stratigraphy of midden and burial sites. Many of the large middens they described are now destroyed, mostly to provide shell for road beds in the first part of the 1900s.

It was a Philadelphia industrialist turned archaeologist, Clarence Bloomfield Moore, whose record of excavations in the southeastern United States, including Florida, laid the foundation of modern archaeological research. Moore, with a crew of laborers and a steamboat named *Gopher*, navigated every major river in the Southeast, located the major mound sites, dug them, and published prompt and full accounts of the results. The St. Johns River was a focus of Moore's attention primarily during the early 1890s, and his publications, principally in the *Journal of the Academy of Natural Sciences of Phila-*

delphia (see Goggin's bibliography for a complete list), have been the starting point for any thorough review of the region's archaeology for more than a century. It is impossible to ignore Moore's work, even though it is dated in many ways, because so many major mound sites are now gone that his results can never be duplicated.

While Moore's excavation reports present a prodigious amount of primary data, the theoretical questions that interested him and his contemporaries are very different from those that concern archaeologists today. It must be remembered that shortly before Moore's work, the American Indian origin of the mounds themselves was in dispute. Such issues as whether copper items could have been made before European contact, and whether mounds were constructed before the appearance of pottery, seem somewhat mundane now, but Moore's recoveries and descriptions of southeastern pottery constituted a significant advance in knowledge. His results contributed greatly to the landmark study of ceramics of the eastern United States by William H. Holmes (1903). Moore's wonderful volumes, long out of print and prized among archaeologists as well as antiquarian book dealers, are now being reprinted and will soon be available to a wide audience.

With the exception of a modest Smithsonian Institution project at Ormond in the 1930s and Civilian Conservation Corps excavations in the Ocala National Forest during the Depression, the St. Johns region received little archaeological excavation and little attention in the literature until World War II ended. In dramatic contrast to the previous half-century, the brief period from 1945 to 1955 marked the birth, growth, and maturity of Florida archaeology. This was one of those rare times when many pieces of a big scientific puzzle, previously nonexistent or apparently unrelated, fell into place. It must have been an exciting time to be a southeastern archaeologist. Several centers of archaeological scholarship turned their attention to Florida and the Southeast, and the result was a synergistic combination of advances in theory, method, and knowledge.

At the University of Chicago, the anthropological and archaeological program begun by Faye Cooper-Cole in the 1920s had trained many of the principal scholars of eastern U.S. archaeology, including John W. Griffin, Charles Fairbanks, and Hale G. Smith, three scholars who would lead Florida archaeology for decades. Foremost among the Chicago products was James B. Griffin. No other single archaeologist had such a wide-reaching impact on the understanding of pre-European Native Americans, and his broad scope naturally extended to the Florida peninsula. James B. Griffin was also instrumental in developing the first consistent taxonomic system for describing archaeological cultures in the eastern United States. Up until the time of the Midwestern Taxonomic Method of Culture Classification, as it was known, much descriptive data had accumulated for many different regions, but there was no agreed-upon framework or vocabulary. Until the McKern system, it was not possible to compare and contrast archaeological units in space or time, because they were all described in different terms (Guthe 1952). Using the new system, Griffin summarized and synthesized St. Johns archaeology in the perspective of archaeology of the whole Southeast.

The Yale University Caribbean Anthropological Program, under the leadership of Irving Rouse, turned its archaeological and ethnographic attention to Florida and beyond. John Goggin, who grew up in Miami and spent his boyhood exploring the Everglades, collecting natural history as well as archaeological specimens, entered Yale following an undergraduate career at the University of Florida and the University of New Mexico, where he received a B.A. in 1938. After the war, he accepted a graduate assistantship at the Yale Peabody Museum, which resulted eventually in an M.A. in 1946 and a Ph.D. in 1948 from Yale (Rouse 1964).

Goggin's dissertation was a synthesis of the archaeology of the whole state of Florida, but the section on the St. Johns region was developed from the data collected by James Griffin for his earlier synthesis. Griffin's new duties at the University of Michigan, where several generations of southeastern archaeologists have since received their training, did not allow him time to develop these materials further, and he suggested that Goggin expand them into an introductory summary of the St. Johns region (see page xvii in this volume).

As Goggin worked on the St. Johns region, Irving Rouse was busy directly to the south in the Indian River region of Florida. Gordon Willey, then of the Smithsonian Institution, was preparing a comparable synthesis of the Florida Gulf Coast, as well as a summary of excavations in South Florida, and within the short space of three years the three founding monographs of modern Florida archaeology were published: *Archeology of the Florida Gulf Coast*, by Gordon Willey (1949); Irving Rouse's *A Survey of Indian River Archeology, Florida* (1951); and John M. Goggin's *Space and Time Perspective in Northern St. Johns Archeology, Florida* (1952). Goggin also produced a comprehensive summary of the southern part of the peninsula, based on his years of exploring and recording in the Everglades and South Florida, but this was never published. It was titled "Archeology of the Glades Area, Southern Florida," but is better known by the enigmatic name "Manuscript B."

Besides the explication of the major area syntheses of Florida prehistory, the other important development of this period was the establishment of archaeology programs within the state. The two principal universities in Florida just after the war were the University of Florida in Gainesville and Florida State University in Tallahassee. At the latter institution, anthropology had been introduced early by Raymond F. Bellamy as part of the sociology curriculum. Bellamy and his radical anthropological notions were repeatedly attacked by religious and government leaders from the 1920s through the 1950s, culminating in the investigations of the infamous Johns committee, a Florida version of the McCarthy hearings. In Gainesville, anthropology also developed initially within the sociology department, and it was not until 1948 that an anthropologist joined the faculty—John Mann Goggin, fresh from Yale and hard at work on the St. Johns archaeology monograph. Anthropology was first listed as a separate department in 1949–50 at the University of Florida, and Goggin remained active in the department to the time of his death in 1963. Similarly, the anthropology program at Florida State University hired Hale G. Smith as its first head in 1949. And John W. Griffin, who was from Daytona and who possessed a wonderful knowledge of northeast Florida archaeology and history, was hired by the Florida Park Service to organize and implement a statewide archaeological program. William Sears, hired around that time by the Florida State Museum, and Charles Fairbanks, who later became chairman of the anthropology department at the University of Florida, were the other two professional archaeologists in Florida during its developmental period. Amazingly, all of these men were connected with the anthropology programs of the University of Chicago and later (after Faye Cooper-Cole retired) the University of Michigan. Indeed, for roughly two decades, anthropology in Florida was primarily archaeology, and all the modern anthropology programs in Florida were developed by archaeologists (du Toit 1986).

Space and Time Perspective is a solid foundation for the study of Florida archaeology; those aspects that appear now as shortcomings nearly fifty years after it was first published were unavoidable when it was compiled. Typical of its time, it is largely a descriptive and classificatory work. This is not a fault, but rather a necessary first stage in understanding the prehistory of any region. Goggin's delineation of the archaeological cultures and their distinctive artifacts in time and space is so well done and so correctly constructed that it has warranted only the slightest revision in the past half-century. His chronological division system, into the St. Johns I and St. Johns II periods and the further subperiods, remains as useful today as when it was devised. In contrast, the chronological schemes for Indian River, south Florida, southwest Florida, and the central Gulf coast have all been revised since their initial publication.

The major change in the northern St. Johns region has been not in the relative age of the archaeological periods, but in their absolute age. Before the advent of radiocarbon dating in the early 1950s, there were few reliable methods of estimating how long ago archaeological events occurred. Through seriation, it was possible to determine the age of remains relative to each other (that is, which was older or younger), but there was no absolute time scale. By comparing archaeological culture traits, it was possible to correlate layers within a site as well as between sites, and a relative chronology could be constructed even where there were no sites with complete cultural sequences. Similarly, comparisons could be made from one culture area to the next, based on the presence of trade or foreign items, and in this way, charts were constructed comparing regional archaeological sequences displayed on a single time scale. These were linked together from one region to another, covering the state, the Southeast, the East, and eventually the West and Central America.

Goggin's Figure 2, "Areas and Periods of Culture in Florida," presents the culture sequences for six different areas comprising the whole state. It is internally consistent, and reflects our modern framework of archaeological cultures, but the time scale is squeezed to a fraction of its real length. This is typical of preradiometric chronologies and reflects a general agreement on time depth among southeastern archaeologists, based more on judgment than hard evidence. The error increases with time, so that St. Johns II subperiods are a few centuries too recent, and the older St. Johns I and Orange periods off by 500 years. For preceramic times (for which no pottery is available to compare among sites), Goggin's vague reference to "Suwannee Points?" at the bottom of the chart where the time scale is discontinued reflects a lack of data in the region as well as a general lack of understanding throughout the continent. Extinct Pleistocene fauna had already been discovered in association with artifacts, but there was no way of accurately dating these remains. We now know that these Paleo Indian artifacts are 10,000 years and older, a time depth not contemplated in the late 1940s.

Goggin's approach to St. Johns archaeology was unusually modern in its ecological orientation. His "Subareas of the Northern St. Johns Area" (Figure 1) reflects mainly geographic differences among northeast Florida landscapes. He counts river basin, interior pine flatwoods, and Atlantic coast as one subarea north of Palatka, but divides these provinces into three parts to the south. Indeed, these areas show distinct patterns of resources, drainage, soils, and related environmental factors, as well as different types of sites and settlement patterns (Miller 1998). Little use is made of Goggin's subareas in modern studies, though they do have descriptive value and do reflect real differences. Goggin's emphasis on the environment was further developed in a short section on ecological changes, a subject that he considered in greater detail in a 1948 paper entitled "Florida Archeology and Recent Ecological Changes." Northeast Florida is an area that is particularly sensitive to changes in sea level, and Goggin was the first to suggest that this factor influenced the availability of shellfish along the coast. He wrote: "Indications are that large populations were not settled on the coast until St. Johns times, possibly because the waters of the coastal lagoons were too fresh for the growth of oysters. With the rise of the sea a balanced salinity was achieved and shellfish flourished in the lagoons" (p. 21).

Goggin described the archaeological cultures of the St. Johns region in terms of traditions, which he defined as a distinct cultural complex that may in the course of time pass through some changes but not enough to alter the basic configuration. As the word suggests, traditions endure over long periods and are readily distinguishable from each other. Ten Florida traditions are defined by Goggin, but only five occur in the northern St. Johns region, of which the Archaic and St. Johns traditions are the two most important. The concept of tradition as it was developed in this monograph was a major methodological contribution by Goggin, especially in showing how important environmental factors were in shaping and conserving cultural tradition (Willey and Phillips 1958: 37 in Rouse 1964: 371). Perhaps it is the obvious significance of such environmental factors as sea-level rise, drainage, and climatic change in the St. Johns basin more than in other parts of the peninsula that led Goggin to this realization.

At a time when the field of historical archaeology was not yet recognized, although a few archaeologists were working on postcontact sites, Goggin extended the tradition concept to include Spanish-Indian and Seminole traditions. The latter was virtually unknown in the region. His interest in Spanish material continued to grow from his early treatment in the northern St. Johns monograph and eventually dominated his research interests in Florida and the Caribbean. Many of the themes that guide Spanish colonial archaeology today were laid out in Goggin's discussion of the Spanish-Indian tradition: missionization, religious conversion, labor conscription, conservatism in subsistence, colono-ware ceramics, and syncretism. The Spanish colonial study for which Goggin is best known is his comprehensive study of the Spanish Olive Jar, a common and distinctive European ceramic type found on sites throughout Latin America.

Since *Space and Time Perspective* was published, much has changed, and the more it changes the more it seems to stay as Goggin originally described it. It is no surprise that archaeological method, theory, and interests have undergone fundamental changes in fifty years. The kinds of work now undertaken in the St. Johns region reflect great growth, not only in research questions, but also in the modern context of archaeological conservation. Who would have guessed that St. Augustine would enjoy a continuous research program of more than two decades' duration in historical archaeology, led by Kathleen Deagan? Who could have foreseen that the Timucuan Ecological and Historic Preserve would be established by Congress to protect archaeological and historical sites near the mouth of the St. Johns River (Russo 1993)?

Since Goggin's time the field of historical archaeology, which he had a hand in developing, has matured. The study of Spanish missions and of St. Augustine, not to mention underwater archaeology, which Goggin literally invented, are now the subjects of sophisticated research programs of many years' duration. Several generations of graduate students have specialized in these areas in Florida and elsewhere, bringing to fruition the many topics he introduced. Goggin was definitely a product of his time, but what a time it was, when one could range freely across the intellectual and geographic landscape and, if one was able, set the course of research for years to come. *Space and Time Perspective* is a fundamental work—that is, it is solid and competently done and stands the test of time. More interestingly, however, it is a work of broad scope by a man of wide interests whose perspective is refreshing in our age of increasing specialization.

James J. Miller

WORKS CITED

du Toit, Brian. 1986. *Anthropology in Florida: The History of a Discipline* (Florida Journal of Anthropology Special Publications, no. 5, Gainesville).

Guthe, Carl E. 1952. "Twenty-five Years of Archeology in the Eastern United States" (in *Archeology of Eastern United States*, James B. Griffin, ed., pp. 1–12, Chicago: University of Chicago Press).

Holmes, William H. 1903. "Aboriginal Pottery of Eastern United States" (Bureau of American Ethnology Annual Report, no. 20, Washington, D.C.)

Miller, James J. 1998. *An Environmental History of Northeast Florida* (Gainesville: University Press of Florida).

Rouse, Irving. 1951. *A Survey of Indian River Archeology, Florida* (Yale University Publications in Anthropology, no. 44, New Haven, Conn.)

———. 1964. "John Mann Goggin, 1916–1963" (American Antiquity 29: 369–375).

Russo, Michael. 1993. *The Timucuan Ecological and Historic Preserve Phase III, Final Report* (Florida Museum of Natural History, Department of Anthropology, Gainesville).

Willey, Gordon R. 1949. *Archeology of the Florida Gulf Coast* (Smithsonian Miscellaneous Collections, no. 113, Washington, D.C.; reprint, Gainesville: University Press of Florida, 1998).

PREFACE TO THE 1952 EDITION

WHEN the cooperative archeological program was arranged between Yale University and the University of Michigan, which resulted in excavations at South Indian Field, Florida, it was planned that James B. Griffin of the latter institution would prepare a summary of the archeology of the adjacent region, now called the Northern St. Johns area (Goggin and Sommer, 1949: 5–7). Unfortunately the press of other work, particularly new administrative and teaching duties, made it impossible for Dr. Griffin to write the St. Johns paper. However, he very generously turned over to me his file on the region for use in preparing my dissertation at Yale, a synthesis of the archeology of all Florida which was presented to the Faculty of the Graduate School of Yale University, in 1948, in partial fulfillment of requirements for the degree of Doctor of Philosophy (Goggin, MS*a*).

Since Dr. Griffin was of the opinion that it would be some time before he could again work on this area, it was subsequently suggested that the part of my dissertation on the St. Johns be used as the basis of an introductory summary. Such a paper complements other results of the Yale Caribbean Anthropological Program in Florida (Goggin and Sommer, 1949; Willey, 1949*a*; Rouse, 1951; Ferguson, 1951; Goggin, MS*b*). As a series, these reports afford archeological summaries of the entire east coast and southern portions of the state and, when combined with Gordon R. Willey's (1949*b*) material on the Gulf Coast, they provide an adequate coverage of most of the state.

The present paper, then, consists of the section on the Northern St. Johns area first prepared for my dissertation, together with introductory and explanatory additions, and certain minor changes. It is not assumed that the archeology of this region is now thoroughly covered, but it is believed that most of the existing data have been arranged in a working cultural and temporal framework.

From 1944 to 1947, archeological research in other parts of Florida in conjunction with the Yale Caribbean Anthropological Program allowed me opportunity to become initially acquainted with this region. The grant of a fellowship, in June, 1947, from the Social Science Research Council, made a general study of Florida archeology possible. Under this fellowship information on the Northern St. Johns area was gathered and organized. Further aid was subsequently received from the Yale Program so that this particular paper could be prepared.

This paper was finished in the fall of 1948. All material available before that time, published papers and manuscripts, was utilized. Information has since been added as the result of the anthropological research program of the University of Florida, aided by a grant from the Wenner-Gren Foundation for Anthropological Research, Inc. (formerly the Viking Fund, Inc.). This enabled the writer to become personally acquainted with many sites in the area and to collect numerous specimens. The bulk of the data available on Seminole archeology and the St. Augustine Period are also a direct result of this program. The generous and timely help of the Wenner-Gren Foundation is gratefully acknowledged.

Like so much of the present work in Florida this paper is a symbol of cooperation between fellow workers in the field. My obligations are very heavy towards Dr. James B. Griffin, who so generously allowed me complete access to his notes on museum specimens from this area. In conversations also he has made many suggestions of value.

My co-workers on Yale Florida archeological projects, Dr. Irving Rouse and Mrs. Vera Masius Ferguson were also generous in allowing me the use of notes, manuscripts, and materials from their work in the adjacent Indian River area. Dr. Rouse has also been very helpful in many other ways, particularly as my dissertation advisor. Both he and Mr. Ripley Bullen, Florida Park Service, Archeological Survey, have read the finished manuscript, making many worthwhile suggestions.

Dr. Gordon R. Willey has, as usual, been very interested in discussing many problems of the area, and those which touch on other regions of the state. In addition we worked together taking notes and classifying specimens in several institutions.

Thanks are also due Dr. Cornelius Osgood for the opportunity to participate in the Yale Caribbean Anthropological Program and for his constant cooperation and help in many ways.

The final writing of this paper was done at the University of Florida. I am grateful to Dr. John Maclachlan, head of the Department of Sociology and Anthropology, for offering me various facilities of that department. Its secretaries, Mrs. Carolyn Kendrick and Miss Louetta Young, cheerfully typed several drafts of the paper, while Miss Lois Watkins and Mr. Bernard Boyle, student assistants, checked many bibliographic items and other details. Their aid is thankfully recognized.

Field experience in the area mainly has been limited to surface surveys in various parts of the area, although some excavations have been conducted. In addition to an organization of published material, I have also attempted to study all the known archeological specimens in various museums. Much of the success of this work is due to the friendly and cooperative staff of the various institutions visited.

It is impossible here to do more than list the people and institutions who were of special help and to whom I am most grateful for their interest: Gordon Ekholm, Junius Bird, and James Ford at the American Museum of Natural History; Matthew W. Stirling, Henry B. Collins, Jr., and Gordon R. Willey at the Bureau of American Ethnology, Smithsonian Institution; Helen McCormick at the Charleston Museum; Paul Martin, Alex Sphoer, and George Quimby at the Chicago Museum of Natural History; Herman Gunter and J. Clarence Simpson at the Florida Geological Survey; Alberta Johnson at the Florida Historical Society Library; John W. Griffin, Ripley P. Bullen, at the Florida Park Service, Archeological Survey; Hale G. Smith at Florida State University; Nile C. Schaffer at the Florida State Museum; Albert Manucy at Castillo de San Marcos National Monument; Donald Scott, J. O. Brew, Phillip Phillips, and Fred Orchard at Harvard Peabody Museum; James B. Griffin and Albert Spaulding at the Museum of Anthropology, University of Michigan; George Heye and E. K. Burnett at the Museum of the American Indian, Heye Foundation; W. D. McKern and Robert Ritzenthaler at the Milwaukee Public Museum; Frederick Johnson at the Robert S. Peabody Foundation for Archaeology, Phillips Academy; W. W. Ehrmann and Julian C. Yonge at the University of Florida; J. Alden Mason and H. Newell Wardle at the University Museum, University of Pennsylvania; Neil Judd, Waldo Wedel, T. Dale Stewart, Marshall Newman, and Joseph Caldwell at the United States National Museum; and Henry B. Roberts at the Wagner Free Institute of Science.

In addition the private collections of Mrs. H. H. Simpson, Sr. of High Springs, Mrs. Zelia Wilson Sweett of New Smyrna, and of John D. Thompson and Harold Ryman, St. Augustine, were kindly made available for my inspection.

The staff of the Museum of the American Indian, Heye Foundation, deserves special thanks for their aid in my long study of the Clarence B. Moore collection now housed at that institution. Grateful acknowledgement is also made for photographs furnished by Hale G. Smith, the United States National Museum, and the Harvard Peabody Museum. All material illustrated from these last two institutions is taken from photographs furnished by them.

Gainesville, 1951.   JOHN M. GOGGIN

ABBREVIATIONS OF INSTITUTIONS*

A.M.N.H.	American Museum of Natural History, New York.
C.M.	Charleston Museum, Charleston, South Carolina.
C.M.N.H.	Chicago Museum of Natural History, Chicago.
D.P.M.	Davenport Public Museum, Davenport, Iowa.
F.S.P.S.	Florida State Park Service, Archeological Survey, Gainesville.
F.S.M.	Florida State Museum, Gainesville.
F.S.U.	Florida State University, Tallahassee.
H.P.M.	Harvard Peabody Museum, Cambridge.
M.A.I.	Museum of the American Indian, Heye Foundation, New York.
M.P.M.	Milwaukee Public Museum, Milwaukee.
R.S.P.F.	Robert S. Peabody Foundation for Archaeology, Phillips Academy, Andover, Mass.
R.O.M.	Royal Ontario Museum, Toronto, Canada.
U.C.A.L.	University of Chicago, Anthropology Laboratory, Chicago.
U.F.A.L.	University of Florida, Anthropology Laboratory, Gainesville.
U.M.M.A.	University of Michigan, Museum of Anthropology, Ann Arbor.
U.P.M.	University Museum, University of Pennsylvania, Philadelphia.
U.S.N.M.	United States National Museum, Washington.
W.F.I.S.	Wagner Free Institute of Science, Philadelphia.
Y.P.M.	Yale Peabody Museum, New Haven.

* Collections from the area have been personally studied at all institutions except the Davenport Public Museum. Where these abbreviations are used in the text it is to refer to this material; when followed by a number, it refers to a specific catalog number.

INTRODUCTION

THE Northern St. Johns area is a region with the longest detailed history of human occupation in Florida, and one of the few such in the Southeast. The region early became known for its large earthworks, and the Bartrams' descriptions of these sites were quoted in many nineteenth-century summaries of American archeology.

Attention was also focused on the area by the work of Jeffries Wyman and Clarence B. Moore (see Bibliography). These authors emphasized the large shell middens which were often stratified, with a preceramic horizon underlying fiber-tempered and later pottery. Then too, certain exotic features noted by Moore in sand mounds have become widely associated with the region: embossed copper artifacts, the varied and unusual pottery vessels, and "freak" earthenware effigies.

These traits were stressed in many later discussions and summaries of Florida or the Southeast (Dixon, 1913; Holmes, 1914; Wissler, 1938: 268–9). Holmes (1914) noted the first regional variations in the state, defining Peninsular and West Florida areas, a classification followed by Wissler (1938). In 1936 M. W. Stirling (1936) divided peninsula Florida into the Gulf Coast, Glades, Northern Highlands, and St. Johns areas. This last, "which includes the drainage of the St. Johns River and the adjacent northeast Atlantic coast," is essentially the unit covered in this paper.

In a recent definition of Florida archeological regions (Goggin, 1947: 122), Stirling's St. Johns Area was further divided into the Northern St. Johns, including only the coast and river valley north of Cape Canaveral, and the Melbourne (now Indian River) Area, which is culturally transitional between the Northern St. Johns and the Glades Area to the south. The boundary between these two was drawn more specifically at Rockledge in Goggin (MSa), primarily for expediency since it was recognized that a further constriction of the area would be made on completion of the detailed analysis of the Melbourne region by Irving Rouse (1951).

As discussed in this paper, the Northern St. Johns Region will be defined as (1) that part of the St. Johns River valley below the outlet of Lake Harney, (2) parts of Okefenokee Swamp, and (3) the Atlantic Coast from the St. Marys River to the southern end of Mosquito Inlet. The southern boundary consists of a line drawn from just north of Allenhurst on the coast westward through the outlet of Lake Harney. The western boundary extends from the Georgia state line, west of Okefenokee, southeast east of Macclenny and west of Penny Farms, thence curving westwards through Grandin to the east of Lockloosa and southwards to the Marion county south line (Fig. 1).

The northern boundary of the area, the St. Marys River is considered to be purely tentative, reflecting mainly our ignorance of that section. Nevertheless, the boundary will probably not be moved too many miles to the northward, although it appears that certain sites between the present line and Brunswick, Georgia, have affiliations with the Northern St. Johns Area. Such a site is the mound at Woodbine on the Satilla River, explored by Clarence B. Moore (1897: 11–14). Ethnologically we have included Eastern Timucua groups living north of the St. Marys.

The southern boundary, as it now stands, is probably as adequate a one as can be

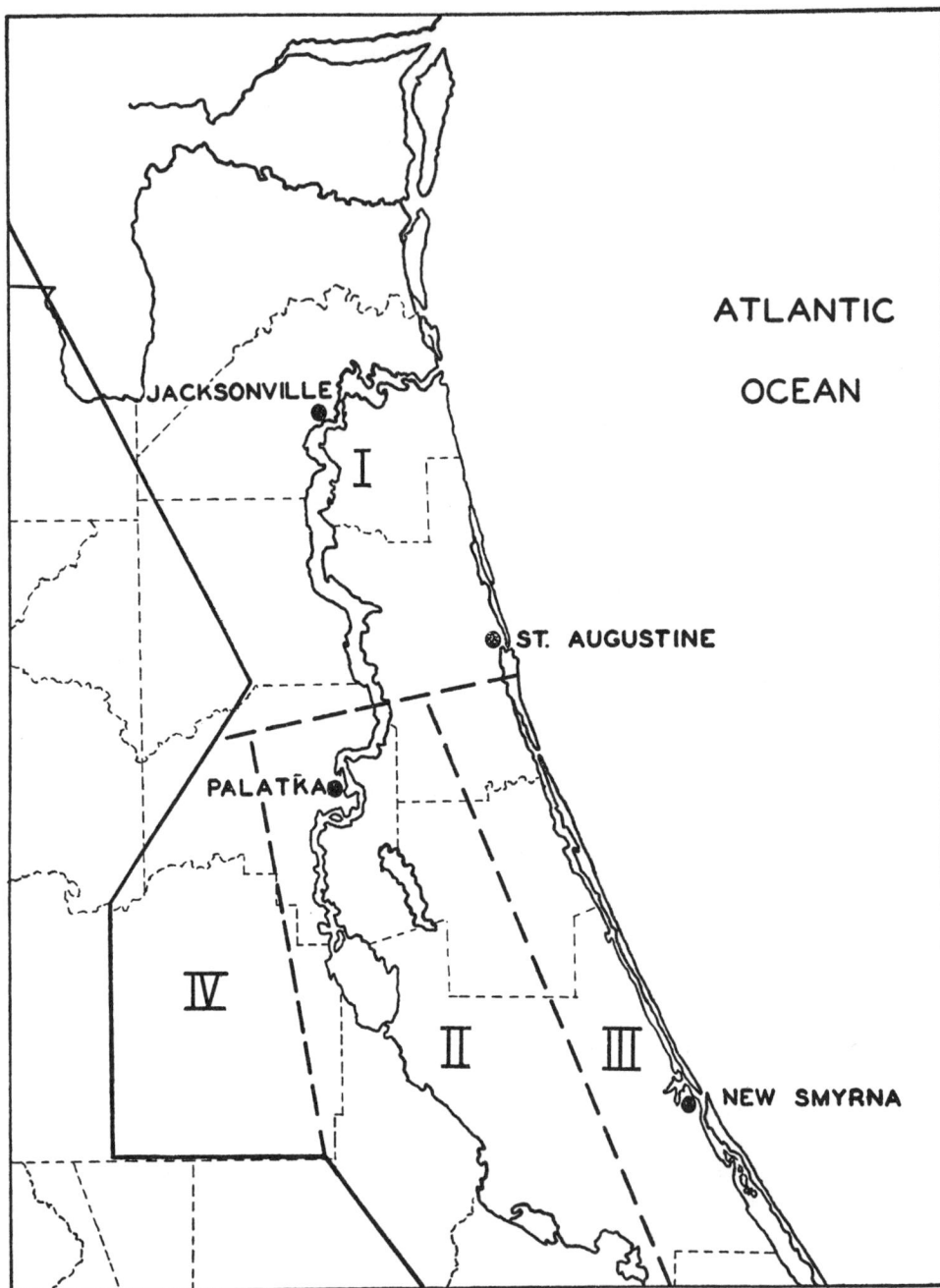

FIG. 1. Subareas of the Northern St. Johns Area.

drawn. Culturally it serves a major purpose since it represents a northern line beyond which little Glades influence passed. The Indian River Area (formerly the Melbourne Region) is thus clearly demarcated as a zone of transition or more properly an area peripheral to two major centers, sharing traits of both. From a physiographic view the boundary is also sound, as it is the southern limit of the Mosquito Inlet on the coast and of high banks on the St. Johns (see also Rouse, 1951).

The western boundary is the least satisfactory of all, the one most subject to future change, and probably the one which will always remain somewhat arbitrary. In delineating this line the procedure has been to draw a line west of known sites in this area but also east of the distinctive sites of Central Florida. Such a technique leaves countless opportunities for future modification. The lack of distinctive physiographic features along this line makes the task more difficult.

Within the region as a whole it has been possible to define four subareas, based in part on geographical features but also distinguished by cultural factors. These are as follows (Fig. 1):

Subarea I comprises the northern coastal and interior sections south to a line drawn from a few miles below St. Augustine southwestward across the St. Johns River about 10 miles north of Palatka. The coast from the St. Johns to north of St. Augustine lacks the distinctive lagoons found elsewhere. On the river the subarea is physiographically noteworthy for the wideness of the stream, which flows between high and dry banks with few of the marshy shores found further south (U.S.C.G.S., 1940, n.d.).

Subarea III consists of the remainder of the east coast north of Allenhurst. This includes the coastal lagoons, Halifax and Mosquito rivers, and the narrow offshore islands. Inland, an arbitrary extension of about 10 miles has been given to the subarea, as the territory immediately behind the shore is poorly known.

Subarea IV comprises the drainage of the Oklawaha River including the bulk of the "scrub" or Ocala National Forest. The southern boundary is the south line of Marion County while the Central Florida region borders it to the west. In addition to the Oklawaha River, a stream characterized by river bottom swamp along its course, the subarea also includes most of the "scrub," a high, dry, rolling, sand country covered with scrub pine, but dotted with unique crystal-clear springs and lakes.

Subarea II, not previously mentioned, comprises the balance of the region, essentially the St. Johns River from the outlet of Lake Harney to just north of Palatka. In this section the St. Johns can be characterized as a series of large lakes connected by intricate and sometimes shifting channels (U.S.C.G.S., 1940a, 1940b, 1940c.).

The distinctive cultural features of these subareas are usually limited to certain periods of time, rather than being constant throughout the whole range of occupation. They will be noted in connection with each cultural period.

NATURAL LANDSCAPE

PRESENT CONDITIONS

The state of Florida occupies a unique position in North America, in that it is a long narrow peninsula jutting towards the tropics from the Southeastern coastal plain. This position has certain disadvantages, particulary in terms of mineral resources, but for the state as a whole it provides many compensatory advantages, especially the mild climate and rich wild life. Unfortunately the Northern St. Johns Area is not too well supplied with compensatory geographical advantages, although certain of its natural features are unique. Perhaps the most distinctive feature of the Northern St. Johns Area is its many miles of shoreline. These are found along the Atlantic coast, the coastal lagoon, and the St. Johns River with its numerous lakes.[1]

The St. Johns River itself is unusual in that it flows from south to north. It rises in the extensive marshes west of Melbourne and Malabar, and flows northward through a region of marshes and lakes. North of Lake Harney the character of the shore changes; from here to south of Palatka, the river is really a chain of connected lakes. In addition to the marshy shores, much river bottom swamp is found. A rough estimate, based on U. S. Coast and Geodetic Survey charts, indicates that less than half of the shore is formed by marshes, the remainder being swamp with occasional bluffs.[2] North of Palatka the river again changes in character, widening and flowing, with few exceptions, between elevated dry banks.

Along the coast, Halifax and Mosquito rivers are distinctive bodies of brackish water paralleling about one-third of the Atlantic shore. These lagoons, ranging from less than a mile to several miles in width, are quite shallow. Inlets, subject to alternate opening and closing, allow access to the ocean. Before modern exploitation and changes these lagoons were rich sources of fish and shell fish. To the north another sixth of the coast has a parallel series of lagoons, the inland waterway lying behind Fort George and Amelia islands.

Geologically the history of the area is simple. Most of the surface is covered with late Pleistocene deposits having elevations of less than 100 feet. With one exception, these deposits are mainly sand. The most important rock in the region, which dates in this period, is the famous coquina rock of the Anastasia Formation found in occasional outcrops along the whole shore line. Certain details of these Pleistocene and Recent deposits are of interest for their associated human remains (Rouse, 1951).

Along the western boundary various exposures of earlier formations are found. These include Ocala limestone of Eocene times; the Hawthorne Formation and Duplin marl of Miocene times; and the Charlton and Citronelle formations and Caloosahatchee marl which date from the Pliocene period (Cooke, 1945). No hard rock deposits are known but flint may be present in the Ocala limestone.

Fine soils are not an outstanding feature of the region, although enough mixed sand soils were available to satisfy the needs of the Indian agriculturist. The successful early development of British and American plantations on the St. Johns testifies to the quality of certain soils.

Vegetation is a difficult subject to present in such a brief consideration since not only

---

[1] This shore line was undoubtedly one of the single most important factors for the Indians. I would estimate a proportionately greater total cubic content of shell refuse for this area than for any other archeological region in Florida—one way of indicating the relative importance of a shore line and associated features to the inhabitants.

[2] Marshes are partially or wholly inundated areas with a grass or water plant vegetation, while the term swamp is generally restricted to a flooded forested area.

is the plant life extensive but it is combined in so many ways because of differences in soil, moisture, and salinity, that the resulting vegetation complexes are very numerous. The flora as a whole is characteristic of the Southeast, being mainly temperate forms. This includes pine and cypress forests and mixed deciduous forests of various oaks, maple, magnolia, ash, gum, cedar, and cabbage palm, among many other trees. A few tropical trees, including the red mangrove, extend sporadically into the southern coastal strip.

Vegetation complexes have been simply defined by Watson (1926: 428–34) as: Grassy Swamp, Savanna, or Marsh; Flatwoods; Scrub; High Pine Woods; and Hammocks. The first is clear; it includes all grass covered inundated areas either fresh or salt. Flatwoods are open pine forest, usually with a water table not far from the surface while High Pine Woods are rolling areas covered with pine, but regions where the water table is not near the surface. Scrub country is usually dry sandy soil covered with scrub oak or scrub pine, both types occurring on old dunes. Hammock is a local term for a group, forest, or assemblage of deciduous trees and palms, usually used in contradistinction to pine woods. More detailed divisions of these complexes are used but these will suffice for our purpose.

Physiographically the area is not too diverse although four natural regions have been noted: Lake Region, East Florida Flatwoods, Peninsular Flatwoods, and the East Coast Strip.[3]

The western border of our area includes part of the Lake Region, specifically the country within archeological subarea IV and parts of subarea II: all the territory west of the St. Johns River below Palatka and a broad strip of land east of the river nearly as far as Lake Harney. This territory is characterized by many large and small lakes and numerous springs, including renowned Silver Springs, one of the largest in the world. Vegetation is diverse. Along the St. Johns and Oklawaha there are extensive stretches of pine flatwoods. Elsewhere west of the St. Johns the topography is one of rolling hills. In places this is covered with a high pine forest, but the large area between the Oklawaha and Lake George known as the "scrub" is a sandy rolling region covered with scrub pine. In favored situations both high and low hammocks occur and much of the Oklawaha is bordered by river bottom swamps.

The East Florida Flatwoods lie almost wholly within our region as a band across the area, north of the Flagler-Volusia county line. The country is in general flat but rises gradually to the west. Shallow ponds and bays are numerous, but springs are scarce. Open forests of long-leaf pine are typical, with areas of scrub vegetation near the coast. Bays contain a swamp complex, as do the shores of many streams. Some hammocks are also found in this last habitat.

Southward, about the north end of Volusia County, these flatwoods gradually merge into another form, Peninsula Flatwoods, Eastern Division. This occupies the remainder of the Northern St. Johns Area with the exception of a narrow coastal strip. Distinctions between this and the preceding region are of a minor nature. Pine flatwoods, various types of marshes, and occasional swamps are the characteristic vegetation forms.

[3] Harper (1914, 1921). The following summary of physiographic areas is mainly taken from these works.

The East Coast Strip extends along the whole Atlantic shore of the Northern St. Johns Area. It is characterized by a combination of offshore islands separated from the coast by a lagoon and includes the mainland west of the lagoon for several miles inland. The vegetation, which is perhaps the most varied of any of the physiographic areas, includes large areas of flatwoods, scrub on dunes, and tidal marshes. In addition much of the west shore of Halifax and Mosquito lagoons is lined with fine hammock. In the latter lagoon the red mangrove reaches its northern limit.

Throughout most of the area wild life was abundant.[4] Mammals included deer, bear, panther, wildcats, raccoons, fox, skunks, muskrats, opposums, marsh and cottontail rabbits, and many minor forms. Birds were common, the numerous wading forms finding abundant food along the miles of shoreline. In their rookeries thousands of individuals were easy prey for the primitive hunter. Reptiles too were abundant, turtles and alligators being present in quantities along the St. Johns, while various snakes were widespread.

In the salt and fresh waters of the region still more life was present. Fish swarmed in the coastal lagoons and streams while shell fish were everywhere abundant. In the salt waters, oysters, clams, and coquinas were easy to obtain while the snails, Ampullaria and Paludina, and various pelecypods inhabited streams and ponds.

A factor of importance for both the plant and animal life is the climate. This is fairly mild during the winter while the summers are not excessively hot. Although frosts visit the northern portion of the region yearly, parts of the south may go some years between severe frosts. This area is classed as Cfa, a humid mesothermal climate (Köppen, 1918). In a modification of Köppen's classification which has proved popular with many American geographers, Thornwaite (1931) classifies the area as CB'r, a sub-humid, mesothermal climate with adequate seasonal distribution of precipitation, although this is one of the driest parts of the state. A large section of the area receives less than 50 inches of rainfall per year and the remainder has a precipitation of 50 to 55 inches (Mitchell and Ensign, 1928).

Ecological Changes

Ordinarily one is not inclined to consider ecological changes to be of any importance within the time considered in this paper—some few thousand years. Nevertheless, evidence indicates that a number of changes have taken place (Goggin, 1948b). It appears, though, that they were of a strictly local nature and that in many respects the area was not too greatly different than at the present time.

Two important factors in these changes are a rising sea level and a fluctuating climate, the first related to the second, but each having distinct local influences. Since the last glaciation the melting ice caps have caused a fluctuating, but constant, rise in sea level. In recent years this has been demonstrated by careful measurement (Flint, 1947: 426–8); and in the Glades (Goggin, MSb) and Indian River (Rouse, 1951) areas of Florida it can be demonstrated in relation to archeological sites.

---

[4] Sources on the fauna include: mammals (Sherman, 1936), herpetology (Carr, 1940), birds (Bailey' 1925; Howell, 1932), and molluscs (Smith, 1937).

In the Northern St. Johns Area this rising sea level appears to have been an important factor in controlling the food supply of the Archaic peoples along the coast (Goggin, 1948b). Indications are that large populations were not settled on the coast until St. John I times, possibly because the waters of the coastal lagoons were too fresh for the growth of oysters. With the rise of the sea a balanced salinity was achieved and shellfish flourished in the lagoons.

The second factor effecting ecological change appears to be climatic fluctuations. These fluctuations were probably of a minor order, yet were locally important because the area was a zone intermediate between the temperate and tropical. With minor climatic changes this zone would move north or south causing considerable local change. The full extent of such changes cannot yet be evaluated, but certainly vegetation was somewhat different at times. The royal palms noted by William Bartram (1940: 113) on the St. Johns, between Astor and Lake Dexter, were probably stragglers left during a climatic fluctuation.

Certain other ecological anomalies have no ready explanation. This is the case with the extinct Great Auk remains found at the Cotten site (Goggin, 1948b).

HISTORICAL BACKGROUND

The first Europeans to visit Florida will probably never be known, but it is generally conceded that visitors touched the state previous to its "discovery" by Juan Ponce de Leon in 1513. One of these, most often given credit for the discovery of Florida, is Sebastian Cabot, who is believed to have coasted the eastern shore of Florida in 1497 (Lowery, 1901: 123).

Another, whose claims are not so well accepted, is Amerigo Vespucci, reported to have visited the southeastern Atlantic coast of North America in the following year. It is also not improbable that other unknown adventurers and slavers visited the peninsula in the last years of the fifteenth century and in the first decade of the sixteenth century.

In any case there is good evidence for some knowledge of Florida previous to Ponce de Leon's visit because it is depicted on early maps. The most famous of these is the Cantino Map made in 1502 (Lowery, 1901: 123). This shows Florida with some accuracy; at least it indicates that Florida was known.

Nevertheless, Juan Ponce de Leon has for many years been given the honor of having discovered Florida. Although this is not properly due him, he does deserve credit for being the first to leave us a detailed account of his visit to Florida.[5] On his first voyage he landed on the northeast Atlantic coast of Florida, undoubtedly somewhere in the region under consideration.[6] Contacts with the Indians here appear to be negligible

[5] Actually the original journals of Ponce have been lost, but such a detailed account of the voyages is given by Herrera (1720) that he must have had original documents on hand in writing his work.

[6] The exact place of landing is under considerable debate. There are a number of people who support the claim that he landed at St. Augustine (Lawson, 1946). Others have suggested the mouth of the St. Johns River. In most cases these claims are based on longitudes and latitudes given by Herrera. Natural features are not well enough described to be of any value. In view of general data suggesting how inaccurate most recorded longitudes and latitudes were at this date it does not appear wise to base his landing place on such information. See Scisco (1913) and Davis (1935).

and very shortly after Ponce sailed southward, rounding the peninsula, and up the west coast. His reception from the natives there was so unfavorable that he shortly afterwards returned to the West Indies.

Other Spaniards followed. Diego Miruelo traded for gold at some unspecified spot in 1516. In the following year Francisco Hernandez de Córdova visited the southwest coast where he was repulsed (Diaz del Castillo, 1927: 35). Others also explored the west coast, especially Francisco de Garay, but the east coast was not revisited except by Lucas Vasquez de Ayllon's expedition, which made a brief attempt at establishing a settlement north of Florida, probably in South Carolina (Lowery, 1901: 153–7).

In the same year, 1521, Ponce de Leon returned to the southwest coast, hoping to establish a permanent settlement. Unfortunately the Calusa Indians attacked the Spanish, driving them off and fatally wounding Ponce himself. A return by Ayllon to his former settlement was of short duration.

For some reason the northeast Florida coast proved still unattractive and the next explorers continued to try their fortunes on the west coast. The first of these, Panfilo de Narvaez, landed at or near Tampa Bay in 1528, and marched northwards, paralleling the coast but some miles inland (Cabeza de Vaca, 1907). Eleven years later Hernando De Soto also landed near the same place,[7] from which he was to make his long expedition through the peninsula and westward to the Mississippi and his death. In the northward march through the state, De Soto must have come very close to the Northern St. Johns Region, but it cannot be ascertained if he was actually in it.[8]

In succeeding years European contact with Florida was marked by a series of disastrous shipwrecks, mainly on the southern coasts (Lowery, 1901: 352–3). Many of the survivors were killed outright; others, like Fontaneda (1944), were taken captive. These wrecks were rich sources of wealth for the Indians in the form of metals, including much gold and silver. The natives of the Northern St. Johns Region did not appear to have had much direct contact with either the wrecks or distressed mariners, yet by trade they had accumulated a considerable quantity of ornaments made of gold and other metals obtained from these wrecks.[9]

Despite the hardships reported by previous expeditions, the lure of Florida was still strong and numerous schemes were devised to exploit it (Lowery, 1901: 351–4). The next expedition on the Atlantic Coast under Angel de Villafañe attempted a settlement at Santa Elena on the Carolina coast (Lowery, 1901: 354–75). But it was abandoned after a short time.

These successive failures of exploration and settlement discouraged the Spanish to such an extent that Florida was officially closed to exploration in 1561 (Lowery, 1901:

---

[7] Like Ponce de Leon's landing place, that of De Soto is also a matter of considerable dispute. Both Charlotte Harbor and Tampa Bay have been considered, and a number of specific points have been suggested in the latter locality.

[8] There are four accounts of this expedition, three of which were written by participants. These sources have appeared in a number of editions and are the basis of numerous secondary histories (Lowery, 1901: 458–60). The route traversed by De Soto has been a source of interest to many scholars. Swanton (1939) has brought many of these conflicting interpretations together.

[9] This is repeatedly attested by the Huguenot sources (see footnote 10 this chapter) and by Sparke (1941).

376). However, this royal proclamation was quickly revised early in 1562 when news came of the first French Huguenot colony, founded by Ribaut on the Florida coast. Spanish authorities in Cuba were ordered to investigate and destroy the settlement, and in pursuance of this order Hernando de Manrique de Rojas coasted the Florida shore in the middle of 1564, capturing a Frenchman and removing one of the stone columns erected by Ribaut (Lowery, 1905: 45-8).[10] However, lack of food and poor planning caused the French to abandon their colony, without having been seriously affected by the Spanish.

In the meanwhile a second French colony was established by René de Laudonnière, about the same time in this year, just inside the mouth of the St. Johns River (presumably at St. Johns Bluff). Here contacts were made with the Indians of the chief Saturiba, who had been protecting and venerating the stone column previously left by Ribaut. Nearby, Fort Caroline, a small triangular structure of wood and sand surrounded by entrenchments, was erected.

Thoughtless and inept leadership on the part of Laudonnière resulted in innumerable problems for the settlement. Brief exploring expeditions up the St. Johns River and westward brought the French into contact with numerous Timucuan speaking tribes, many of which were bitter enemies. By double dealing Laudonnière alienated most of these despite the initial friendliness of certain groups. In addition, he was overbearing towards the settlers. As a result dissatisfaction grew and a serious mutiny developed, with thirteen men sailing off in one of the ships for a brief career of piracy preying on the Spanish.

Lack of foresight in bringing sufficient provisions, and a too heavy dependence on the natives for the balance, resulted in near starvation for the colony in the spring of 1565. This was only relieved by the fortunate arrival of Sir John Hawkins who generously sold and gave the Frenchmen necessary goods and a ship (Sparke, 1941).

In the meanwhile preparations were being made in France for a third expedition, and

---

[10] Primary sources on the French colony and its later destruction by the Spanish are detailed. They were early organized by Fairbanks (1871), Parkman (1880), and Shea (1884–89, 1886), and more critically and in greater detail by Lowery (1905). The last work includes a good annotated bibliography of primary materials available at that time.

More recently, new original accounts have become available, while others have been translated into English. Among the French material is the book of Ribaut (1927), and the accounts of Le Moyne and Le Challeux, together with the valuable drawings of the former which recently appeared in Lorant (1946).

Spanish sources include Solís de Merás' (1923) and Barrientos' (1902), accounts of Pedro Menéndez de Aviles' activities, and various documents translated by Connor (1925, 1930). Other documents dealing with the period are published and annotated by Zubillaga (1946); however, the Latin annotations are not usable by most students. A less critical biography of Menéndez has been recently written by Camin (1944).

Zubillaga (1941) has also prepared a general account of the Spanish and French in Florida during the years 1566–1572. This parallels Lowery's work to a great extent but benefits by the use of some of the Jesuit letters not available to him. These letters are reproduced in Zubillaga's previously mentioned work and in part by Vargas Ugarte (1940) in the original Spanish. An English translation of selected letters appears in Vargas Ugarte (1935). A critical analysis of the strategic significance of the sixteenth-century Spanish settlement has been made by Chatelain (1941). His bibliographical annotations are of value for any interested student.

before Laudonnière could leave Fort Caroline five ships under Jean Ribaut arrived there in August, 1565. Ribaut brought more colonists and was also commissioned to investigate Laudonnière's behavior.

During the development of French interest in Florida the Spanish Crown had paid careful attention to the progress of the colony, remonstrating with the French about this invasion of their territory. However, after news arrived of the depredations inflicted by the mutineers of Laudonnière's colony, Philip of Spain acted quickly, appointing Pedro Menéndez de Aviles, an experienced admiral and soldier, as Adelantado of Florida with powers to colonize the land and to expel any foreigners from Spanish territory.

Menéndez arrived in Florida shortly after Ribaut and, following an initial reconnaisance, established himself near the present St. Augustine, fortifying the town of the Indian cacique Seloy. Shortly afterwards Ribaut sailed down the coast to attack the Spanish but was driven away by a heavy storm.

Taking advantage of Ribaut's absence from Fort Caroline, Menéndez marched north along the coast and captured that fort. Over half the garrison was killed, and a number of women, children, and musicians were captured. The balance of the French escaped to the forest where they joined the Indians, or else made their way to the coast to be rescued by several small French vessels which had lain down the river during the fighting. The captured fort was renamed San Mateo by the Spanish and manned by a garrison.

Ribaut, who had left St. Augustine, sailing southward with the storm, fared badly. His ships were wrecked on the coast and many of the survivors killed by the Indians. The remainder, including Ribaut himself, surrendered to Menéndez, who ordered them all, with few exceptions, put to death. The French threat to Florida and the route of the Plate Fleets was thus crushed.

Menéndez immediately consolidated his position by exploring Florida and adjacent Georgia, establishing a fort in the latter territory, San Felipe, and other small posts to the south in the territory of the Ais, Tekesta, and Calusa Indians. Most of these posts suffered various vicissitudes and some were later abandoned. Internal troubles, mutinies, and local Indian uprisings plagued all the posts, as well as St. Augustine itself. Nevertheless, the Spanish were firmly established in Florida for the next two hundred years. Even the destruction of San Mateo by Gourgues, a French reprisal for the death of their countrymen at Menéndez's hands, and the later sacking of St. Augustine in 1586 by Sir Francis Drake, had little effect on the Spanish position.

The relations between the Europeans and Indians appear in general to have been badly handled. Laudonnière in particular played various groups against each other but reaped the just reward for his unfaithfullness when he was foresaken by his earlier allies. Menéndez himself tried to treat the Indians fairly, making special efforts to settle disputes between them and giving no aggressive cause for displeasure on his part. Despite all his care soldiers at one post after another antagonized the natives, necessitating withdrawal of the Spanish in some areas. In many of these cases missionaries reaped the main results of the soldiers' actions with the loss of their converts. An early recognition of this situation by the clergy determined them on a new course of action—missions with few or no lay members present. This policy was to be one of immediate fruitfulness for the church, but in the long run it was one of the basic causes for the loss of Florida by the Spanish.

During the seventeenth century the Spanish colony in Florida centered around St. Augustine and isolated parts to the north. Except for occasional threats from English pirates and several Indian uprisings, life in the colony appears to have been uneventful although there were constant pleas from the governors to the Crown for more attention. Eventually, after a number of previous forts had fallen apart from decay, the impressive masonry fort of San Marcos was built at St. Augustine in the last quarter of the century, a massive monument which was to keep the Spanish power in Florida for many years.

But it was also during the seventeenth century that the great chain of missions was established north along the coast and inland across northern Florida by the Franciscans. The first intense mission activity in Florida was begun by the Jesuits, introduced by Menéndez. They founded missions at Tekesta, Carlos, and Guale, but none in our region, apparently because the natives at St. Augustine and San Mateo were too upset by the Spanish (Lowery, 1905: 347). Also abandoned for this reason, was a plan to instruct children from Saturiba and Tactacuru at St. Augustine (Lowery, 1905: 353; Vargas Ugarte, 1935: 65). The Jesuits finally withdrew in 1572, with the Franciscans entering the territory in the following year, although their concentrated activity did not begin until 1583 (Geiger, 1937: 46).

At first much attention was given to the Guale missions (Santa Elena), although some stations were also established in the Northern St. Johns Area. A revolt among the Guale in 1597 briefly stopped work there, but it was shortly resumed (Oré, 1936). Work among the Western Timucua was begun at Potano in 1606 and spread westward to the Apalachee soon afterwards (Geiger, 1937). Even before this, missions had been established on the St. Johns well up the river. Some of these lasted with interruptions throughout much of the century.

It is very difficult to discover details concerning missions in the territory under consideration. Occasional references are made to some, and certain mission lists are available roughly indicating their locations. But in general, the exact location, physical nature, and duration are not recorded. In an attempt to answer the last question the literature was analyzed for references to missions during the period from 1597 to 1697. This has been a fruitful project for it does give some indications of the time range of many missions (Table 1). For most of these missions very little information other than their existence is available. Perhaps a more detailed study of many unpublished documents will add to our knowledge.[11]

Shortly after 1700 the English from Georgia and the Carolinas began a series of raids on Florida which eventually destroyed most of the Indian population in the northern part of the state. The first attack in 1702 directed towards St. Augustine failed to take

[11] Tentative identification of certain archeological sites can be made at this time. There is reasonable probability that Du 53 may have been one of the sites of San Juan del Puerto and that Wrights Landing (SJ 3) was the site of Nuestra Señora de Guadalupe de Tolomato. It is also possible that Mount Royal Village (Pu 35A) was the site of San Antonio de Enacape.

TABLE 1. SPANISH MISSIONS, 1597–1697

Geiger (1937) 1597	Lanning (1935: 239) 1597–1602	Ybarra (Geiger, 1937:186) 1605	Geiger (1937: 234–5) 1610	Oré (1936: 126) 1616	Díaz de la Calle (Serrano y Sanz, 1913: 132–3) 1655	Calderón (Wenhold, 1936) 1675	Lowery MS b (Chatelain, 1941: 124) 1680	Anon. 1680–1700?	Various 1696–1697
						Coastal Missions			
Nombre de Dios	Nombre de Dios	Nombre de Dios	Nombre de Dios		Nombre de Dios	Nombre de Dios	Nombre de Dios de Amacarisse	Nombre de Dios Pº de Thomas de Xpños	
									Sta. Cruce[e]
	San Mateo San Pablo								
					Nuestra Señora de Guadalupe	La Natividad de Nuestra Señora de Tolomato[a]	Nuestra Señora de Guadalupe de Tolomato		
	San Juan	Moloa San Juan	Moloa San Juan		San Juan del Puerto	San Juan del Puerto Santa María	Senor San Juan del Puerto	"Xpños"	St. Wans[e]
						San Phelipe	San Felipe de Athuluteca	Isla de S. Phelipe con Pob. de Xpños	Santa María de Sena[d] (St. Marys)[e] St. Philips[e]
	San Antonio Socochuno								
San Pedro Ibi	San Pedro	San Pedro	San Pedro		San Pedro Mocamo				
					Interior Missions				
	San Sebastian				San Salvador de Macaya		Senor Salvador de Maiaca, conversión nueva	Mayaca	Mayaca[e]
					Santa Lucía de Acuera				
					San Luis de Acuera				
				Avino S. Antonio de Enacape	San Antonio de Nacape		Senor San Antonio de Anacape, conversión nueva		
	Antonico Tocoy San Julian	Antonico Tocoy							
					San Diego de Laca	San Diego de Salamototo	Senor San Diego de Eçalamatoto	Salamatoto	

[a] This should not be confused with the Tolomato on the Georgia coast.
[b] The next available list of Florida missions, Fernandez de Florencia's of 1675 (Boyd, 1948) is not as complete for this area as Lowery, so is not reproduced.
[c] Dickinson (1945).
[d] Swanton (1922:328).
[e] Swanton (1922:339).

the fort, although the town itself was burned. Two years later, Colonel Moore, with Creek allies, attacked and destroyed the Apalachee. Within a short time further raids decimated the Western and Eastern Timucua, driving the remnants of the latter to the environs of St. Augustine. In reciprocation, the Spanish encouraged the various refugee groups to raid the Carolina colonies. Further raids by the English included one led by Colonel Palmer which destroyed the Indian settlements around St. Augustine in 1727, Oglethorpe's futile investment of the same town in 1740, and his final raid of 1743.

A treaty of peace between Spain and Great Britain in 1748 resulted in a cessation of hostilities. However, in 1762 Havana was lost to the English, and was regained in the following year by the ceding of Florida to the English. They retained Florida for twenty years, when it reverted back to Spain. That country held it until 1820, when Florida was ceded to the United States.

The first half of the eighteenth century was a period of waning for the Indians, for by the end of that time once numerous tribes had melted away. After 1706 the Timucua and Apalachee mission provinces were abandoned, and the few remnants of those Indians who escaped the English joined the Eastern Timucua, Yamasee, Mayaca, and other groups east of the St. Johns River.

There the civil and ecclesiastical authorities made many attempts to help them. Natives from the same area were gathered together, when possible, in villages often retaining their old names, and were served by mission priests who spoke their languages. Some towns were even fortified by the priests for protection from attacks by Creek warriors from the north.

One factor or another, perhaps most of all the cultural uprooting, caused the once numerous Indians to dwindle rapidly (see successive mission lists in Geiger, 1940: 132–9). Those left blended together as a few miserable "Indian" camp followers, many of whom departed from Florida with the Spanish in 1763, settling in Guanabacoa, a suburb of Havana. During the subsequent British period they were no longer recognized.

The beginning of the British occupation is a time of importance in our consideration of the Indians in the region. After that time all trace is lost of the Timucua and a new group, the Seminole, appear. These were a composite people mainly formed of Hitchiti, Oconee, and other Muskhogean tribes who moved into the population vacuum of Central Florida about 1750. They centered around Alachua (Paynes) Prairie, south of Gainesville, and later expanded east of the St. Johns. Extensive trade was conducted with them through English trading houses on the St. Johns (W. Bartram, 1940), the two most important in 1773 being located near the present town of Astor and at Stokes Landing above Palatka.

Very shortly after the American occupation of Florida, the desirable Seminole lands attracted the attention of the new settlers and agitation was soon on foot for their removal. The majority left this area, either being moved to Oklahoma or escaping into the unexplored parts of South Florida. A few small bands still remain near the headwaters of the river, in the Indian River Area.

ETHNOLOGICAL BACKGROUND

At the time of European contact in the sixteenth century the Northern St. Johns Region was rather densely populated by a group of Indians who will be called the Eastern Timucua. Properly speaking, the cultural term Timucua has no direct reference to this group, being the name of a single Central Florida tribe. Also, unfortunately, the name has a linguistic connotation which can be legitimately applied to Indians who lived over all of northern Florida west to the Aucilla River and apparently southward to Tampa Bay.[12]

The town or confederacy of Utina or Thimoga, from which the term Timucua is derived was probably not situated in this region, although its exact location is uncertain. Most students place it west of the St. Johns River, Swanton (1922: 328) locating it as far west as Santa Fe Lake but extending its territory east of the St. Johns River. Various French accounts suggest that the tribe was centered somewhat closer to the St. Johns and further south, in which case it would fall within the region under consideration. However, following Swanton, and taking into consideration the De Soto Expedition chronicles, the western location is accepted.[13]

The inadvisability of continuing the use of the term Timucua as a cultural designation was realized in the analysis of the archeology of Central Florida (Goggin, MSa). Here was found an archeological culture pattern which can be attributed to Timucuan-speaking peoples, but a pattern quite distinct in some respects, especially ceramics, from the Northern St. Johns region inhabited also by a Timucuan-speaking group. No appropriate collective term can be found for the Central Florida Indians so the terms Western Timucua and Eastern Timucua were coined, the former to apply to the inhabitants of the Central Florida region and the latter to those people dwelling in the Northern St. Johns region.[14]

The term Eastern Timucua Indians will be used to include a number of tribes extending along the coast from Cumberland Island, Georgia to Mosquito Inlet in Florida, and inland along the St. Johns River. The most important of these were the Saturiba centered around the mouth and some distance up the St. Johns River. A large number of towns included in this tribe, or else subject to it, were later served by three missions. On Cumberland Island the Tacatacuru were an important group, while the Yui, Icafui,

---

[12] This distinction in terminology was clearly recognized by Gatschet (1877: 626–7), but has apparently been ignored by other writers. Swanton appears to be aware of this usage and speaks of the various tribes separately when considering their history, but he does tend to group these all together under the term Timucua in discussing their culture (Swanton, 1946).

[13] Le Moyne (1946: 42) locates Utina on the "main channel" of the St. Johns. It was noted that the French in traveling to Potano (near the Alachua Prairie) could avoid Utina territory by leaving the St. Johns River on one of the small streams coming in below (that is north of) Utina territory (Le Moyne, 1946: 52). This would hardly be feasible if Utina was situated almost directly north of Potano, where the Santa Fe Lake location would place it. Gatschet (1877: 627) locates the town on Lake George. See a further discussion in Goggin (MSe).

[14] Spanish usage is of no help because their Timucua Province extended to Apalachee (Swanton, 1922: 322–3; Boyd, 1939: 257; Chatelain, 1941: 122–4). As will be seen in Goggin (MSe), the designations Southeastern, Southern, and isolated Timucua were also coined to include other Timucuan-speaking groups, beyond the scope of this study.

and Yufera lived to the west on the mainland. This last may have been a Muskogee tribe.

Southward along the St. Johns River were a number of towns collectively known as the Fresh Water Indians, among which the Mayaca were often mentioned. Whether the coastal Indians were included in that Fresh Water group is not certain, but a number of towns were situated on the coastal lagoons. The southernmost tribes were the Surruque and Urubia, living on Mosquito Lagoon.[15]

Population figures are very inadequate, nothing being known of the size of the Surruque or Yufera. The Saturiba were reported to include 500 Christians at one time (Swanton, 1946: 179), surely an incomplete enumeration for the tribe. In the Huguenot period Cacique Saturiba visited the French accompanied by 1200 or 1500 men (Le Moyne, 1946: 38). If such an enumeration were accurate it would indicate a population for that group of some 3500 to 4500 individuals.

Records of Utina population are not available but the tribe was reported to be more powerful than Saturiba, and thus must have been at least as large. In 1602 some 300 Christians or instructees were reported for the Fresh Water Indians (Swanton, 1946: 194), but these probably represent only a fraction of the total members of those tribes.

The Tacatacuru comprised 792 Christians in 1602 while 1100 were under instruction in Icafui. In the same year a population of 1000 is given for the Yui (Swanton, 1946: 194).

Although these population figures are not clear, an estimated population of 5000–8000 people in the sixteenth century would probably be close to the actual number. From this peak the tribes rapidly lost numbers until only 17 individuals were reported in 1736 (Swanton, 1946: 194).

Despite their political diversity these people apparently all spoke intelligible dialects of the same language, Timucua. Gatschet (1880: 479), deriving his information from Pareja's works, notes seven Timucua dialects. Those spoken here include that of Timoga in the lower St. Johns River, the Icafui, the Fresh Water District, Tacatacuru, and that of Santa Lucia de Acuera on the upper St. Johns.[16] The dialect of Mocama was spoken on the northernmost coast of our region. The sole remaining dialect was outside of our area to the west in the Potano region.

Considerable ethnographic data are available for these people, mainly the Saturiba and Utina, in the writings of the various French Huguenots and later Spanish missionaries.[17] Certain aspects of the Eastern Timucua culture will be noted; other summaries can be found in Ehrmann (1940), Gatschet (1880), and Swanton (1922).

The Timucua people were intensive agriculturists, producing large crops of maize.

[15] Many of the St. Johns River towns can be seen on Le Moyne's map of Florida (Lorant, 1946). Most are listed by Swanton (1922: 323–30) and the major tribes are briefly discussed in his later work (Swanton, 1946). Some of the coastal towns are located by Mexia (Rouse, 1951).

[16] Not "a short distance south of Cape Canaveral" as Gatschet (1880: 479) has stated.

[17] The main sources are Le Moyne, Laudonnière, Ribaut, Le Challeux, Sparke, and Pareja. These accounts have appeared in many editions; see Ehrmann (1940), Murdock (1941), Rouse and Goggin (1947), or Swanton (1922, 1946) for specific references.

Pareja's works are very rare but some of his material has been reprinted in part by Gatschet (1877, 1878, 1880). The valuable ethnographic information in these works has not been adequately exploited.

In addition much wild plant foods, fish, and game were utilized. During three winter months the towns were deserted while the people moved into the country, living on wild plants and game. Along the coast they were reported to live on oyster-shell mounds.

The towns were groups of round, beehive-shaped, thatched houses surrounded by a log stockade. A rectangular chief's house was in the center of town. In some instances large communal dwellings appear to have been utilized, although these may have been confused with the chief's house. Small sentry houses guarded the entrance of the stockade. Apparently each house included a number of families, perhaps a single sib.

Men wore breechclouts of skin, while woman covered themselves with brief girdles of Spanish moss. Many ornaments were worn: feathers in the hair; inflated and dyed fish bladders in the ears; strings of animal teeth, shells, or pearls; and copper, silver, and gold disks or plates. The metal for making these, or perhaps the ornaments themselves, were obtained from the South Florida Indians, who salvaged the metal from Spanish wrecks. The descriptions of these ornaments and the depictions in the French drawings, coincide closely with the archeological specimens. Ornaments made from conch shell columella were confused by an early chronicler with unicorn horns.

Body painting with red pigment was extensively practiced as part of the war complex. At other times, red, blue, and black pigment was applied. Tattooing seems to have been common but limited to the chiefs and their wives.

Square-ended dugout canoes were an important means of transportation in this well-watered country. Litters were used for carrying the sick, wounded, and dead, as well as the important nobles, who rode in litters shaded with green boughs.

Social organization was intricately developed, with powerful chieftians collecting tribute from the common people. Chieftianship was hereditary and female caciques were reported. There were two castes or classes, the common people and the nobles. The latter apparently belonged to one phratry, while among the lower class there were five phratries containing a number of sibs. Class distinction seems to have been patrilineal, while the exogamous sibs were matrilineal.

Politically the people were grouped together in small towns, each ruled by a minor chief. Several towns formed a confederacy, or what we have called a tribe, and these were controlled by an important chief, such as Saturiba or Utina. Apparently there was considerable fluctuation in the relationships of the confederacies with each other, all striving to be the dominant group.

This dominance was achieved by war, which here reached an elaborate development in fighting, mainly between neighboring groups. Stockaded towns and ever present sentries, indicate the constant orientation of the culture towards these conflicts. The war complex was well developed, with regular battle tactics and camping order while en route to battle. Weapons included spears, darts (?), bow and arrows, and clubs. The slain enemies were scalped and dismembered. On returning home the victorious Indians held a ceremony in which the arms, legs, and scalps of the enemy were displayed.

Shamans apparently controlled a well-organized religion which depended much on magic. Soothsaying and curing were other activities of the shamans. As constant associates and advisors of the caciques, they were in a position to wield considerable political influence.

ARCHEOLOGICAL RESEARCH

Perhaps the earliest recognition of archeological remains in the region was made by Mexia in his journey down the Halifax, Mosquito, and Indian rivers in 1605.[18] To him the sites in question were not archeological remains but hills or mounds of oyster shells occupied by Indians. These large shell heaps along the Halifax and Mosquito lagoons served as landmarks for seamen until well into the nineteenth century.

However, it is not until the period of British occupation that any note was made of the antiquities as such. Early in this period, in the winter of 1765–66, the noted Quaker botanist, John Bartram of Philadelphia, and his son, William, made a collecting trip well up the St. Johns River. Many Indian sites were noted (24 identifiable), especially midden sites, which the Bartrams called shell bluffs. The aboriginal origin of these middens was apparently not realized, although they were considered to be old Indian fields because of the presence of potsherds on the surface. However, a sand mound at Murphy Island was recognized as being of Indian construction, as was the famous Mount Royal.[19]

William Bartram subsequently returned to Florida in 1773–74, traveling up the St. Johns River, then cutting westward to the Seminole town of Cuscowilla on Alachua Prairie and thence to the Suwannee River. On this trip he also noted many Indian sites, describing a few, particularly Mount Royal.[20] Subsequent travelers to the region have left few details of their journeys, but like many early travelers they probably camped on the Indian sites, whether or not they were recognized as such. Some desultory digging may perhaps have been attempted in sites by army people during the Seminole Wars period, as was done in southern Florida (Goggin, MSb) and in the Indian River region (Rouse, 1951), but specific details are lacking for the Northern St. Johns.

Although the origin of coastal shell mounds was debated for some years following, as early as 1824 their artificial origin was noted by James Pierce. He contrasted them with natural shell deposits in the north where the shells were often found with the two valves together (Pierce, 1825: 122).

In the winter of 1848 Augustus Mitchell partially excavated a mound on Amelia Island (Mitchell, 1875). He reported burials and a few artifacts and, as a medical man,

[18] A transcription and a translation of his account are in Rouse (1951).

[19] The diary of this trip has been recently published with annotations by Francis Harper (J. Bartram, 1942). However, the section dealing with the St. Johns River portion of the journey has never been found, so the account which was published by Stork is inserted in the diary.

William Stork's early description of East Florida (Stork, 1767) included Bartram's description of the St. Johns journey in the second and following editions of that work. An excerpt from the third edition describing Mount Royal appeared in the Annual Report of the Smithsonian Institution for 1874 (J. Bartram, 1875).

[20] William Bartram's account appeared in his *Travels*, first published in 1791 and subsequently in many editions, not only in English but also in the German, Dutch, and French languages. This work is known for its literary significance as well as for being a source of much natural history information. A description and figure of Mount Royal were subsequently included by William Bartram (1853) in another paper.

A manuscript report of this trip, apparently the source for the *Travels*, has been recently edited and annotated by Francis Harper (W. Bartram, 1943). It should be consulted by anyone interested in details of this region.

offered a few comments on the crania found. Apparently this is the first recorded excavation in the area and one of the earliest in the state.

In 1848 Count F. de Pourtalés (1868) discovered human bones imbedded in "calcareous conglomerate" at the foot of a shell bluff on Stone Island, Lake Munroe. This find was never published in detail but was communicated to Louis Agassiz who dated the material as being as much as 10,000 years old (Haven, 1856: 86–7; Nott and Glidden, 1860). This opinion was included without comment by Lyell in his classic work on the antiquity of man (Lyell, 1863: 44–5).

Wyman (1875: 15), in his final report, noted that Pourtalés' finds are from the Stone Island midden and cites Pourtalés as having recognized the artificial nature of the site—a fact certainly not recognized by Agassiz. Hrdlička (1907: 19) later discussed the find but drew no conclusions except that fossilization itself means little in Florida. In light of more recent work in the region it seems clear that the bones found by Pourtalés can probably be attributed to one of the early shell midden horizons, possibly Mt. Taylor or the Orange period.

Daniel G. Brinton's book, *Notes on the Floridian Peninsula, its Literary History, Indian Tribes, and Antiquities*, published in 1859, is a classic landmark in the field which it so broadly covers. In this work Brinton notes many archeological sites of the region and recognizes the artificial nature of the coastal middens, although he considers the river middens to be natural formations. However, in a later paper (1872), he recognizes the St. Johns River middens as being formed by Indians.

In the immediate decades following the War Between the States there was a tremendous upsurge of interest in Florida archeology, particularly in this area, due mainly to the increase of tourist and invalid visitors. During this period Jeffries Wyman, Curator of the Peabody Museum at Harvard University, stands out above all others and is certainly the first major figure in Florida archeology.

Wyman apparently made his initial visit to the region in 1860 but it was not until 1867 that he began the first of a series of systematic studies of archeological remains on the St. Johns River and parts of the Atlantic Coast (Wyman, 1867, 1868a, 1868b). He made subsequent trips in 1869 and 1871 (Wyman, 1870, 1872), and the results of the work were brought together in a final report (Wyman, 1875).

The work of Jeffries Wyman cannot be over-praised. For its time it was most competent and unusually advanced. He was an excellent observer and noted many features which have only recently been recognized as worthy of more detailed study.

Various news articles based on Wyman's work appeared in contemporary American and British journals, but they are of no great significance (Anon., 1872, 1873, 1876b). In 1876 excavations were made in a sand mound on Murphy's Island. Fantastic stories of the finds were printed in the *Palatka* (Florida) *Herald* and later reprinted in the *Scientific American Supplement* (Anon., 1876a). These concerned a chamber within the mound and seem to be without foundation.

R. E. C. Stearns a naturalist who traveled over much of Florida in the late 1860's noted many sites in the state. Of interest to us are his comments on Amelia Island sites (Stearns, 1869: 282–3).

In the closing years of the century numerous brief articles on the archeology of the region appeared. These were mainly the records of amateurs, usually naturalists, medical men, or tourists. Most are only of casual interest although some contain certain details of significance to the specialist. They include Lente (1877), Calkins (1878), Mayberry (1878), Harrison (1878), Haldeman (1878), Dall (1885), Shepard (1886), and Hale (1887).

However, two figures of the 1880's deserve special note for they made genuine contributions. Andrew E. Douglass, an amateur archeologist of New York, conducted numerous excavations in sand mounds along the Atlantic Coast. His publications and specimens, now in the American Museum of Natural History, are some of the most valuable sources of information for this type of site in the region (Douglass, 1882, 1883, 1884, 1885).

The other figure is J. Francis LeBaron, a civil engineer interested in the antiquities of Florida, who spent much time in this region leaving us a detailed site survey (LeBaron, 1884). The specimens he collected and a site map are in the Harvard Peabody Museum.

LeBaron's site material formed the basis of the Florida section of Cyrus Thomas' *Catalogue of Prehistoric Works East of the Rocky Mountains* which appeared in 1891. However, there was included additional material obtained by the Smithsonian's widespread circulation of a request for information concerning sites, which was begun some ten years previously. Certain of the answers to this request had already appeared (Clarke, 1880; Biddle, 1880).

The last decade of the century is dominated by the work of Clarence B. Moore, who made his first visit to the region about 1875 although he did not begin serious archeological work until 1892. From then until 1895 he tested many midden sites and excavated a large proportion of the sand mounds along the St. Johns River. The coastal region was not intensively worked, apparently because of his belief in the thoroughness of Douglass' work. Moore's results were published in a series of papers in the *American Naturalist* (Moore, 1892a, 1892b, 1892c, 1893, 1894c) and in the *Journal of the Academy of Natural Sciences* (Moore, 1894a, 1894b, 1895a, 1895b, 1895c). A report on his brief work along the lower St. Johns and on the Atlantic coast was privately printed in 1896, but this edition is very rare. Fortunately it has been reprinted (Moore, 1922a, 1922b, 1922c).[21]

Moore's contributions in the St. Johns region are perhaps the most significant of all his work in the Southeast. It certainly represents vigorous analysis in contrast to the simple descriptive nature of much of his later work.

[21] The material collected by Moore is now found in a number of institutions. That from his first work, in the St. Johns shell heaps, was deposited at the Wagner Free Institute of Science, Philadelphia, where it is still on display. The bulk of the material from his later work, particularly the more unique specimens, were deposited in the Academy of Natural Sciences, Philadelphia. A few years ago this collection was obtained by the Museum of the American Indian, Heye Foundation, where it is now on display and in storage. The third major group of Moore specimens is in the Robert S. Peabody Foundation, Andover, Massachusetts.

However, Clarence Moore was generous in distributing his material and there is scarcely a major or minor contemporary institution that did not receive some specimens from him. These include the American Museum of Natural History, the Charleston Museum, Chicago Museum of Natural History, Davenport Academy of Science, Harvard Peabody Museum, Milwaukee Public Museum, Royal Ontario Museum, University Museum (Pennsylvania), United States National Museum, Yale Peabody Museum, and others.

Moore's position is a peculiar one. He is alternately condemned or praised by present workers, both amateur and professional. In terms of his period, though, he was considered good—a competent worker whose results were respected (Putnam, 1896). Although our present standards are more critical, we cannot casually dismiss Moore's work. By using his publications and specimens with care, considerable information can be derived from them. He was a careful recorder and a cautious interpreter, but one who was, nevertheless, willing to back his postulates. Considering the problem from another viewpoint, it is quite probable that if Moore had not excavated the sites he did, many would have been lost to science through the efforts of treasure hunters and pothunters.

Aside from the mere recording of data, some of Moore's postulates have been important and have stood the test of time. These include the recognition of historic as well as prehistoric burial mounds, proof of the existence of prehistoric Indian dogs, the confirmation and further elaboration of Wyman's stratigraphy, and the recognition of the prehistoric use of copper (Moore, 1903a). These points are all accepted as a matter of course now, but in the 1890's they were sources of controversy.

As a by-product of this work, Harrison Allen described and discussed crania obtained by Moore (Allen, 1896) and W. H. Holmes wrote a paper on Moore's pottery finds (Holmes, 1894). The ware classifications of this paper are still basic to any pottery study in the area. Holmes' ideas about pottery and its value as a chronological time marker were far ahead of his period. In Holmes' later general paper on eastern United States pottery he again discusses material from this region (Holmes, 1903).

As in the years following Wyman, there was a similar period after Moore's time when the sole work in the area consisted of brief descriptive papers usually by amateurs (Webb, 1894; Brower, 1906; Butler, 1917). Some brief attention was focussed on the Hernandez site near Ormond (now the Cotten site) when bones of the extinct Auk were found there (Blatchley, 1902; Hay, 1902; Hitchcock, 1902). The significance of this find, however, was not appreciated and such a ridiculous explanation as that of F. H. Lucas (1903) went unchallenged. He attributed their presence to preserved birds brought down from northern regions as food by early Europeans and traded to the Florida Indians. The indubitable occurrence of the finds in a fiber-tempered pottery horizon would have made this explanation valueless to any interested contemporary archeologist—but none seem to have considered the problem.

Indications of stratigraphy constantly attracted the attention of students here. Both Wyman and Moore found clear cut evidences of ceramic changes on the St. Johns, but it was Gleck (1894) who first noted them on the coast. His accounts are vague but appear to indicate a real stratigraphic situation.

However, it remained for N. C. Nelson, fresh from his new stratigraphic ceramic approach in the Southwest, definitely to point out a ceramic sequence at Oak Hill on the Atlantic Coast. This was done by controlled collecting from the exposed face of a shell mound being removed for road metal (Nelson, 1918).

As in other parts of Florida, there was little interest in archeology during the 1920's, but here, as elsewhere, the botanist John K. Small made numerous references to archeological sites in his many descriptive papers (Small, 1920, 1921, 1923a, 1923b, 1925, 1927, 1929).

Mrs. Zelia Wilson Sweett, an interested amateur archeologist, recovered a large collection of artifacts from sites in the vicinity of New Smyrna which were being removed for their shell content. She generously helped various interested individuals, such as Amos W. Butler and N. C. Nelson, in their work and prepared one paper which includes archeological data (Sweett and Marsden, 1925).

The various Federal relief projects of the 1930's had both a direct and indirect effect on the archeology of the area. One Smithsonian project, under the direction of Jesse Jennings, excavated a site at Ormond (Stirling, 1935). Both as part of his special interest in Florida and in his supervisory capacity over the Federal archeological project, Matthew W. Stirling visited the area, making collecting trips around DeLand. This familiarity with the region was undoubtedly of aid in his formulation of a "St. Johns Area," a concept basically the same as used in this paper (Stirling, 1936).

Indirectly Federal projects affected archeology in the Ocala National Forest. Here, members of the Civilian Conservation Corps made numerous excavations in their spare time, gathering a large number of artifacts which were eventually deposited in the United States National Museum. Three mimeographed papers give brief accounts of their work and simple drawings of many of the specimens (Abshire et al., 1935; Potter and Taylor, 1937a; Potter and Taylor, 1937b). Fortunately the men ceased their digging when they realized the extent of their inexperience in archeology. Nevertheless, they did rescue valuable information and specimens from sites being destroyed for their shell content.

During 1939 and 1940 excavations were made by W. J. Winter in St. Augustine. Sponsored by the St. Augustine Restoration Society and the National Park Service, the work was carried out in the older parts of the city and in the moat of Castillo de San Marcos. Abundant Indian material was revealed in association with Colonial artifacts (Smith, 1948).

A possible association of an artifact with extinct mammal remains was reported at Bon Terra farm about 29 miles south of St. Augustine (Connery, 1932). Further investigation by E. B. Howard (1940) failed to verify the find and did not reveal any other artifacts, although numerous mammal bones were found.

For some years members of the Florida Historical Society have been interested in archeology and eventually in 1939 an archeology committee was formed within that organization. To date their one project of interest to us is a detailed mapping of sites on the south end of Fort George Island (Winter, 1940: 168-9).

About this same time Vernon Lamme, former State archeologist, conducted some excavations at Marineland in connection with a commercial archeological exhibit. This work does not appear to have been either of an extensive or intensive nature (Lamme, 1941).

The contemporary period of modern archeological study in this region begins with James B. Griffin's reappraisal of the St. Johns region in connection with broader problems of the Southeast (J. B. Griffin, 1945a, 1946). In addition he defined the more important pottery types in the region, bringing to attention the significant early occupation of the region by users of fiber-tempered pottery (J. B. Griffin, 1945b). The chron-

	NORTHWEST GULF COAST AREA	CENTRAL GULF COAST AND MANATEE REGIONS	GLADES AREA	INDIAN RIVER AREA	NORTHERN ST. JOHNS	CENTRAL FLORIDA
1800	Seminole	Seminole	Seminole	Seminole	Seminole	Seminole
1700	Leon-Jefferson		Glades III c	St. Augustine	St. Augustine	Potano
1600		Safety Harbor			II c	
1500	Fort Walton		Glades III b		II b	Alachua
1400				Malabar II		
1300	Weeden Island II	Weeden Island II	Glades III a		St. Johns II a	Hickory Pond
1200						
1100						
1000	Weeden Island I	Weeden Island I	Glades II c		St. Johns I a	Cades Pond
900						
800			Glades II b, late			
700				Malabar I'		
600		Santa Rosa-Swift Creek	II b, early			Pre-Cades Pond
500	Santa Rosa-Swift Creek				St. Johns I a, late	
400						
300		Perico Island	Glades II a			
200						
100						
0					St. Johns I a, early	
100		Deptford ---?---	Glades I			
200	Deptford			Malabar I	Orange late	
300						
400		?	?		---?---	↑
500						S a n t a
600						
700						
800	Orange?	Orange?		Orange	Orange	Orange
900						F e
1000						
1100						C o
1200						m p
1300						l e
1400						x
1500						
1600						Preceramic
1700	Preceramic?		Pre-Glades (Preceramic)			
1800				Mt. Taylor	Mt. Taylor	
		Suwannee Points?				Suwannee Points?

FIG. 2. Areas and Periods of Culture in Florida.

ological culture picture presented by Griffin has been adopted by Martin, Quimby, and Collier (1947).

Renewed interest in other phases of Southeastern archeology, particularly the Southern cult, has also focused attention on the St. Johns region. Waring and Holder (1945) discuss Southern cult objects from the area, recalling affiliations noted previously by Webb and Dodd (1939).

Modern excavations in the regions were only begun in 1947 by John B. Griffin and Hale G. Smith of the Florida Park Service. Their work consisted of site surveys and surface collecting in Volusia County and excavations in three sites—the Cotten site, an early fiber-tempered pottery site; Nocoroco, a late prehistoric and historic site (Griffin and Smith, 1949); and Green Mound, a large shell midden occupied in St. Johns I and II times (J. W. Griffin, 1948a, 1948b).

A small stratigraphic test was made late in 1947 by Lois Watkins, a University of Florida student, at Kauffman's Island, Lake Kerr, in the Ocala National Forest. The results of this work were so promising that further stratigraphic tests were made in the fall of 1948 (Watkins, MSb).

In an endeavor to obtain details of Seminole archeology, the University of Florida commenced excavations in 1949 at Stokes Landing (Goggin, 1949b). This is the site of Spaldings Lower Store, a late eighteenth century trading post for Seminoles residing in the vicinity and to the west. In 1950 and 1951 stratigraphic tests were dug at Fort San Francisco de Pupo (Goggin, 1951). Rounding out the University's program of historic archeology, test excavations were also made in 1950 and 1951 at Rollestown, revealing a long sequence of occupation from Mt. Taylor to St. Augustine times.

A graduate student, Miss Lillian Seaberg, has been studying the "Fountain of Youth" site organizing notes made when an historic cemetery was uncovered there some years ago. Stratigraphic tests in the adjacent midden have yielded background data (Seaberg, MS).

In addition to the excavations noted, we conducted intensive site surveys and made surface collections around St. Augustine and on the St. Johns south of Palatka, and at the same time covered superficially the whole area from Cooks Ferry on the south to Amelia Island on the north. This has resulted in the discovery of many new sites, some with surface sherd and artifact collections of several thousand specimens, affording much new data for analysis. In some cases these data have given information for poorly known periods and in other cases, such as at Mt. Royal, they have widened our viewpoint of a site known for its burial mound material.

A summary of the archeology of the region has been included by the author in a paper covering the entire state (Goggin, 1947). The present report represents a further development of that project. An unpublished summary, similar to that prepared by the author, has been written by John W. Griffin, who has also prepared a ceramic chronological analysis of several coastal sites (J. W. Griffin, 1948a). The prehistoric cultural traditions found in the area are summarized by the writer in a paper presented at the Rollins Conference on Florida prehistory (Goggin, 1949a). Temporal charts incorporating successive revised conceptions of the culture sequence in the region have appeared since the 1947 summary (Goggin, 1948c, 1950a). The latter is reproduced here with changes as Figure 2.

CULTURAL SEQUENCE

DEVELOPMENT OF CHRONOLOGY

THE following discussion of the archeology is presented in terms of temporal periods which are also considered to be cultural or subcultural units as the case may be. This is in accordance with previous practice in Florida (Willey and Woodbury, 1942: 238; Willey, 1949b; Goggin, 1947: 116; Rouse, 1951).

In view of the fact that there are few modern stratigraphic excavations in the region, and that they do not reveal the complete sequence, it is perhaps worthwhile to discuss the method by which the present chronology was developed. As presented here, it represents a combination of sequences found by several workers plus information derived from a seriation of burial mound sites.

Table 2 shows in simple form the "periods," "cultures," "horizons," or ceramic differences noted by various early workers. These are chronologically arranged from left to right, with my first combined sequence on the right. The earliest student, Wyman, clearly noted non-pottery levels underlying pottery-bearing strata. He also recognized the differences between the different basic pottery wares, but seemed to have little awareness of their chronological position, although he did recognize certain geographical distinctions in pottery distribution, especially the greater frequency of sand-tempered pottery (with its accompanying complicated-stamped designs) on the lower St. Johns River.

Somewhat later Moore was able stratigraphically to define fiber-tempered pottery as being early in contrast to chalky ware pottery. Even more important, he was able to prove that fiber-tempered pottery is nowhere associated with burial mounds except accidentally and to show that burial mounds were a later trait than fiber-tempered pottery because of the chalky ware pottery in that type of site (Moore, 1894b: 212–13).

Nelson in 1918 demonstrated the superimposition of check-stamped over plain chalky ware pottery. Underlying the latter was a non-ceramic horizon.

The final sequence on the right in Table 2 is a combination of the previous three. Here is a reconstructed sequence of horizons as follows: preceramic, fiber-tempered pottery, plain chalky ware, and check-stamped chalky ware. Modern excavations corroborate this sequence in part. The Cotten site excavation on the Halifax river (J. W. Griffin, 1948a: 51) and the Kauffman's Island excavation (Watkins, MSb) both reveal a sequence of fiber-tempered pottery overlain by check-stamped chalky ware.[1] An identical sequence was found at South Indian Field in the Indian River region (Ferguson, 1951). Deep stratigraphic tests at Spaldings Lower Store reveal a similar situation with fiber-tempered material under check-stamped pottery, capped by historic material, and this is even better demonstrated at Rollestown and the "Fountain of Youth" site (Seaberg, MS).

At this point the sequence of preceramic, fiber-tempered ware, and check-stamped chalky ware horizons seems well established. However, the existence of a plain chalky

---

[1] At these sites plain chalky ware accompanies the check-stamped type, but a horizon characterized by the former type alone cannot be distinguished.

ware horizon preceding the check-stamped chalky ware horizon was at first based only on Nelson's Oak Hill sequence. To the south though, Rouse (1951) has been able to demonstrate the existence of a similar plain chalky ware horizon between the fiber-tempered pottery and check-stamped chalky ware horizons in the Indian River area. This gives considerable support to the existence of such a period here. The Rollestown and Spaldings Lower Store excavations also support this separation; at both sites plain chalky ware has a high frequency point below the maximum concentration of check-stamped chalky ware.

Final evidence for the local existence of such a period has been found by a detailed study and seriation of the sand mounds excavated by Clarence B. Moore. These were all known to be from post-fiber-tempered times both because of their occasional superimposition on sites of that horizon and because of the absence of any fiber-tempered pottery in sand mounds.

A careful analysis of the contents of the sand mounds indicated that some contained check-stamped chalky ware while others lacked this pottery, although containing an

TABLE 2. DEVELOPMENT OF CHRONOLOGY

Wyman	Moore	Nelson	Combined
Ceramic (including check-stamped chalky ware and fiber-tempered pottery)	Chalky ware pottery	Check-stamped chalky ware pottery	Check-stamped chalky ware pottery
		Plain chalky ware pottery	Plain chalky ware pottery
	Fiber-tempered pottery		Fiber-tempered pottery
Preceramic	Preceramic	Preceramic	Preceramic

abundance of plain chalky ware. Certain exotic specimens in these latter mounds could be correlated with similar materials found on the Florida Northwest Gulf Coast.

There, a sequence of Santa Rosa-Swift Creek, Weeden Island I, and Weeden Island II periods is recognized (Willey and Woodbury, 1942; Willey, 1949b). The latter horizon is distinguished by an abundance of check-stamped pottery and a relative absence of complicated-stamped pottery. The first two of these horizons have an abundance of complicated-stamped pottery, but the second lacks check-stamped pottery. Distinctive ceramic specimens, as well as exotic Hopewellian copper objects, indicated a contemporaneity of many of the plain chalky ware sites of the St. Johns River with the Santa Rosa-Swift Creek and Weeden Island I periods. Other mounds in the Northern St. John Region which contained check-stamped pottery were correlated with Weeden Island II. Thus it appears from the total sum of evidence that the existence of a plain chalky ware horizon in the Northern St. Johns Region is substantiated, although detailed stratigraphic evidence is not yet available.

The first basic sequence discussed here appears in a summary paper on the archeology of the whole state (Goggin, 1947). At that time most of the horizons were given culture names. The earliest period was simply called "non-ceramic," but the following fiber-tempered pottery horizon was named "Tick Island" because of the concept advanced by James B. Griffin (1945b) that Tick Island Incised pottery was the important fiber-tempered pottery type of the region in contrast to Orange Incised, thought to be more important in the Indian River region to the south. The plain chalky ware period was called St. Johns I and the subsequent check-stamped chalky ware horizon, St. Johns II.

After the first draft of that paper was written, the monumental survey of Eastern archeology by James B. Griffin (1946) appeared. This paper, written several years previous to publication, presented a sequence for the St. Johns River area of the following periods, from late to early:

> Mount Royal
> Murphy Island
> Racey Point
> Tick Island

These four periods were similar to those proposed by myself. Tick Island is the same as my horizon of that name, but both Racey Point and Murphy Island fall within the St. Johns I Period. Mount Royal was coeval with or included within St. Johns II.

Subsequently, in a more detailed analysis of the archeology of the whole state, my cultural sequence was even more modified (Goggin, MSa, 1948c, 1949a, 1950a). It is used as the basic framework in this paper and reads as follows, from late to early:

> St. Augustine
> St. Johns II a, b, and c
> St. Johns I a, early; a, late; and b
> Orange
> Mt. Taylor

The Mt. Taylor Period is the preceramic horizon, while the term Orange replaces Tick Island for the fiber-tempered and early incised chalky ware horizon. St. Johns I remains the same but has been divided into three parts, two of which correspond to James B. Griffin's Racey Point and Murphy Island periods. St. Johns II has been divided into three parts and in addition a terminal part has been separated as the St. Augustine Period on the basis of new evidence presented by Hale G. Smith (1948). This period has been culturally substantiated by our surface surveys and stratigraphically placed above St. Johns II by excavations at Rollestown

MT. TAYLOR PERIOD

The Mt. Taylor Period is the earliest era of occupation on the St. Johns River. Previously this has been simply known as the preceramic or non-ceramic horizon (Goggin, 1947: 123), although James B. Griffin (1946, Fig. 2) included it in his Tick Island Focus.[2] However, my previous distinction between non-pottery and pottery periods

---

[2] The term Tick Island Culture is also used by Martin, Quimby and Collier (1947: 391) to include "Tick Island," a pre-pottery horizon, and "Late Tick Island," a fiber-tempered horizon. The use of the name Tick Island is not very appropriate for the preceramic level since only the fiber-tempered horizon is recognized at the Tick Island site.

still seems valid and the name Mt. Taylor has been given to the pre-pottery horizon on the St. Johns. This term is taken from the site of that name, from which the greatest amount of cultural data for this horizon are available.

Little modern archeological work has been done in sites of this period; nevertheless, the data of the pioneer workers are fairly clear and useful, although limited. Jeffries Wyman (1868a, 1875) first pointed out the presence of sites, or levels within sites, which lacked pottery. Clarence B. Moore followed this lead and carefully demonstrated that there were sites in which pottery could be shown to be present only in parts (Moore, 1892c, 1893, 1894b, 1894c). Although he did not dig with a system of arbitrary levels, he nevertheless noted by measurement, in a number of sites, the extreme depth at which he found pottery. This varied from the surface foot or so at some sites to the bottom and various intermediate depths at others. It is on the work of these men that the present summary for the period is mainly based. Their published reports and museum specimens have been studied and analyzed.

On the east coast, stratigraphic work of N. C. Nelson (1918) at Oak Hill indicated a preceramic horizon which preceded plain pottery and check-stamped pottery periods. This non-ceramic period should be correlated with the Mt. Taylor Period and is probably only a coastal extension of that culture.

Recent work bearing on this problem includes a surface survey by A. J. Waring (letter to Irving Rouse, 7/4/44). There are also suggestions that this horizon underlies the Kauffman Island site recently tested by Lois Watkins (MSb).

Most sites of the period are freshwater shell middens, which are situated close to the banks of the St. Johns River or its tributaries. Sites occur from a point not far north of Palatka well up the river, beyond the limits of the area and into the Indian River region (Rouse, 1951). Most of the sites are fairly large, covering several thousand square feet of surface and ranging from 6 or 8 to 15 or more feet in thickness.

Middens are composed of the shells of Ampullaria, Paludina, and sometimes Unio, plus varying amounts of sand, humus, ashes, and bones of most of the locally found mammals, reptiles, birds, and fish. There is some stratification in the deposits but it apparently has little cultural significance. Hearth areas are marked by fire places (undescribed) and lenses of compacted crushed shell, but in other parts of the sites the shell may be loosely deposited. In parts of many shell heaps, usually near the bottom, there are levels or lenticular masses of breccia formed by the consolidation of the midden material which is cemented by lime leached from other material by acidic ground water. The Ampullaria and Paludina found in sites and levels of this horizon are of the small size (Goggin, 1948b).

The material possibly dating from this horizon at Kauffman Island lies in a sand matrix accompanied by a few fragments of animal bone. This possible horizon at Oak Hill is found in a typical refuse deposit of that region—a predominantly oyster shell midden.

Judging from the material remains found, the cultural complex must have been simple, with a general scarcity of artifacts as well as few defined forms. Neither Moore nor Wyman described materials from this horizon in any detail and not all specimens mentioned by them could be located in their collections. The following summary of artifacts is based on the few specimens examined and published descriptions of others, which are not usually precise. Only those artifacts were considered in this analysis which were positively placed in a non-pottery horizon by the finders. Mt. Taylor and Horse Landing had the largest number of specimens.

Chipped stone points are some of the most abundant objects cited for the period, 16 specimens or fragments being noted. No particular form is common, but most are medium to large sized variants of stemmed triangular points. The form is usually crude and often asymetrical (Moore, 1893, Fig. 3; 1894c, Figs. 2–6). A single "bunt" or stemmed scraper is noted (Moore, 1893, Fig. 1). A square-shaped flint blade from the base of the Horse Landing site may be the oldest specimen recognizable in this period (Wyman, 1868, Pl. 10: 10; 1875, Pl. 2: 7). Another large blade or scraper is illustrated by Moore (1893, Fig. 2).

Miscellaneous stonework includes a flint hammerstone and a smoothed piece of coquina. The latter was probably a grinding stone for shaping shell or bone tools. An unusual specimen from the site two miles north of Palatka is a "small piece of greenstone cut into the form of a pyramid" (Moore, 1893: 9).

Shell implements were not abundant but four Busycon gouges are reported. Two of these have been examined and there seems little question about the identification of the others called "shell gouge" and "triangular shell chisel" respectively.

Bone objects were fairly numerous but the references are so vague that they are of little help. They include 14 "bone awls" or fragments, 5 "bone implements," 2 pieces of "worked bone," 1 fragment of "sawed bone," and a shaped tooth. Splinter awls come from the northern site on Huntoon Creek and the shell midden two miles north of Palatka. Some of the "awls" or "implements" may be bone pins; in fact two bone pins are in the Moore collection and catalogued from Mt. Taylor. One is incised and the other has an unusual carved top, but it seems odd that Moore did not figure them or at least comment on them as he so usually did with specimens of interest. A sawed and broken antler fragment is illustrated by Wyman (1875, Pl. 2: 3). A long bone projectile point and parts of other bone points or possible bone pin fragments are in the collection from the shell midden two miles north of Palatka.

Ornaments, except for possible bone pins, were scarce. A grooved shell pendant was found at Mt. Taylor (Moore, 1893, Fig. 4) only 1.5 feet below the surface. It may pertain to a later occupation. The drilled mammal phalange from Horse Landing (Wyman, 1868, Fig. 7; 1875, Pl. 4: 5) may have been an ornament.

The absence of certain objects is worthy of comment. Both Wyman (1875: 58) and Moore (1893: 720–1) definitely state that whole shell, Busycon picks or tools are not found in the early shell heaps, a term they use for this period.[3] Wyman (1875: 57) also comments on the absence of Busycon dippers. Neither Wyman nor Moore mention the presence of steatite vessels in pre-pottery times. Nevertheless the possibility that they were present cannot be dismissed since they occur in the following Orange Period and, although Moore collected steatite sherds, he makes no references to them in his work on the fiber-tempered pottery horizon.

[3] It should be noted, though, that a possible Busycon pick X came from a preceramic level at Kauffman Island (Watkins, MSb).

Data clearly indicate that part of midden 2 at Salt Springs Run was occupied in this period. In view of the large collection of artifacts from this site it is perhaps significant to list the types, although it is not known which came from the Mt. Taylor horizon: chipped stone points, chipped stone scraper, hammerstone, bannerstones, Busycon gouge, Strombus celt, short bone projectile point, socketed antler point, bone awl or pin fragments, bone bead, incised bone fragment, perforated columella pendant, and circular Busycon gorgets (1-, 2-, and 4-central-hole types).

Burials were made in middens. Remains of two skeletons were found "mingled" at a depth of 9 feet in the Osceola Mound. One femur showed evidence of sawing (Wyman, 1875: 63). The skull from here is of interest because it appears to be of a long-headed form, although the specimen should be reconstructed and re-measured (Wyman, 1875: 64–5).

Because of the scarcity of good camping or dwelling spots along the river most sites have been occupied many times, as the following list will indicate:

Only three sites are reported to have no pottery at all: La 32, Vo 44, Se 5.

Sites with pottery only on the surface or in the surface loam are most common and include: Pu 4, Pu 27, Mr 2, La 16, Vo 19, La 36.

Several sites have pottery only in the upper two feet: Vo 4, Vo 7.

Another group of sites have pottery in the upper parts but none in the lower two-thirds or one-half: La 21, Vo 125.[4]

Two sites appear to have no pottery in the very bottom levels: Pu 64, Mr 40.

ORANGE PERIOD

This horizon, characterized by the use of fiber-tempered pottery, has been previously called the Tick Island Period (Goggin, 1947). It was thought that a form of fiber-tempered pottery, Tick Island Incised (J. B. Griffin, 1945), was characteristic of the area, distinguishing it from a region using Orange Incised pottery to the south. However, more detailed study indicates that Orange Incised is also typical of this region with Tick Island Incised a minor form occurring in only 6 sites[5] (out of 46 early Orange Period sites) and usually associated with Orange Incised. In all places it is a rare form and even at the type site it is not as abundant as Orange Incised. Therefore, the term Orange Period, used for the culture to the south (Fig. 2) has been extended to this area.

The population was mainly concentrated on fresh water shell middens along the St. Johns River, with a sparse population on the east coast. The greatest concentration of

[4] Although this site (Oak Hill) is included here as dating in part from the preceramic horizon, it is possible that such an apparent occupation may be the result of a small sample rather than a true lack of pottery. The total sherd sample from the site is not large, and the section thought to be preceramic is not extensive. The presence of oyster shells as the dominant material in this part of the midden also tends to suggest an error in dating. If our evidence from other sites along the coastal lagoons is correct, oysters did not appear until St. Johns I times, being absent in the Orange Period (Goggin, 1948b). Of course a fluctuating environment, with oysters in the Mt. Taylor Period and no oysters in the Orange Period, followed by the return of oysters in St. Johns I times is possible, but we have no other evidence for it.

[5] These are Bluffton, Mt. Royal, Enterprise, Tick Island Midden, Black Hammock, and Silver Glen Spring Midden.

sites is in subareas II and IV. In subarea I, the prehistoric levels of Forts San Carlos and Pupo, St. Johns Bluff, Clay Bluff, Fort George Island, Shellbluff Landing, Wrights Landing, South of Wrights Landing, the "Fountain of Youth" site, Crescent Beach Bridge, and Summer Haven were occupied; while in subarea III the Cotten site is definitely of this culture, and Rock House Mound shows some evidence of occupation at this time.[6]

The criteria used as diagnostics of the period are the following pottery types: Orange Plain, Orange Incised, St. Johns Incised, and Tick Island Incised. Although exact stratigraphic evidence of their relationship is lacking in this region it is assumed that the first three have the same relationship as in the Indian River area (Ferguson, 1951; Rouse, 1951), where Orange Plain and Orange Incised are present for an extensive period with St. Johns Incised and St. Johns Plain following for a briefer period. The temporal relation of Tick Island Incised to Orange Incised is not clear; James B. Griffin (1945: 222) once suggested that it is later. As he now recognizes (Sears and Griffin, 1950), if such were true, the St. Johns Incised motifs should be like Tick Island; instead they are more like Orange Incised.

A problem of culture terminology should be discussed here. In this paper I have designated the time when St. Johns Incised (and its accompanying St. Johns Plain) is found as the last stage of the Orange Period. In the neighboring Indian River region where a similar sequence is present, Rouse (1951) makes a different cultural division. He considers St. Johns Plain and St. Johns Incised as the markers for the beginning of a new major culture unit, Malabar I (equal to Orange late) and the precursor of the Malabar I' period (the Indian River equivalent of St. Johns I).

In part, this difference in terminology is taxonomic. Rouse and I recognize generally similar ceramic sequences, but emphasize different criteria in naming our periods. Rouse (1951) feels that the change in ceramic ware is most significant, whereas I consider it more important that the incised designs survived the transition from Orange to St. Johns ware and that the ultimate disappearance of these designs coincides with the arrival of sand mounds in the Northern St. Johns Area. Throughout this study my major period distinctions have been partially based on ceramic factors and partially on other cultural factors, in this case sand burial mounds. In contrast, Rouse (1951) consistently uses ceramic traits to distinguish his periods. It is hoped that my inconsistency with respect to the ceramic factor is justified by an attempt to evaluate other cultural aspects.

There may, however, also be a factual basis for the difference in terminology. In the Indian River Area, Rouse (1951) bases his sequence on the situation at South Indian Field, where a layer containing only Orange Plain and Orange Incised pottery underlies one with only St. Johns Plain and St. Johns Incised. Ferguson (1951), too, obtained indications of a sharp break between Orange and St. Johns pottery at South Indian Field. The writer, looking at the same material, admittedly with a less intimate acquaintanceship, is not so impressed with the evidence for an abrupt change.

[6] South Canal may possibly be included if the presence of a doubtful St. Johns Incised vessel is used as a criterion.

In the Northern St. Johns Area, the writer lacks a stratigraphically detailed situation similar to that found at South Indian Field. Nevertheless, the broad mass of material suggests a gradual ceramic change with much experimentation producing fiber-tempered chalky ware and fiber-tempered gritty ware before fiber tempering was finally abandoned. Drawing a line on the basis of ceramic paste is indeed difficult.

The question of decoration is another matter. It appears that the designs originated on Orange Incised and continued through various fiber-tempered experiments with chalky and gritty wares onto pure chalky ware, St. Johns Incised. When these incised designs disappeared there was no other common decorated pottery in the region for many years. Coincidental with their disappearance was the appearance of sand burial mounds.

Shell middens are the best known sites of this culture. Those on the St. Johns River are composed of freshwater gastropod and pelecypod shells plus other refuse such as ashes, sand, and animal bones. Many of the sites represent continuation of earlier middens, which in turn were occupied by later peoples. Exact measurements are not available, but some middens cover several acres and may be many feet thick. The only coastal midden from which detailed data are available is the Cotten site (formerly the Hernandez site). This is a large site with 12 feet of deposits mainly coquina (*Donax variabilis*) shells. Evidence suggests this shell was the main form of molluscan food available at this time, and for that reason the coast was relatively unoccupied until later times when changing ecological conditions favored the growth of oysters in the coastal lagoons (Goggin, 1948*b*). Crescent Beach Bridge midden is also formed of coquina shell and dates in part from this time. Material from Shellbluff Landing, Wrights Landing, and South of Wrights Landing (all midden areas with abundant oyster shells) was picked up on the beach, not *in situ*. However, the deep water of North River may not have been effected by sea-level stages significant for oyster growth in the shallower lagoons to the south, or the oysters may be wholly due to later occupation.

On the other hand the situation at those sites might, on excavation, turn out to be similar to the "Fountain of Youth" site. Here, an extensive oyster-shell midden with later material overlays Orange refuse in a sand matrix (Seaberg, MS).

Refuse in sand also appears on the St. Johns River, in all cases in the lower levels of sites with other periods of occupation. These are Fort Pupo, Rollestown, and Spaldings Lower Store.

The analysis of the Orange Period sites, and sections of sites occupied in Orange times, has not been satisfactory. Since most specimens were not excavated in a manner permitting the cultural segregation of the materials, it is difficult to draw conclusions about the total artifact complex, much less the non-artifactual features. Non-ceramic artifacts which can with confidence be assigned to this period include Busycon gouges, Strombus celts, a possible columella chisel, a thin grinding stone, bone awls, plain and incised bone pins, bone projectile points and incised turtle bones. Steatite vessel fragments occur in three sites of multiple occupancy, and in one site certainly of this culture, but it is probable that most examples pertain to this period. The large collection from the Cotten site, which has only been briefly described (J. W. Griffin, 1948*a*), will add considerable to our knowledge of the period. However, we can assume that Orange Period traits of the Indian River Area were probably present in our area.[7]

One artifact type can be discussed as a possible marker for the period. This is a form of incised bone pin with an intricate angular geometric design of numerous parallel lines, many of which are bordered with small ticks.[8] One pin fragment has been stratigraphically placed in this horizon at the Cotten site and another comes from Ginns Grove (Pl. 8, s). A similar example occurs at South Indian Field in the Indian River Region (Rouse, 1951). Incised turtle bone, covered with a detailed maze-like design of lines was found at the Cotten site. This was a fragment of a large worked piece of unknown function. A similar specimen dates from the same time at South Indian Field (Rouse, 1951). Busycon pick X has not been noted in the above list but possible examples come from the Cotten site and Kauffman Island.

Weaving is definitely known at this period, judging from a few textile impressed sherds. They indicate both plaiting or twilling as well as a twined textile. In one instance the former appears to be a mat made of narrow splints woven in a four-over four-under herringbone pattern (Pl. 1, B). The twined textile consists of a number of broad elements held together by widely separated, knotted traverse elements (Pl. 1, D).

Midden burials have not been found in any sites, but in view of their extensive occurrence directly to the south (Rouse, 1951) it is probable that they will also be found here. Human bones in the Old Site, Eaton Creek (Abshire et al., 1935: 24) may date from this horizon. Putnam (1896) refers to a cranial specimen from the Hawkinsville Midden which may pertain to this time level.

Of the 53 sites recognized (including two questionable ones) most were also occupied either previous to this period or subsequently. In the following tabulation of sites the term *late* will be applied to sites at which St. Johns Incised is present, while the term *early* will be equated with the presence of the fiber-tempered types.

The following sites were occupied only in the Orange Period: Pu 26, Pu 40, SJ 46.

In the following sites an important part, but not all of the occupation was in the Orange Period: Na 10 (early), Du 5 (early), SJ 32 (early), SJ 33 (early), SJ 31 (early), SJ 43 (early), Du 41 (early), Pu 8 (early and late), Pu 18 (early), Pu 64 (early), Mr 2 (early), La 2 (early and late), Vo 22 (early and late), Vo 24 (early and late), Vo 29 (early and late), Vo 30 (late), La 26 (early ?), La 28 (early and late), La 34 (early and late), Vo 55 (early and late), Se 6 (late), Se 11 (early and late), Vo 62 (early), Vo 83 (early), Mr 13 (early), Mr 14 (early), Mr 16 (early and late), Mr 26 (early and late), Mr 27 (early), Mr 40 (early and late).

Occupation in some sites at this period was short or temporary, or in any case is indicated by relatively few sherds, often only a single sherd. These sites are: SJ 1 (early), SJ 3 (early), Du 8 (early and late), Cl 10 (early), Pu 4 (early), Pu 23 (early), Pu 35 (early and late), Pu 46 or Pu 47 (early), Mr 4 (early), Vo 4 (late), La 17 (late) La 29 (early and late), Vo 34 (late), La 39 (late), Vo 42 (early and late), Se 9 (early), Se 12 (early), Se 13 (early?), Vo 101 (early), Vo 113 (late).

[7] In addition to certain of the above-mentioned artifacts, stemmed flint points and numerous steatite vessel sherds, some with incised lips, were also present at South Indian Field. A red jasper tubular bead from a mixed culture level may pertain either to the Orange or a later horizon (Ferguson, 1951).

[8] The use of ticks is diagnostic, since geometric designs on bone pins have an extensive time range in Florida.

Several of the sites in the last group perhaps should not be included, as the presence of Orange Period pottery is probably fortuitous. The Orange Incised sherd (H.P.M. 74-26/12681-4) in the Cooks Ferry Mound (Se 13) is probably accidental.

ST. JOHNS I PERIOD

Following the Orange Period, interest in pottery decoration by incision declined, although a new development of red slipping became widespread.[9] Some local incised and stamped forms occur but they are relatively rare, and an important proportion of the decorated material is either direct trade ware from the west or local copies. Because of the lack of distinctive local forms, it is not easy on the basis of available collections to point out midden sites occupied at this time.

Stratigraphic evidence for the period has been shown at Oak Hill (Nelson, 1918), Green Mound (J. W. Griffin, 1948a), and at sites in the Indian River Area (Rouse, 1951). This clearly indicates a predominantly plain chalky ware period preceding the extensive development of check-stamped chalky pottery. Moore's work on sand mounds, to be considered in detail, substantiates this.

Doubts have been raised as to why (or how) a cultural development could exist at this time without being influenced by the early expansion of regular and linear check stamping to the north and west. However, these influences did reach the northern St. Johns and imported types, as well as a few local experiments in simple, check, and linear-check stamping on chalky ware, are found; but apparently the local conditions were not favorable at this time for acceptance of check stamping. This subject will be further discussed in another section.

Certain divisions are possible within the period. James B. Griffin, (1946, Fig. 2) first pointed out that Racey Point and Murphy Island represent different horizons. Later a third and final division was noted (Goggin, 1947: 123). On further examination these units still appear to represent different temporal and/or cultural horizons but, rather than indicating local changes of importance, they seem to reflect the more distinctive changes taking place in other parts of the Southeast and Florida. The units can, on the basis of trade items and cross cultural ties, be roughly correlated with three horizons occupying the same general time on the Gulf Coast (Fig. 2). Differences are much less sharp between the first and second, than between those two grouped together and the last. Therefore, two broad subperiods will be made, Ia and Ib, but early and late divisions will be recognized within Ia, and these will be considered as cultural and temporal levels potentially of divisible equality.

Sites of the period include both middens and low sand burial mounds, but few of the former have been recognized on the basis of surface surveys because the distinctive ceramic types are so scarce that they were not obtained in the desultory midden collecting of Wyman and Moore. The burial mounds were often completely excavated, resulting in a more adequate sample. The few middens listed here are included only because of the presence of tetrapod vessel fragments or Deptford series pottery types, except in rare cases where the sample of St. Johns Plain is large enough to suggest that check-stamped pottery was not present.

[9] For a discussion of differences in the interpretation of the beginning of this period, see pp. 44-5.

The distribution of sites is such as to indicate that the population was definitely localized at times. The available data suggest that the main concentration was on the St. Johns with only a few people on the coast. However, it is possible that this reflects our scanty knowledge of the coastal area more than the actual situation. Levels dating from this period are probably present in many of the Atlantic Coast shell heaps.

Of particular interest is the apparent shift in population during the course of the period from the upper St. Johns and Oklawaha rivers (subareas II and IV) to the lower St. Johns (subarea I). Of 16 burial mounds in subareas II and IV only 3 can be ascribed to occupation in Ib times, while of 21 mounds in subarea I, 16 date from Ib times. Five of the sites in subareas II and IV are only tentatively placed within the whole period. There does not seem to be any appreciable cultural variance between these subareas at any given time level.

In the analysis of cultural traits of the period, ceramic types were used to classify sites into the following categories: Ia; Ia, early; Ia, late; Ia and Ib; Ib; I?. However, cultural summaries will be given only for the divisions Ia, early; Ia, late; and Ib.

Certain cultural traits which cannot be handled by subdivisions will be first considered. A study of burial mounds and their associated traits reveals a fairly wide range of size and form, and presence and absence of traits. In terms of the temporal subdivisions used here, none of the variations appear to have much significance. Most mounds are low, only three being 8 feet or more (ranging up to about 12 feet) in height, while 15 are less than 4 feet in elevation, in a series of 31 measured. Mounds are generally truncated cones or low rises, but several are series of intersecting mounds, with both a ridge and a V-shaped mound showing other developments. Intersecting mounds date from Ia, early, and Ib times. Sub-basal excavations were reported in two instances and pockets or stains of hematite were noted in ten cases at all periods.

Data are so incomplete and uneven on burials and burial features that it does not appear significant to present tabulations. Moore did not consistently record features, his excavation methods were not precise, and lastly the skeletal remains were often so decayed, and at times intermixed, that an accurate count or even estimate of numbers was impossible. Interments were most commonly secondary bundle burials, although in some cases, as at Tick Island Mound, all the methods of interment used were not carefully determined. Here, and at two other sites, of Ib times, primary burials accompanied secondary interment. Evidences of cremation were noted in the larger mound at Beauclerc. The number of individuals buried in a site varied from 2 to well over 100, but in general the number was less than 25. However, in view of the problems of preservation these figures are no more than guides. Burial offerings were not commonly placed with the remains, deposition of artifacts throughout the site being more typical. Vessels, when found, were more often killed than not, and both pre-fired and post-fired basal perforations occur.

St. Johns Ia, early. This division is characterized by a majority of St. Johns Plain pottery with Dunns Creek Red as close numerical second in burial sites. St. Johns Plain vessels with tetrapod, and less commonly tripod and bipod, bases are found consistently, although not commonly, and one boat-shaped vessel of this ware is known. Minor local forms include Oklawaha Plain, Oklawaha Incised, and St. Johns Red on Buff. Trade wares include Deptford Linear Check Stamped, Deptford Bold Check Stamped, Deptford Simple Stamped, and an associated cord-marked type. Tetrapodal base forms of the two former types have been found. More significant perhaps are the local attempts at copying these Deptford forms. At Tick Island (both midden and mound) there have been found chalky ware sherds with simple stamping,[10] linear check stamping, and cord marking. These forms are very rare, only 34 sherds occuring among the 661 sherds and vessels from the site, and they appear at few other sites. For this reason it may be best not to give them type names at the present time.

Artifacts other than pottery exhibit a wide variety of forms but in general most are not widespread. Fortunately, the Tick Island Mound gives us a good sample, which can be considered typical of the horizon. Most of the material is ceremonial or ornamental, but tools include stone and Strombus celts, Busycon gouge, stone chisel, extra large socketed bone point, chipped flint points, bone awls, bone needle, and Busycon dippers. Shell ornaments are numerous including beads, columella beads, perforated disks, flat shell pendant, double grooved columella pendant, and an ellipitical shaped ornament. There are also bone pins, quartz plummet pendants, a double grooved stone plummet pendant, and a coral pin. Miscellaneous material includes mica, galena, and two clay elbow pipes. Copper ornaments include a covered mammal jaw, tubular bead, and a covered wooden turtle effigy. A copper disk found near the surface may be intrusive, as the pattern is closer to later forms than those of this period. Clarence B. Moore often refers to potsherds shaped like arrowheads, some of which are noted here. However, the few seen in his collections do not impress one as copies of stone points.

Artifacts from other sites of the period include a shell chisel, Strombus celts, stone chisel, flint points, pebble hammers, mica, and another clay elbow pipe.

St. Johns Ia, late. It is this division which is most difficult to isolate at the present time. As in previous periods, St. Johns Plain is the dominant form, sometimes represented by tetrapod vessels. Dunns Creek Red continues to be important in burial sites, but the Oklawaha types do not appear to be present. Deptford forms are occasionally found, as is early Swift Creek Complicated Stamped pottery. Apparently this horizon equates with the Santa Rosa-Swift Creek period to the west, so it is of interest to see that the site with strongest Hopewell influences, North Mound on Murphy Island, fits in here.

The question of Hopewell contacts or influences in Florida is of considerable general interest and is discussed in other papers (Goggin, MS*a;* 1949*a:* 27, 38). However, certain details bearing on the St. Johns will be considered here. Emerson Greenman (1938) pointed out Hopewellian traits in Florida and noted a number of sites which he considered to be of this period. A further evaluation of data suggests that certain sites which he dates as of this time—Shields Mound, Grant Mound, and Mt. Royal— are in part, if not wholly, later; and one site—Tick Island Mound—appears to be slightly earlier. The data for including Broward Mound are not completely satisfactory, but Greenman compares a vessel from here with Hopewell forms and J. B. Griffin (unpub-

---

[10] Well in St. Johns II times there is another development of simple stamping on this paste. Therefore, it cannot be used as a marker for St. Johns Ia.

lished notes) comments that it is suggestive of the Alexander series of this same general time level. However, its resemblance to the later Englewood series is also strong.

Murphy Island (North Mound) can perhaps be considered typical of the period, although it lacks complicated stamped pottery. St. Johns Plain and Franklin Plain (?) tetrapod vessels do occur. The site itself is unusual in being the largest mound of the whole period, measuring 80 feet in diameter and about 12 feet in height, with the form of a truncated cone. Copper objects are the outstanding specimens from here and include wooden artifacts overlaid with repoussé copper, copper disks, a cymbal-shaped ear spool, a conjoined tube, and a crescent-shaped ornament. At the base of the mound was found a small fragment of iron. This is probably of meteoric origin and is another tie with the Ohio Hopewell to the north.

Other objects include a flanged, spool-shaped clay object; elbow pipes of clay, one a bird effigy; and two unique pendants or ornaments of clay. Shell beads were rare, but stone-pendant ornaments of several types are present including single- and double-grooved stone pendants, grooved quartz crystal, ringed stone tube, and steatite beads. Five shell pins, found within 2.5 feet of the surface, are probably intrusive, as is European trade material found as deep as 3 feet from the surface. Circular Busycon gorgets are present.

As in many mounds of a slightly later date, groups of pebbles, pebble hammers, and flint chips were common. Some of the pebble groups may represent the rattlers from decayed gourd or wood rattles. Stone celts, chipped points, and Busycon dippers were very abundant and Strombus celts, stone hones, worked fossil bone, a hammerstone, a shell bannerstone (?), and mica were also present.

Other sites had little else that is different. Mica or copper is often present, but the copper lance point from Monroe Mound is unusual (Moore, 1895a, Fig. 24).

St. Johns Ib. Late occupation in St. Johns I times is distinguished by trade wares from the west, mainly late variety Swift Creek Complicated Stamped and Weeden Island pottery, including Tucker Ridge Pinched. Together with the lack of check-stamped pottery these forms suggest that this period can be equated with Weeden Island I. St. Johns Plain and Dunns Creek Red are the local forms of pottery.

Most of the common minor artifacts continue to be present including stone celts, chipped points, grinding slabs, stone hones, and hammerstones. Clay elbow pipes are still found, as is mica, but copper seems to be proportionately less common. Pebbles, chips, and pebble hammers occur in many sites.

As is to be expected, certain sites probably range well into the end of the period and perhaps an even later occupation is indicated for some.

Sites of the period. In addition to sites which have been placed in one or more parts of the period there are several others which appear to belong somewhere in the period but lack sufficient data for precise placement. They are indicated on the site list by I?. One of these, Gamble Mound, Ia?, is worth noting because J. B. Griffin (1946: 49) has assigned it to this general period, presumably because of a St. Johns Plain tetrapod vessel fragment. The presence of check-stamped pottery of an unknown type raises a question as to this allocation of the site.

The following list of sites is arranged by subarea. Unless otherwise noted all are sand burial mounds:

Subarea I: Wa 2 (Ia, late), Wa 3 (Ib), Wa 4 (Ib), Du 6 (Ia, early), Du 10 (Ib), Du 11 (Ia), Du 13 (Ia, late to Ib), Du 15 (Ib), Du 19 (Ib), Du 20 (Ia, late), Du 21 (Ia, late), Du 24 (Ib), Du 25 (Ia, late to Ib), Du 31 (Ib), Du 32 (Ib), Du 33 (Ib, very late?), Du 36 (Ib), Du 38 (I?), Du 39 (I), Du 40 (Ib), SJ 25 (Ia, early to Ib). There is a single midden site, SJ 31 (Ia).

Subarea II: Pu 9 (Ib), Pu 20 (Ia, late), Pu 22 (Ia), Pu 38 (I?), La 6 (I?), Vo 14–18 (Ia), Vo 24 (Ia to Ib), Vo 25 (Ia, early), La 25 (Ia), La 34 (Ia), La 36 (I), Vo 41 (I?), Se 4 (Ib), Se 6 (Ia). Two midden sites are Pu 64 (Ia), Pu 23 (Ia).

Subarea III: Vo 125 (I), undescribed sand mounds in coastal Volusia county (personal communication, John W. Griffin).

Subarea IV: Mr 12 (I?), Mr 25 (I?), Mr 33 (Ia to Ib), Mr 39 (I?).

Unclassified complex (?). Three sand mounds excavated in this region exhibit a strong similarity of contents but yet cannot be placed in any of the recognized cultural or temporal classifications. The date of these is not known, although internal evidence suggests that they are somewhat early and so they will be considered within this period.

The first of these sites, on the Atlantic Coast, is Mt. Oswald on the east bank of Tomoka Creek, about two miles from its mouth. The site is a large sand mound situated on the point of a sand ridge. A summit plateau 28 feet in diameter rises 14 feet above the basal ridge. Douglass' excavation removed a large portion of the center of the mound revealing the structure to be composed of sand with occasional coquina shells scattered throughout (Douglass, 1882, 1885: 82). With the exception of two caches of bannerstones "no other objects of interest or importance whatever were found . . . no indication of any burial, nor were there any vessels or fragments of pottery" (Douglass, 1882: 104). One pendant was found on the surface.

The bannerstones were of three forms including five examples of Type 1, one of Type 2, and two of Type 3. A single bannerstone wing pendant was found on the surface of the mound.

Without the usual criterion of pottery it is difficult to date the site, and the scanty material present makes it difficult to determine the mound's function. From its general description there do not appear to be any factors present which would hasten the decay of bones if burials had been present, so unless the mound is of far greater antiquity than seems reasonable, it would appear that no burials were ever placed in the site.

The occurrence of the bannerstones themselves is of little value in interpreting the site. In fact it is not clear whether the artifacts represent intrusive caches or original deposits. Douglass favors the former idea but his evidence is not clear. The largest cache of five bannerstones was found 14 inches deep, about 2 feet northeast of the center of the summit plateau. The second cache was 3 feet below the first.

Bannerstones themselves are known to appear very early in the Southeast, dating back to preceramic times, when they were used as atlatl weights. Typologically, then, they might be early. A relatively early age for the mound itself is suggested by Douglass, who notes the absence of any oyster shells in the mound, while many oyster shells are scattered on the sandy surface around the mound. Presumably they were deposited later than the building of the mound or else some would have been included in the site, as it was apparently constructed of nearby sand.[11]

The other two sand mounds, at Thornhill Lake on the St. Johns River, were excavated by Clarence B. Moore (1894a: 88–9, 1894b: 167–73). The larger, which will be called No. 1, was about 11 feet high, while the smaller, No. 2, was about 9 feet high. Both mounds contained primary burials, over 50 in the first, but only about 7 in the second (not completely dug). With some of the burials were various ornaments, beads, pendants, and several bannerstones.

In Mound 1 five bannerstones were found in association with burials: one of Type 2; three of Type 3 (2 miniature); and one of Type 5. Two pendants were made from broken wings of bannerstones.

Other artifacts included numerous small shell beads which lay along the forearms of burials, some large tubular shell beads, and tubular red stone beads of a material which Moore calls catlinite. These appear, though, to be jasper, as they are quite hard. A double-perforated shark's tooth, a small bone projectile point, and four chipped points make up the other material found.

Three bannerstones were found in Mound 2, all of Type 2. These, lying with shell beads on the breasts of three skeletons, were the only artifacts noted in this mound.

Neither of the mounds can be temporally placed. In the smaller, no sherds were found and in the larger, despite careful attention, only two sherds with "ordinary stamped decoration" were obtained about four feet from the surface. There seems no reason, according to Moore, to believe them intrusive and he postulates an accidental deposition during the course of the mound's construction.

A collection from Coontie Island, in the Matanzas River south of St. Augustine, should perhaps be grouped with material from the three sand mounds.[12] The specimens were washed from the sandy shore exposed at low tide. It is reported that there was no mound or burials and no refuse here, so the deposit may have been a ceremonial offering. Included were three bannerstones, red jasper beads, massive hard stone beads of various forms, and numerous large beautifully chipped stone points up to 7 or 8 inches long.

Few other bannerstones have been reported in the area, although more come from here than from all the remainder of Florida.[13] Along the St. Johns one was found at Dillon's Grove (W.F.I.S. 15056), another of shell at Mt. Taylor (surface, Moore, 1898), one from Stokes Landing Midden (U.F.A.L.), two at the main shell heap (Midden 2) on the north side of Salt Run (U.S.N.M. 378329), and three from the Shields Mound (Moore, 1895a: 461–2). These last three are the only datable specimens, as the Shields Mound is placed in St. Johns IIa times.

[11] Although this suggests an early age for the mound relative to surrounding surface deposits, it is interesting to note that oysters were not present or at least common on the nearby Halifax River during Orange times (Goggin, 1948b). At that period the middens were formed of coquina shells (*Donax* sp.). At this site coquina shells were present in the mound.

[12] Specimens in the possession of John D. Thompson and Harold Ryman of St. Augustine.

[13] Elsewhere in the state two specimens occur in the Indian River Area, one in the Manatee Region, one in the Glades Area, two in Central Florida, and five in the Central Gulf Coast Area (Goggin, MSd). However, only one of all these comes from a datable site, Lewis Place on the Aucilla River, placed in Weeden Island I Period.

Considering the four sites first discussed, the one thing they have in common is nineteen bannerstones, three being the least found in any site. This suggests a definite position of the artifact in the complex, when it is seen that only nineteen other specimens have been found in all other Florida sites. With the exception of two sites in the Northern St. Johns Area which had two and three specimens respectively, the others are all single finds. A second shared trait is red jasper beads, which are found at two sites, Coontie Island and Thornhill Lake 1, in each case in considerable quantity, while elsewhere in Florida they occur only very sporadically, usually as single specimens. Pendants made from a broken bannerstone wings were also found in two sites. They are reported elsewhere only at Orange Park (U.P.M.) in this same region. The almost total absence of pottery is another common feature.

It is perhaps worthwhile to consider in some detail the distribution of the red jasper bead, for it may be of significance in placing the Florida finds, since the beads were not locally made; at least the material is not locally found. On the preceramic level this form of bead has been found at Indian Knoll, on the Green River in Kentucky ("red claystone," Moore, 1916: 449), at Poverty Point in Louisiana (Moore, 1913: 70; Webb, 1948: 229), and in the Pickwick Basin (Webb and DeJarnette, 1942: 71, 197, Pls. 95, 96, 220: 2).

Dating the sites as a whole is not possible. However, certain objects such as bannerstones, red jasper beads, and massive stone beads are all very early, dating from preceramic times. On the other hand, sporadic examples of these have been found in sites which can be dated later. But the concept of sand burial mounds is apparently post-Archaic or at least only recognized in this part of Florida in St. Johns I times. The pottery from Thornhill Lake 1 may be either early St. Johns I, if a Deptford check-stamped form, or St. Johns II, if a later form.

In summary it appears that these sites may date from sometime in the St. Johns I Period. They could possibly be later, but the clustering of the early traits and the numerical concentration of examples of these early types, which is not found in demonstrably later sites where a few specimens sporadically occur, suggests that here is some sort of a carry-over from very early times. This represents one of the most interesting problems of the region.

ST. JOHNS II PERIOD

The St. Johns II Period is a continuation of the preceding horizon, distinguished mainly by the introduction of St. Johns Check Stamped pottery. Many midden sites and burial mounds occupied or used in St. Johns I times, continued to be used during this period. For this reason it is not easy to separate some sites of the period from those of preceeding times. Within the period as a whole the changes in pottery types and other artifacts were of a minor nature and are only now beginning to be worked out, which makes subdividing the period difficult. Foreign pottery types, helpful in the previous period for defining subperiods, are not as numerous during St. Johns II, although some are present. Such foreign influences as do occur seem to have been localized in only a few sites. Because of the above factors, neither a well rounded picture of the whole period nor of the subperiods is available.

Stratigraphic evidence for the period has been derived from Nelson's (1918) work at Oak Hill and the Florida Park Service study at Green Mound (J. W. Griffin, 1948a). At both sites St. Johns Check Stamped pottery overlies St. Johns Plain. This was previously recognized in a general manner by Moore (1894b) on the St. Johns but he did not carefully describe the sequence. Supplementary evidence from the Cotten site (J. W. Griffin, 1948a), Spaldings Lower Store, and Kauffman Island, (Watkins, MS b) in this region, and South Indian Field (Ferguson, 1951) and other sites (Rouse, 1951) in the Indian River region confirms the late position of St. Johns Check Stamped pottery.

Three divisions have been defined on the basis of seriation and cross correlation of artifacts. None are completely satisfactory and all are open to future change. St. Johns IIa is presumably coeval with Weeden Island II in time and includes sites which have trade material of that general horizon, including Weeden Island pottery. One site, Grant Mound, is placed here because of the presence of "long nosed god" copper maskettes similar to those of the Gahagan Focus in Louisiana, which dates from this time level (Webb and Dodd, 1939; Krieger, 1947).[14] Further evidence for the general time position of Grant Mound is seen in the presence here of a bi-conical, copper covered wooden ear plug (Moore, 1895a, Fig. 38) identical with those from the Powell Mound in Illinois (Kelly and Cole, 1931: 322, 335). However, another specimen from Spiro (Boudeman Collection, Kalamazoo) presumably is somewhat later (reported by James B. Griffin, personal communication). James B. Griffin (1946: 88) also points out similarities between Powell Mound material and late Coles Creek, with which Gahagan has relations.

St. Johns IIb is placed coeval with early Fort Walton and tentatively includes sites, as Mount Royal, that contain Middle Mississippian traits. It has been suggested that a single complex is represented at both the Grant and Mt. Royal sites, and that an agreement on the date for one of these sites should closely date the other. However, while the sites are in general of the same culture, they do not appear to be of the same period, Grant Mound being placed in St. Johns IIa and Mt. Royal in St. Johns IIb. Distinctive artifacts in these sites can be placed in a sequence west of the Mississippi, where the "long nosed god" maskettes fit in the Gahagan Focus, and the "forked eye" plate of Mt. Royal (Fig. 6) is almost identical with one from the Spiro Focus (Waring and Holder, 1945, Fig. 11, d-e). Krieger places Middle Spiro (from which the Spiro plate probably dates) about a hundred years later than the Gahagan Focus (Krieger, 1946, Fig. 26). There is no reason to suspect that the relative position or time interval of these objects should be different in Florida.

St. Johns IIc comprises early historic sites dating previous to the middle seventeenth century, which marks the beginning of the St. Augustine Period. In general, IIc is best known from intrusive burials. One village site of the period is Mt. Royal. Recognizable diagnostics appear to be a lack or scarcity of San Marcos pottery types and the presence of Fig Springs Polychrome and related majolica types, along with Spanish olive jar fragments.

The "Fountain of Youth" site in St. Augustine possibly belongs to this horizon (Seaberg, MS). Burials here are extended, flat on back, face to east, with hands often

---

[14] A general discussion of these objects is in preparation (Goggin, MSc).

crossed on chest. Grave goods are rare; only a few child burials have glass beads. This site suggests a Christian Indian community.

Midden sites of St. Johns II are quite numerous and include some of the largest and most spectacular shell heaps in Florida. Along the St. Johns River and its tributaries the middens are formed of fresh-water shells, both pelecypods and gastropods, but contain much other refuse, such as animal bones and lenses of sand, ashes, and black dirt. Many middens of this horizon tend to be shallower and more extensive. The term "shell fields" has been applied to this type of site, although it is also used less frequently in reference to deeper deposits. Coastal shell heaps are almost entirely composed of oyster shell, with only small quantities of other species. Some sites in Volusia County over 25 feet high are impressive landmarks along the flat coast.

Sand burial mounds differ little from the preceding period, although some are quite large. Out of 13 mounds with measurement data, seven were more than 10 feet in height, ranging up to 32 feet (Spruce Creek Mound). The smallest was only 2.5 feet high and five were less than 6 feet in height. Diameter varied considerably in relation to size; for example, of two 10-foot high mounds, one was 95 feet in diameter and the other 210 feet. The smaller mounds ranged from 35 to 55 feet in diameter.

Mounds are usually dome shaped or conical, sometimes as in case of Grant Mound, a truncated cone. Shields Mound is a fine example of a truncated pyramid with a ramp leading up one side. The well known Mt. Royal site has an "avenue" leading to a pond about a half mile distant. This "avenue" consists of a pair of low parallel ridges 1 to 2 feet high about 50 feet apart (J. Bartram, 1942: 74–5; W. Bartram, 1940: 101–2, 1853, Fig. 6; Brinton, 1859: 168–9; Moore, 1894a; 17–18). Although not as prominent as when first noted by the Bartrams, these ridges stand out quite clearly in air photos. They are unlike any other earthwork in the region but are similar to the paired ridges so widespread in the northern Glades Area (Goggin, MSb).

South Mound on Murphy Island also has associated earthworks (Moore, 1895b: 515–16). They were apparently rather indistinct in Moore's time; at the present, previous excavation makes it difficult to trace their exact nature. No internal structures have been noted in any mounds of the area.

Burials were reported in all mounds, but as a rule were not numerous and often were badly decayed. Several sites had 30 or so interments and one, Shields Mound, had over 150. At two sites, Point La Vista and Dunns Creek, primary burials were the common form; at all others secondary burials were characteristic. Burial offerings, except with period IIc burials, were not typical. Occasional artifacts were found throughout the mounds in no association with burials.

The period IIc burials, previously mentioned, are mainly intrusive burials in either St. Johns I or II mounds. They are primary interments, usually only two or three in a site, and are normally quite shallow, being about a foot below the surface. Accompanying grave furniture commonly includes iron tools, sometimes found with stone celts, glass beads, and other European ornaments and coins, as well as copper, silver, and gold ornaments of Glades Area types. Spruce Creek Mound is either a burial mound of St. Johns IIc times or else intrusive burials were quite deep.

Pottery found in the mounds usually has a basal perforation or killing. This has sometimes been made previous to the firing of the vessel. Perforated Busycon dippers have also been found.

Even though certain sites can be assigned to subperiods it does not seem advisable to attempt to break the whole artifact complex down for each subdivision. Because of the tentative nature of these subdivisions the artifacts will be summarized for the whole period and certain distinctive forms of the subperiods will be noted.

Pottery is most commonly St. Johns Plain and St. Johns Check Stamped. An unnamed plain gritty ware, of late date, is present in many of the northernmost sites, particularily coastal middens. Dunns Creek Red is found sporadically throughout the area.

Chalky ware types with simple stamping and scoring are found. Apparently simple stamping appeared late in St. Johns II; perhaps it is characteristic of IIb (Griffin and Smith, 1949: 346-7). Sometimes it is confused with scoring, which may be found with either wide or narrow marks. Small fragments of the former are often hard to distinguish from simple-stamped pottery.

"Freak ware" or "extemporized ware," terms mainly used to include various animal effigies and odd clay objects, are most typical of this horizon. Although the animal forms are often cited as being characteristic of the Northern St. Johns Region, they actually are not widespread even in this horizon, the one large cache from Thursby Mound overshadowing the many sites where they are not found. A few crude animal effigies, not exactly like the Thursby specimens, have been found in other sites. Clay spool-like objects have been noted at three sites and flanged earthenware tubes at two sites. One example of a miniature vessel shaped like a four-legged stool was found.

Pottery types characteristic of earlier horizons are very rare; they may represent mixed sites or else the specimens are heirlooms or carryovers. These include Oklawaha Plain, St. Johns Red on Buff, St. Johns Punctated, and unclassified complicated stamped forms.

Most Weeden Island trade types are uncommon but include Weeden Island Plain, Wakulla Check Stamped, Thomas Simple Stamped, Carrabelle Punctated, Weeden Island Incised, Weeden Island Punctated, and Papy's Bayou Punctated. However, certain types of the Weeden Island culture are fairly widespread and although never common, occur with surprising frequency in burial mounds and midden sites. These are Little Manatee Zoned Stamped and Little Manatee Shell Stamped, as well as Sarasota Incised of the Englewood culture.

Later trade types include single examples of Pt. Washington Incised, Safety Harbor Incised, and Moundville Black Filmed as well as what appear to be local expressions of Fort Walton Incised on St. Johns paste or chalky ware. Cord-marked forms occur in northern sites, especially those from the mouth of the St. Johns River north. Some appear to be Prairie Cord Marked, others are probably Georgia types, Savannah Fine Cord Marked being noted. A single Gainesville Linear Punctated sherd has been found, and Alachua Cob Marked examples are known from a single site (Mr 44). More widely found, but never commonly, are examples of the related St. Johns Cob Marked.

A pottery form difficult to interpret is an unnamed series, characterized by sherd tempering. Plain forms are most abundant but decorated types include fabric-marked, complicated-stamped, simple-stamped, check-stamped, and cob-marked examples. This latter is the most common technique of decoration, at least at Du 53. Sherd-tempered ware occurs as far south as Mount Royal on the St. Johns River and to the St. Augustine area on the coast, but is more abundant northward. Its stratigraphic position is clearly St. Johns II (Seaberg, MS). Judging from its distribution, the form is either a trade ware from Georgia or was inspired by forms of that state.

An analysis of the sites has revealed an extensive artifact complex, many types represented by numerous examples. Both in quantity and number of occurrences, stone celts and chipped stone points are the most abundant artifacts in the sand mounds. Over 130 celts were found in a single mound, no small number when it is realized that they are all made of hard igneous or metamorphic rocks foreign to the state.

Certain flint points of interest are small triangular, and the Cahokia-type specimens (Moore, 1894a, Fig. 5). The former appears to be typical of part of the period, but the latter is known only from Mount Royal.[15]

Tools and implements include Strombus celts, Busycon gouges, and hammerstones, and less commonly stone chisels, flint celts, pebble hammers, shell scraper, flint blades or scrapers, and hones. There are also grinding slabs, grooved stone weights, bone awl, bone splinter awls, and a socketed bone point. Vessel forms include Busycon dippers, but they are not so common as previously, and, in two instances, steatite vessel fragments. It is questionable whether these last pertain to this horizon.

Ornaments are especially numerous in terms of variety, but shell beads, plummet-form pendants, plain and incised bone pins, and copper ornaments are the only forms which occur in any frequency. Other types include red jasper beads, steatite beads, sandstone beads, pearl beads, shell pendants, perforated stone pendants, boat shaped pendants, perforated pebble pendant, and a stone two-holed gorget. There are also stone tubes, a boat stone, bannerstones, perforated canine teeth, and shell replicas of perforated canine teeth. Copper objects are mainly embossed sheet copper plates and ornaments. Sheet metal beads, copper pins, and copper overlaid wooden specimens are found.

Miscellaneous objects and artifacts include mica, pebbles, hematite, galena, clay wedge, and curved clay tube. Stone and clay elbow pipes are very common.

There is another group of artifacts, some of which are ornaments, others perhaps both ornamental and ceremonial. Many of these forms have been included within the Southern Cult artifact complex (Waring and Holder, 1945). They include shell pins, a hoe-shaped implement (Moore, 1903b), spuds or spatulate celts, a discoidal stone, copper-covered stone ear plug, and a copper plate with an embossed forked-eye design (Fig. 6). Other artifacts not necessarily part of the cult are "long nosed god" copper maskettes and biconical, copper covered wooden ear plugs. All of these forms were found in prehistoric sites, dating from St. Johns IIa and IIb.

[15] Small triangular flint points are also characteristic of the Alachua Period to the west in Central Florida, and the Safety Harbor Period on the Gulf Coast.

In St. Johns IIc times European or European-derived artifacts are present. A variety of trade objects are found with burials. They include mainly iron tools or ornaments. Glass seed beads are the most numerous of the latter, but chevron beads have also been found. Copper, silver, and gold ornaments are all simple, cut or embossed sheet-metal forms typical of the Glades and Indian River areas to the south. A single gold coin bead has been reported. Two silver ornaments are apparently of European origin.

Iron axes, chisels, and knives, are represented, as well as a horseshoe. Glass fragments, a bone comb with scroll decoration (Fig. 7), hawk bells, and silver coins also occur with burials.

Spanish pottery includes both olive jars and majolica. Certain types of the latter ware, Fig Springs Polychrome, Ichtucknee Blue on White, and Ichtucknee Blue on Blue, can be used as time markers for St. Johns IIc. They appear to reach their peak before 1650.

Midden sites of this period are especially numerous, but burial mounds are not proportionately as common as in previous periods. The temporal position of the listed sites will be indicated by the designations II, II?, IIa, IIb, IIc following the name. The following are burial mounds:

Subarea I: Cn 1 (II), Du 12 (IIa), Du 14 (IIa), Du 37 (II), Cl 3 (II), Du 48–50 (II?).
Subarea II: Pu 6 (II?), Pu 14 (IIa, IIc, intrusive), Pu 20 (intrusive burials, IIc?), Pu 21 (IIa), Pu 35 (IIb), Vo 5 (II?), La 9 (II), La 10 (II), La 11 (II), Vo 25 (intrusive burials, IIc?), Vo 36 (IIa, IIb, IIc intrusive), Vo 39 (II), Vo 49 (IIc, intrusive?), Vo 50 (II), Se 4 (intrusive burials, IIc), Se 13 (intrusive burials, IIc).
Subarea III: Vo 75 (II), Vo 99 (intrusive? IIc).
Subarea IV: Pu 50 (II?).

In addition to the burial mounds, a series of midden sites were occupied at this time:

Subarea I: Na 1 (II?), Na 5 (II), SJ 36 (II), SJ 38 (IIc?), SJ 7 (II), SJ 8 (II), SJ 39 (II)' SJ 41 (II), SJ 42 (II), Du 34 (II), Du 45 (II), SJ 27 (II).
Subarea II: Pu 15 (II), Pu 59 (II), Pu 66 (II), Pu 16 (II), Pu 19 (II), Pu 24 (II), Pu 34 (II), Pu 37 (II), Pu 39 (II), Pu 43 (II), Mr 1 (II), Mr 3 (II), La 5 (II?), Vo 2 (II), Vo 12 (II), Vo 21 (II), La 24 (II), Vo 32 (II), Vo 52 (II), Se 25 (II), La 42 (II), Vo 53 (II), Se 2 (II), Vo 60 (II), Se 8 (II), Vo 61 (II).
Subarea III: Fl 2 (II, IIc), Fl 6 (II), Vo 82 (IIc), Vo 85 (II), Vo 90 (II), Vo 91 (II), Vo 92 (II), Vo 95 (II), Vo 100 (II, IIc), Vo 103 (II), Vo 105 (II), Vo 106 (IIc), Vo 109 (II).
Subarea IV: Pu 51 (II), Mr 9 (II), Mr 10 (II), Mr 44 (II), Mr 41 (II), Mr 42 (II).

In addition to the above sites, 45 others which had been occupied during earlier horizons continued to be inhabited. In all, 119 sites date completely or in part from this horizon.

ST. AUGUSTINE PERIOD

In later historic times new cultural influences appeared in the Northern St. Johns Area. Excavations in the city of St. Augustine and in the moat of Castillo de San Marcos have turned up considerable quantities of this material. That from the Castillo must be post-1683 in time, but the other excavations suggest that the period's beginning was earlier. The definition of the period and a preliminary description of the culture, based on these data, were given by Hale G. Smith (1948).

Since this section was first written in 1947, our rapidly expanding knowledge of historic times has resulted in much new light on the period. Smith (1948) suggested an initial date of 1565 for the period; a modification to 1650 was proposed by Goggin (1948c, Fig. 12). Subsequent data indicate that this estimate is close.

Exactly how to define this period as we learn more about Spanish activities, is something of a problem. Inasmuch as there are considerable indications of earlier Spanish contacts with the Indians, the question is whether all such contacts should be placed in a broadened historic period. It is probably best not to do so. Such data can be effectively considered in cultural terms in the Spanish-Indian tradition. By restricting the St. Augustine Period to the elements defined originally by Hale Smith (1948), we set aside a definite historical segment of the Spanish-Indian tradition defined by cultural criteria and retain its usefulness for historic analysis. The marker for the period, then, is San Marcos Stamped and related wares.

As an archeological complex the period includes sites basically Spanish in culture and inhabitants, such as Castillo de San Marcos; sites of mixed Spanish and Indian occupation, as Fort Pupo; and those basically Indian with few actual resident Spaniards (probable mission sites), such as Wrights Landing, Du 53, and Rollestown.

With one possible exception, all sites include refuse deposits, but descriptions are not available for most localities. In St. Augustine the site consists of a refuse layer some 18 to 22 inches deep which underlies much of the center of town. Other sites, such as Shellbluff Landing and Palm Valley, are shell middens; shell fields, like Du 53 and Wrights Landing; or a sand midden area partially overlying shell, as at Rollestown. Refuse at Fort Pupo is scattered deeply in a sand matrix. There is a significant shift at this time from the deep midden pattern of the earlier periods to an extended midden area.

Structural remains include an elaborate Spanish stone fortress, Castillo de San Marcos, as well as the remains of a wooden blockhouse with earth embankments, Fort Pupo (Goggin, 1951). The entrenchments and ridges reported by John Bartram (1942: 46) at Rollestown were probably similar to the last structure but we have no historical documentation for them and they are not apparent at the present time, probably having been eroded away by the river. Excavation elsewhere will undoubtedly reveal remains of mission structures, or other Spanish buildings. As late as 1766 such remains were still visible on Fort George Island (J. Bartram, 1942: 48).

No adequate burial data are available. Burial mounds are unreported; but since subsoil interments were practiced in the previous period it is probable that this style of burial continued.[16]

[16] A single burial mound, Bayard Point on the St. Johns River, can be mentioned here, although the site is probably later. Guns and powder horns were not generally available to Indians in Spanish Florda, yet mounds are not known to have been made by the Seminole. This mound, 4 feet 9 inches high and 45 feet in diameter, appears to have been built to hold the burials; Moore (1894b: 188–9) states clearly that they are not intrusive. Its proximity to Fort Pupo poses the possibility that it was constructed by Yuchi or other Muskogean warriors during their various engagements at that fort. However, the presence of a female burial somewhat discounts this possibility.

At the present time the period is basically known by its ceramic complex, especially the marker type San Marcos Stamped. This is a grit and/or limestone tempered ware impressed with either simple, cross-simple, check, or complicated stamping or a combination of those forms. The rim is often folded, with reed or other punctations at the base of the fold. Smith (1948) notes that simple stamping (including cross-simple stamping) is the majority type of decoration in the latter part of the period, post-1686. Excavations at Fort Pupo clearly substantiate this, but on the other hand material from Wrights Landing, thought to be pre-1686, does not have a large percentage of complicated-stamped material.

Along with San Marcos Stamped are other wares including the related San Marcos Plain and San Marcos Red. Chalky wares continue to be represented by St. Johns Plain, St. Johns Check Stamped, St. Johns Scored, and St. Johns Simple Stamped. Trade material in the collection from the Castillo de San Marcos moat includes Fort Walton Incised and Lamar Complicated Stamped.

In all sites with this material, there is found substantial quantities of Spanish pottery which commonly includes the coarse storage vessels, usually called olive jars, and sometimes fine, tin-enameled majolica. Even more important than Spanish pottery itself, is the influence it exerted on local ceramics. One San Marcos Stamped sherd from Castillo de San Marcos moat has a vitreous green glaze on the interior. On San Marcos types, ring foots, inspired by Spanish forms, are not uncommon. Some St. Johns Simple Stamped ware from early in the Spanish occupation at Fort Pupo has the typical Spanish plate form with a flat base. This shape is common in San Marcos pottery.

Certain Majolica types are clearly associated with the horizon. These include Puebla Polychrome, Abo Polychrome, and San Luis Polychrome. They apparently have a 1675–1700 date (and perhaps later) in Florida. On the other hand the dominant early or middle seventeenth century forms, Fig Springs Polychrome and several associated types, are not typically present.[17] It is interesting to see that at a basically secular site such as Fort Pupo, majolica is very rare (1 small sherd). It is very likely a luxury associated with the mission areas (at missions or mission influenced sites) or with governmental executives (Castillo de San Marcos and St. Augustine proper).

As was mentioned, little is known of the non-ceramic features of the period. At Bayard Point, in association with three primary burials, were flint lock guns, lead bullets, powder horns, red pigment (European), flint and steel (?), bone-handled iron awl, glass beads, silver earrings, and glass fragments. This artifact assemblage is very similar

---

[17] At Mt. Royal village (St. Johns IIc and earlier) it is the dominant Majolica type while San Marcos Stamped is very rare. Wrights Landing with Fig Springs Polychrome, San Luis Polychrome, a few Puebla Polychrome sherds, and abundant San Marcos series pottery could be construed as an early St. Augustine Period site bridging the time gap between the two Majolica groups' points of greatest frequency. However, the insignificant proportion of complicated stamped varieties of San Marcos Stamped (2.23 per cent of 2688 sherds) would rule out such an early date in view of Smith's data for complicated-stamped importance in pre-1686, St. Augustine times. Nevertheless, it is not impossible that this complex is a mixture resulting from two Spanish-influenced occupations; if the site is Tolomato mission there were at least two late occupations.

to one found in Central Florida and considered to be Seminole (Goggin *et al.*, 1949). Thus this may very well be Seminole also.

The total Indian ceramic picture of the St. Augustine Period is such a unique contrast to the previous periods that one is inclined to wonder if some completely new influence was not in the area. The possible source of such an influence is quickly apparent when material from Georgia is examined. There, a late period, the Lamar, shares a remarkable number of similarities with San Marcos Stamped, and one Late Lamar ceramic development is close in all details. This pottery, King George Malleated (personal communication, Joseph Caldwell) is from the historic Huspaw Indian (a Yamasee group) occupation at Fort King George in 1715.[18]

However, the development in Florida dates previous to this time so an earlier source must be found, although in any case it is probably Georgia, most likely southeastern Georgia. The question has also been advanced whether this period represents the taking over of new ceramic ideas by the historic Timucua or the actual presence of Georgian peoples. It seems most probable that both situations existed; the widespread and significant occurrence of the San Marcos types indicates their adoption by the Timucua.

Who the carriers of the new types were is not certain. The group most often suggested are the Yamasee (J. W. Griffin, 1949; Rouse, 1951), although the earliest movement of these people into the Timucua area was not until after 1680 (Swanton, 1946: 209). However, even earlier, by 1658 (Lanning, 1935: 210) the Guale Indian town of Tolomato had been moved to only three leagues north of St. Augustine (perhaps the present Wrights Landing site).[19] It is most probable that these Indians brought the San Marcos types with them, if indeed the types themselves did not actually precede the Georgia Indians. Not only are these types common enough to suggest such an adoption but the San Marcos decorative styles were even, on occasion, applied to local types. St. Johns Check Stamped sherds from Fort Pupo bear the usual San Marcos rim treatment with a fold and reed punctations (Goggin, 1951).

The following sites are included in this period. All except the last three are in subarea I; those are in subareas II and III respectively:

Na 4, Na 10, Du 53, Cl 8, Cl 10, SJ 1, SJ 14, SJ 38 (?), SJ 32, SJ 3, SJ 33, SJ 34, SJ 40, SJ 31, SJ 9, SJ 10, SJ 10A, SJ 11, SJ 12, SJ 43, SJ 44, Pu 23, Pu 64, SJ 28.

A few sherds resembling San Marcos Stamped from the upper levels at Kauffman Island (Watkins, MS*b*) suggest a sporadic occupation there at this time.

[18] Since the above was written it has been possible to visit and make surface collections at the Fort King George site near Darien, Georgia, as well as to examine the material from Caldwell's excavations, now in the custody of Miss Bessie Lewis. Individual sherds of King George Malleated cannot be distinguished from San Marcos Stamped, but some distinctive vessel forms of Georgia are not found in Florida. Like the Florida material the Georgia sherds accompany Spanish olive jar and majolica fragments. These latter include only an unidentified plain type in Caldwell's collection, and one Ichtucknee Blue on White specimen from our surface collecting.

[19] Interestingly enough, the Fort King George site in Georgia is considered by some to have been the original, early seventeenth century, Tolomato mission (Coulter, 1937, end paper map). However, others attribute the site to the Tupique or Espogache mission.

SEMINOLE PERIOD

Although the area had an important occupation by the Seminole Indians from some time around the 1760's to the 1870's, only one archeological site has definitely been identified with them. However, the Bayard Point mound must be considered as a possible second site. It is only a matter of detailed work until more Seminole sites are recognized.[20]

The Indians commonly known as Seminoles are of a rather diverse origin but initially were of Hitchiti and Oconee derivation. These people first moved to Florida about 1750, centering on the Alachua Prairie. Later various refugees, including some Yuchi, Yamassee, and Creek groups, swelled their ranks and finally, after 1800, the Creek element became numerically dominant.

During the British occupation the Seminole were not numerous on the St. Johns, although groups were noted by William Bartram (1940). However, several trading houses for their convenience were established on the river, the best known being near Astor (J. Bartram, 1942: 71) and at Stokes Landing (J. Bartram, 1942: 70; U.F.A.L.).

After the English departed from Florida many of their plantations on the St. Johns were abandoned and perhaps it was for that reason more is then heard of the Seminoles there. One of the earliest mentioned towns is Oklawaha, reported by Hawkins in 1799, and subsequently in 1821 and 1822 (Swanton, 1922: 400, 404, 405). It is said that this group represented the last element of the Yamassee (Cohen, 1836: 64 ff.), a possibility which Swanton (1922: 402) accepts.

In 1821 two additional towns were also noted, one on the south side of Okefenokee Swamp and the other at Spring Garden near Volusia (Swanton, 1922: 407). This last is a well known town of Yuchi Indians under Chief Billy. At times the town appears to have been located at Beresford (Williams, 1837: 274).

Our most complete list for the river dates from 1823. At that time five towns were listed: Etanie, a settlement west of the St. Johns near the head of Rice Creek; Yalacasooche, at the mouth of the Oklawaha; Ahapapka, at the head of the Oklawaha; Talahassee (the Yuchi town), on Spring Garden Creek; and Yulaka (under Chief Philip), about 35 miles above Volusia on the west bank of the river. This last is very likely King Philips Town or Cooks Ferry, as it has been called in this paper.

In the next few years, with the development of hostilities, most of the large towns appear to have been abandoned. In any case when John J. Audubon visited Spring Garden in 1832 he saw only an active American plantation and he gives no report of Indians (Audubon, 1926: 168). However, some camps remained or were established from time to time, those noted being at Salt Spring in 1835 (Williams, 1837: 215) and

---

[20] Since this paper was written field surveys have been made around Middleburg on Black Creek in Clay County. Abundant American-European material was found dating from the 1830–40's. At that period the area was a major military post, quartermaster's depot, hospital, rest camp, and refuge center during the second Seminole War.

The single Indian sherd found is a brushed form, related to Stokes Brushed, but more like material from Pine Bluff and Manatee Springs on the Suwannee River. It is probably Seminole and indicative of what will be found by continued intensive search.

at Lake Jessup in 1837 (Williams, 1837: 55). It is quite probable too that Philips Town remained occupied at this time, for occasional references are made to Philip himself.

Following the Seminole Wars, after the 1840's, most of the Seminoles probably left the area. It is somewhat of a surprise to find that Philips Town was still occupied at the time of Le Baron's visit in 1869 (Le Baron, 1876: 39). This undoubtedly was the northernmost Indian settlement in Florida at the time and must have been abandoned soon after, as no record of it is given by numerous following travelers.

Archeological data are limited to the rather small sample recovered at Spaldings Lower Store, the present Stokes Landing, an English trading post *circa* 1763–84. Certain potsherds found there can probably be classified as Seminole. The most common form, Stokes Brushed, is a coarse, heavy, grit-tempered ware with a surface strongly striated by deep brush marks or scoring (Pl. 12, L to P). From the nature of the large quartz inclusions it is possible that this pottery (or its tempering) was an import from either western Florida or regions to the north of that area.[21] Other presumed Seminole imports are a few sherds of a fine smooth ware with mica inclusions (Pl. 12, J). Incised sherds of this paste (Pl. 12, K) appear related in a general way to Ocmulgee Fields Incised, a very late Georgia type.[22] None of these types appear to have been locally made, but further work should reveal local pottery since the Seminole in Central Florida are reported to have been making it as late as the 1820's (Pierce, 1825: 135).

A flint point from Spaldings Lower Store possibly dates from this horizon, although stone points probably were not in general use at such a late date. A heart-shaped silver brooch (Pl. 12, G) and a silver ball earring were probably intended for Seminole trade. Another possible Seminole artifact is a conical piece of rolled copper (Pl. 12, H), a "tinkler" made to be attached to a bag, leggings, or other accoutrement.[23]

Few details are available for other aspects of Seminole culture. However, the picture given for Cuscowilla town to the west would probably describe the Seminoles here (W. Bartram, 1940: 163 ff.).

[21] This type also fits well in the general pattern of historic brushed surface types in the West Florida-Georgia area, i.e., Chattahoochee Brushed, tentatively identified as Seminole (Bullen, 1950); Walnut Roughened, attributed to the Hitchiti (Anon., 1940); and an unpublished type, Ocmulgee Fields Brushed Roughened, from Kasita town on the Chattahoochee River (Willey, MS). Creek ethnological specimens are similar in many respects (Schmitt, 1950).

[22] This similarity is of more than passing interest since that pottery is attributed in part to the historic Hitchiti in Georgia (Jennings and Fairbanks, 1939c; James B. Griffin, 1946, Fig. 2) and it is known that those eighteenth-century Indians in Florida called the Seminole were of Hitchiti derivation.

[23] Omitted from consideration are numerous colonial artifacts used alike by whites and Indians.

CULTURAL TRADITIONS

IN the foregoing cultural summary the picture presented has been one of discrete cultural and temporal units succeeding each other. The relationships between some of these are clearly indicated; in other instances they are inferred. However, it is apparent that certain of these units are related expressions of broader cultural configurations, which will be called traditions. As used here, the term tradition refers to a distinct cultural complex which may in the course of time pass through some changes but not enough to alter the basic configuration.[1]

Ten cultural traditions have been recognized in Florida (Fig. 3): Paleo-Indian, Archaic, St. Johns, Malabar, Gulf, Glades, Florida Mississippian, Alachua, Spanish-Indian, and Seminole (Goggin, MSa). Of these the first three and the last two are represented in our area. Unfortunately our knowledge of these cultural configurations is not even, but the general nature of the two most important in this region, Archaic and St. Johns, can be seen. The Paleo-Indian and Seminole traditions are apparently not well represented because they were not important here.

PALEO-INDIAN TRADITION

DEFINITION

The Paleo-Indian Tradition is that of a simple nomadic or seminomadic group depending on hunting and, probably to a lesser extent, on gathering of wild foods, and fishing.[2]

DISTRIBUTION

Occurrences of this tradition are limited to questionable sites which do not tie in culturally with expressions of the tradition elsewhere in Florida, particularly in Central Florida, where the tradition is apparently present in preceramic sites, associated with the Suwannee Point, a large stone point suggestive of Plainview forms.

In the Northern St. Johns Area, there are two possible examples of the tradition. The first is the supposed association of extinct mammal remains and an artifact at Bon Terra farm, some 29 miles south of St. Augustine (Connery, 1932; E. B. Howard, 1940). Unfortunately this association remains to be proven by more detailed evidence.

The second site, about which little is known either, is at New Smyrna (Gidley, 1929: 491, 493). Here there was a possible association between extinct mammal remains and artifacts, similar to occurrences of those materials at Vero and Melbourne sites in the Indian River Area to the south. Another similarity with the last mentioned sites may be seen in the ecological situation of the New Smyrna material. On the basis of this factor alone, New Smyrna may perhaps be disqualified for any antiquity in terms of

---

[1] The concept is discussed in greater detail in Goggin (1949a).

[2] The term *Paleo-Indian* includes only the early preceramic cultures, as used by Roberts (1940). It is not the same as James B. Griffin's (1946) usage of the term, which includes the late preceramic cultures, here considered in the Archaic Tradition.

Rouse's (1951) interpretation of the geological history of the Melbourne and Vero sites.

A third possible Paleo-Indian expression is represented by a single flint point from Watson's Landing on the St. Johns River (Pl. 7, R and S; Wyman, 1875, Pl. 2, Fig. 6;

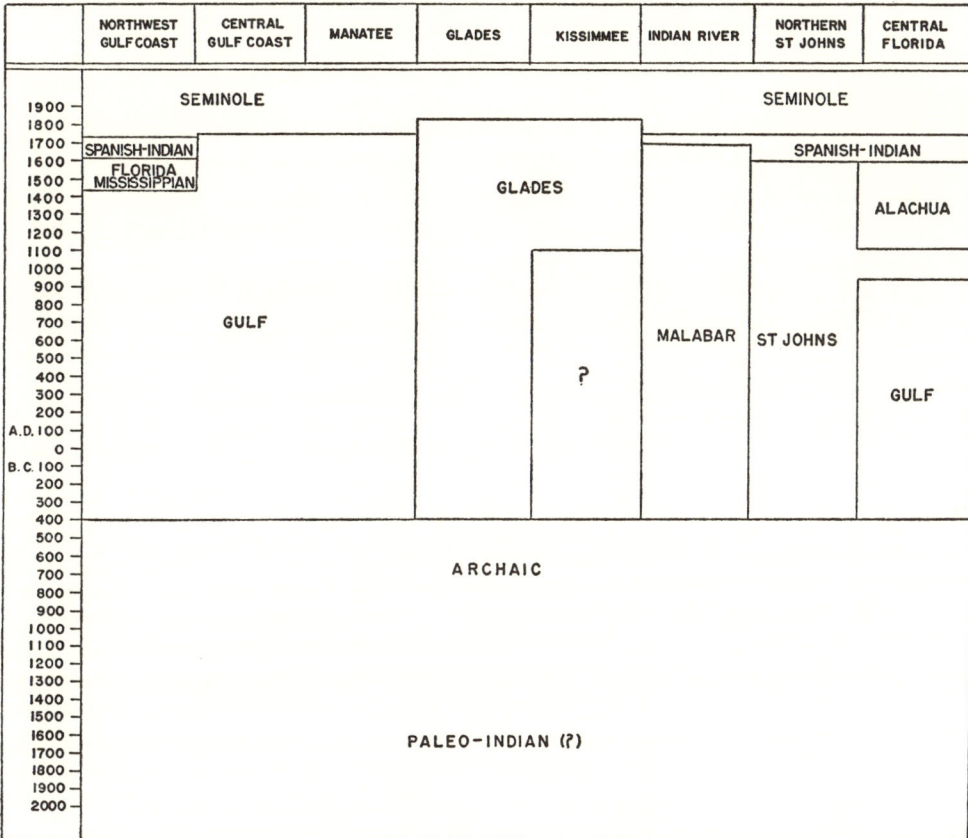

	NORTHWEST GULF COAST	CENTRAL GULF COAST	MANATEE	GLADES	KISSIMMEE	INDIAN RIVER	NORTHERN ST JOHNS	CENTRAL FLORIDA
1900	SEMINOLE						SEMINOLE	
1800								
1700	SPANISH-INDIAN			GLADES			SPANISH-INDIAN	
1600	FLORIDA							
1500	MISSISSIPPIAN							ALACHUA
1400								
1300								
1200		GULF						
1100								
1000								GULF
900								
800							ST JOHNS	
700				?		MALABAR		
600								
500								
400								
300								
200								
A.D.100								
0								
B.C.100								
200								
300								
400								
500				ARCHAIC				
600								
700								
800								
900								
1000								
1100								
1200								
1300								
1400								
1500								
1600				PALEO-INDIAN (?)				
1700								
1800								
1900								
2000								

FIG. 3. Cultural Traditions in Florida.

H.P.M. 67-1/2898). This has a channel flake removed from one side and is like the Suwannee form in general outline. It bears a very heavy patina. Other material from the site indicates a long range of occupation from Orange to historic times.[3]

ENVIRONMENTAL RELATIONS

Possible expressions of this pattern are too few and too poorly known to draw any conclusions as to special ecological or environmental relations.

[3] A new site near Silver Springs yielding several fluted Suwannee points has been reported since this paper went to press (personal communication, Dr. Wilfred T. Neill). The Florida Park Service plans an excavation here.

HISTORY

Our data are too scanty to allow any interpretations. The evidence only suggests a possible presence of this pattern here; it is not improbable that the two reported sites will be eventually discounted or, in the case of the New Smyrna site, placed in the Archaic pattern. On the other hand the early complex characterized by Suwannee points in Central Florida may be found to extend into this region.

ARCHAIC TRADITION

DEFINITION

The Archaic Tradition[4] is characterized by a semi-sedentary group of people obtaining their food by hunting, fishing, and gathering. Pottery was absent in the earlier part of their history, but later, fiber-tempered ceramics appeared. Sites of the period consist of large shell middens occupied for a long time.

The ceremonial life does not appear to have been complex. Primary burials were made in middens. However, the presence of many scattered human bones in these sites suggests that little interest was felt for the remains; perhaps, as Wyman (1875: 67–71) has suggested, there was even cannibalism. This indifference towards the dead is emphasized by the lack of burial offerings.

Technical skill was fair; the few artifacts from the preceramic level of this pattern are not notable, but they include much worked bone in the form of projectile points, antler projectile points, awls, pins, and miscellaneous worked fragments. Most of these forms are present only in the latter part of the period of existence of the tradition.

Stone work consists mainly of chipped points, usually of a stemmed triangular form. Large blades and scrapers are also present. Some of these blades appear to resemble the *coup de poing* in form (Wyman, 1875: 49) and are similar to other early blades of this shape found elsewhere in Florida. Busycon gouges occur in the earliest phase of the pattern; additional types of worked shell, Strombus celts in particular, appear later. Steatite vessels are known from the later phase and were probably also present earlier.

Art is not distinctive in the earlier level, but when pottery appeared, simple incised geometric decoration was applied to it. More tasteful and intricate incised motifs appear on the late bone pins.

DISTRIBUTION

The Archaic Tradition is found in this area in its most characteristic form. Elsewhere it occurs in the Indian River Region (Rouse, 1951) and, less typically, in other parts of the state (Goggin, 1948c, MSa).

Within the Northern St. Johns Area this tradition appears to be most typical inland in subareas II and IV. Here the earlier phase, the Mt. Taylor Period, is well developed while its presence on the coast appears to be rare. The later phase, Orange Period, is

---

[4] The use of the term *Archaic* follows Ford and Willey (1941: 332). Criticisms against this usage of the term have been made by James B. Griffin (1946: 42) and more recently by Sears (1948). See Goggin (1949a).

also most commonly found on the river although a few sites are reported on or near the coast.

ENVIRONMENTAL RELATIONS

The concentration of the Archaic Tradition in this area (and in the adjacent Indian River Region) does not appear to be an historical accident. The subsistence complex was apparently based on a river-marsh habitat where extensive food in the form of fish, freshwater molluscs, numerous reptiles, wading birds, and other game could be easily obtained. The most suitable area of any size of this nature is along the St. Johns River from its head waters to about Palatka. In this section of the river's course most of the banks are low, and extensive marshes, many entering spring runs, and large lakes are found. It is here that the pattern can be seen in full development.

Few traces of the tradition have been found on the coast. Why the coast was not more heavily occupied in view of the extensive use of molluscs there by the later inhabitants is somewhat of a puzzle. However, a study of the rare coastal sites of the tradition indicates that the main food supply, at least as expressed in midden remains, was derived from coquinas (*Donax* sp.). Although these are very abundant on the ocean beach, they are very small molluscs and, as far as is known, can only be used for broth. They could hardly be an important food supply. The lack of other shells in coastal sites of the tradition, particularily oysters and ribbed clams (*Chione* sp.) suggests that these molluscs were not living in the vicinity, probably because of an unsuitable habitat in the coastal lagoons. A slightly lower sea level, even only a few feet, would have produced a different salinity in the shallow lagoons, making them unfavorable habitats for certain molluscs. The inference, then, is that the Archaic Tradition is no more than scantily represented on the coast because the food situation was poor there in comparison with the St. Johns River (Goggin, 1948*b*).

HISTORY

Presumably the Archaic Tradition is related to similar cultural expressions in the Southeast, and was either derived from or very strongly stimulated by one of them. The possibility that the Florida center was the source of the others does not seem probable in view of the variances among them and the simplicity of the culture found in Florida at the earliest level. From which of the various Southeastern centers the Mt. Taylor Period was derived or influenced cannot be said at present.

However, by the Orange Period, when fiber-tempered pottery appeared, specific resemblances to various centers can be noted. In pottery itself we can turn north to the nearby Stallings Island center in Georgia. The pottery there is somewhat different in paste and finish, and is commonly decorated by linear punctation instead of the incision of the Florida center. But if the nature of the decoration on the Savannah River pottery is ignored, much similarity between the basic designs of the two will be seen. In northern Alabama, there is another fiber-tempered pottery center but the designs do not exhibit a great similarity to the Orange Incised pottery of Florida. This is interesting because it seems probable that the large steatite vessels of the St. Johns were traded from

Alabama. Certain similarities in rim decoration have been noted between these vessels and the contemporaneous (?) Poverty Point specimens of northern Louisiana (C. H. Webb, 1948; Ferguson, 1951).

At the end of the Orange Period the first important change since the introduction of pottery took place. This was the shift from fiber-tempered to chalky ware with the same designs being carried on. It was apparently an internal development of short duration. Just previous to the change the prototypes could be seen in hybrid chalky-fiber-tempered ware. While this experiment was being made, another ware was also being tried. This was made by adding sand to the fiber temper. However, this second experiment did not achieve cultural favor and was abandoned.

The exact nature of the end of the tradition is not clear. Nevertheless, there appears to be a clear-cut distinction between this and the succeeding St. Johns Tradition.

ST. JOHNS TRADITION

DEFINITION

The St. Johns Tradition can be briefly characterized as a pottery using, mound building, semi-sedentary complex probably with agriculture. It is notable neither for its technology and material culture nor for its ceremonial aspects, as expressed in archeological remains.

The pottery is simple and seems to have been relatively unimportant, plain and check-stamped ware being dominant. Crude clay effigies of plant products and animals for funeral offerings, and other unusual artifacts such as flanged clay spools and funnel-like objects, are found. Smoking pipes of stone and clay now appear, and stone celts of foreign materials were imported.

Ceremonialism does not seem to have been developed in terms of mortuary customs as elsewhere in Florida. In fact, obligations towards the dead seem to have been met at times in a very matter-of-fact manner by specially preparing poorly-made pottery vessels with pre-fired basal perforations. The Mt. Royal earthworks are distinctive and unlike anything else.

In many respects the tradition is a reflection of the dominant mound-building complex on the Gulf Coast. For some unknown reason this tradition was highly selective, in terms of adapting foreign influences, especially in ceramics. Nevertheless, various influences from many Southeastern centers are found here and they stand out more sharply than in any other region in Florida. I cannot perceive as yet the underlying current or "psychology" of this pattern. Perhaps the lack of a good detailed cultural sequence may be part of the difficulty; by seriation a series of cultural blocks have been arranged in a sequence but they do not give a smooth feeling of cultural continuity.

DISTRIBUTION

The St. Johns Tradition is centered in the Northern St. Johns Region, where its earliest period, St. Johns I, followed the Orange Period. Succeeding the earlier level was St. Johns II, which continued into early historic time, apparently to the middle of the seventeenth century.

During the range of this tradition it exerted strong influences to the south in the Indian River Region. The importance of these influences cannot be properly evaluated at present. Central Florida, to the west, was also strongly influenced, and at least one period, Cades Pond, can be considered a western extension of St. Johns Ib. In the subsequent period, Hickory Pond, the St. Johns Tradition can be recognized as an influence but not the dominant one.

ENVIRONMENTAL RELATIONS

The tradition is found on both the coast and in the interior along the St. Johns River. It is especially strong in the former area, where the people seem to have depended greatly on molluscs. This may represent a shift in population from the river valley to the coast to take advantage of the increasing oyster beds which apparently developed there about the beginning or sometime along in the St. Johns I Period. Yet at the same time the food-rich swamp habitat along the St. Johns was not abandoned.

Although there are many data on this region I believe they are highly selective, concentrating on middens and mounds. Historic ethnological data indicate the presence of large villages, and archeological sites of this nature are found to the west in Central Florida. Since that type of site leaves only a thin refuse layer over a large area, it was not noted by the early investigators. It is probable that sites of this nature will be found in regions with good soil for agricultural purposes, perhaps below Lake George on the St. Johns River.

HISTORY

Although the St. Johns Tradition succeeds the Archaic Tradition, it cannot be positively demonstrated to have developed out of it. However, such a development is a very strong possibility.

In its earliest period, St. Johns I, the tradition is characterized by sand burial mounds and an abundance of plain chalky ware pottery, St. Johns Plain and Dunns Creek Red. Some incised and decorated pottery, Oklawaha Plain and Oklawaha Incised, is found but it is not common. The chalky ware is a local development which spread to many parts of Florida at this time. Red painting may have either come from the Gulf Coast or have been developed locally and thence spread outward.[5] Certainly it reached its greatest importance here.

Throughout the period there was apparently little change in the general cultural tradition. Yet, on the basis of foreign traits three temporal divisions can be made. The earliest of these, St. Johns Ia, early, is equated with the Deptford Period (and perhaps also with Tchefuncte and Adena)[6] because of the presence of tetrapod vessels and of Deptford Bold Check Stamped, Deptford Simple Stamped, and Deptford Linear Check Stamped trade pottery. These three types all had a momentary influence on the local ceramics, their decorative techniques being experimentally copied on local

[5] A third center on this same time level was the Hope Hull Focus of Alabama (J. B. Griffin, 1946: 50).

[6] Similarities have been noted by J. B. Griffin (1945a: 240).

chalky ware. However, for some reason they did not take hold, and check-stamping disappeared here for several hundred years until the St. Johns II Period. Podal bases, though, achieved considerable local popularity.

St. Johns Ia, late, is not as clear-cut a period as the previous, but seems to be a continuation of the basic pattern with influences from the Gulf Tradition. These consist of Swift Creek Complicated Stamped pottery and Hopewellian traits, including many copper objects, monitor pipes, and even a fragment of probably meteoric iron. The exact nature of this relationship is uncertain. It is expressed in a number of typical artifacts, but they are concentrated in a few sites and appear to have had little influence as a whole. St. Johns Ib is a continuation of the basic pottery, distinguished only by some examples of Weeden Island I pottery types.

St. Johns II carries on the tradition and is marked only by the introduction of check-stamped pottery. As before, temporal sub-divisions have been made solely on the basis of foreign influences. St. Johns IIa is marked by Weeden Island material and, strangely enough, has connections with the Gahagan Focus in Louisiana. Among other similarities are "long nosed god" copper maskettes, which occur in the two cultures and at Aztalan in Wisconsin (M.P.M. 26888-9), while similar examples in shell come from northern Alabama (Holmes, 1883, Pl. 70, Fig. 103) and Tennessee (M.A.I. 15/8078). Another of copper is reported from the St. Louis Mound, dating from Old Village times (personal communication, James B. Griffin). St. Johns IIb contains Middle Mississippi influence in the form of trade pottery, temple mounds, and Southern Cult objects, one of which, a copper plate with a forked-eye design (Fig. 6), is identical with a plate from the Spiro Focus in Oklahoma. Another St. Johns trait widely and sporadically found is the flanged tube. On the St. Johns it is limited to Mt. Royal. Other occurrences widespread in the Southeast, unfortunately cannot be dated.[7] The final horizon, St. Johns IIc, is only distinguished from the former by European material.

In the course of the history of the tradition, there was constant trade and interchange with neighboring northern and western cultures. Throughout the deposits of the tradition exotic material, such as copper, galena, mica, and foreign stone celts, is constantly found. Although the tradition itself changed very little through its course it appears to have adopted briefly many new innovations. For some reason none of these were integrated and appear to have been only brief fads. Thus constant interest in new traits was uniquely combined with a conservatism in avoiding their integration into the tradition. In early historical times the tradition can be correlated with the Eastern Timucua Indians.

[7] A cursory survey of the literature and museum collections reveals specimens from the following states: Georgia (A.M.N.H. 2/119; M.A.I. 1/31, 4/4167, 19/2989), Alabama (Anon., 1923b; Brannon, 1926: 45; Brannon, 1928); South Carolina (A.M.N.H. 2/120); Tennessee (Holmes, 1884: 454; M.A.I. 2/5120, 4/5297, 4/6331, 6/7698, 20/4883; A.M.N.H. 584 Terry); North Carolina (Anon., 1923a); and Pennsylvania (A.M.N.H. 202/2202). As was previously mentioned the only date attributed to these is in Tennessee where they are placed in the Candy Creek Focus (personal communication, James B. Griffin). Such a date does not correlate with the supposed date of the Florida finds.

SPANISH-INDIAN TRADITION

DEFINITION

Throughout much of Spanish America, the impact of Hispanic culture on that of the Indian resulted in a new development, a unique combination of cultural elements of both. This was true in Florida, although certain circumstances, such as the brief period of time involved and the limited and special contacts between Indians and whites, resulted in a new complex which was perhaps not so well defined and integrated as similar patterns elsewhere in Spanish America.

The Spanish-Indian Tradition varied somewhat in different parts of Florida depending on the basic Indian culture and on the type of Spanish contact, religious or secular. Both types of contact were found in the Northern St. Johns Area working on the basic agricultural St. Johns Tradition. The lack of excavated sites limits our knowledge of the Spanish-Indian Tradition, but it is clear that Indians were subject to both secular and religious influences, probably more of the former. Nevertheless many mission sites, and perhaps plantation sites, yet to be located and excavated in our area, will shed considerably more light on other phases of the pattern.

The background for the development of the Spanish-Indian Pattern lies in the typical Spanish attitude of the time towards the natives. The Spanish were interested in them as subjects for religious salvation, but they also wanted contented peon labor for agriculture, fishing, and other exploitative projects needing quantities of unskilled labor. This was in contrast to the practice of the English, and to some degree the French, who converted the Indians into a market for European products in return for furs, hides, vegetable oil, etc. The English, in addition, considered the natives either as potential enemies or allies, and through trade, armed the latter with European weapons. The Spanish never did this, and probably lost Florida for that reason.

The Spanish approach was to pacify the natives in the most feasible way, graft Roman Catholic doctrine upon the local religion when possible, keep the native culture relatively unchanged in terms of subsistence, and take them under the wing of the Spanish Crown in a typically feudal manner. In Florida this was accomplished fairly well, often with some of the understanding of cultural problems which is now called Applied Anthropology. Particularly in the matter of native religion, the Spanish, religious and secular alike, displayed considerable restraint, not attacking it until a propitious time (Vargas Ugarte, 1935).

As a result of this approach the aboriginal culture pattern remained relatively unchanged, and the culture had few traumatic experiences. A large amount of material culture, and probably also non-material culture, persisted with only the introduction of a few simple steel tools and, in places, a new religion and social customs.

Certain features resulting from this pattern are of interest and were generally widespread. The making of pottery, for example, continued in the pattern, although Spanish vessel forms were sometimes copied. This parallels the picture in New Mexico (Kidder and Shepard, 1936: 273), Cuba (Rouse, 1942: 144), and elsewhere at the same time.

Some experimentation was even tried in combining European and aboriginal techniques. One sherd has been seen of aboriginal ware with San Marcos Stamped type of decoration on the exterior and a vitreous green glaze on the interior (Smith, 1948: 316).

The retention of pottery under European acculturation is a trait mainly restricted to areas of Spanish domination in the New World, appearing to some extent also in areas under French influence, as in the Lower Mississippi Valley, but absent in areas under Northern European domination. This undoubtedly stems from the importance of earthenware vessels in the basic Spanish or Mediterranean peasant economy, while vessels of metal or wood appear to have been more important in Northern Europe. In turn, local Spanish cooking ware was influenced by that of the neighboring Indians, a parallel to the situation in New Mexico, where the Spanish plain wares appear to be derived from Mexican Indian wares (Hurt and Dick, 1946).

In other respects introductions were more divergent from aboriginal traits, as for example in the case of metal tools. As in the Indian River Area (Rouse, 1951), the most common of these appear to have been scissors, adzes, and axes. The latter two did not differ in function from those of the Indians, but they did in form. However, even the old type was not immediately rejected, as iron celt-like axes are found as well as the perforated type, the tool fitting in a hole in the handle rather than the haft fitting in a hole in the tool.

European weapons are not common in any sites of this pattern. Probably this is a result of the Spanish policy against arming Indians, but also it reflects the basic Spanish New World pattern in which few Spaniards and fewer Colonials had firearms. They used weapons similar to their Indian neighbors; in other places, for example, they perfected the use of the spear, lasso, and bola.

As was mentioned, one of the developments in Hispanic-American civilization is a blending of European and Indian elements to produce a unique culture. We have mentioned the Spanish influence on the Indian, so the reverse acculturation should be considered. It appears to have been strong, especially on the soldier or peasant level. The archeological sample from Spanish Fort Pupo could easily have been interpreted as an Indian occupation if historical sources did not list the personnel (Goggin, 1951). For example, the soldiers must have depended to a great extent on Indian pottery for ordinary cooking and eating purposes.

Only enough details are now known to indicate the nature of this interesting picture. Future work in archeological sites of the historic period will add many details.

DISTRIBUTION

The Northern St. Johns Area was undoubtedly one of the major centers of the Spanish-Indian Tradition, equalling the other centers of the Western Timucua and Apalachee. Within the area the tradition was localized around Spanish missions, in St. Augustine, and possibly later in European plantations.

The temporal range was probably from very late in the sixteenth century to early in the eighteenth century. A broken remnant of the pattern continued well past the middle of the eighteenth century but it was hardly an integrated culture.

ENVIRONMENTAL RELATIONS

There is a clear relation in most cases between the pattern and its particular geographical environment. The northern centers developed because of a two-fold Spanish interest in proselytising the natives and later in building up a good source of food supplies for the Spanish garrison at St. Augustine. These two purposes went well together, because missionary activity was easiest in densely populated regions where people were concentrated in large towns. In general such a concentration and population is possible only when agricultural skill is well developed and when the country is suited for farming. Such was the case in Northern St. Johns Area.

The relationship of the tradition to good farming lands is clearly indicated by our method of locating historic sites. English plantations of the eighteenth century, which appear on certain maps, generally are found on examination to have been situated on an earlier historic or prehistoric Indian site, for example Wrights Landing, Mt. Royal, and Rollestown.

HISTORY

The actual beginning of the tradition varied. In general, European artifacts came in early, even before Europeans were seen, in some cases by the middle of the sixteenth century. However, these appear to have been mainly ornaments and perhaps a few tools. The aboriginal culture pattern was little altered by these introductions.

But with the introduction of missions in the sixteenth century the pattern took form. Pressure was applied on the Indians to change religious customs and certain social traits such as polygyny. At the same time, to make their exploitation more effective, the Spanish introduced better tools.[8] This seems to have been a deliberately selective process on the part of the Spanish and was especially enforced in terms of forbidding the Indians firearms. However, at the same time there seems to have been little effort to change aboriginal customs purely for the sake of conformation to Spanish pattern, in part perhaps because there were strong parallels between Spanish-peasant and Indian cultures.

Despite some Indian rebellions, this pattern developed peacefully and became more thoroughly integrated until the end of the seventeenth century. Then raids by Creek and other Indians, who were accompanied in some cases by the English, became more numerous and disrupting. Having only primitive weapons, the Florida Indians were ineffective against the flintlock muskets of their foe, while the Spanish were unable to offer sufficient protection. For sometime these raids were disruptive but not too bad; however, the raid of Colonel Moore on the Apalachee towns in 1704 was completely shattering, as most of the villages and crops were destroyed and over 1000 captives were taken to South Carolina. From this time on the natives of the Northern St. Johns

---

[8] In contrast, where no exploitation was involved, the Spanish appear to have systematically kept iron and tools away from the Indians. See the account in Dickinson (1945: 63) of the thorough search by the Spanish coastal patrol of an Ais town for all metal objects, even including nails. Royal instructions, in 1687, reminded the Spanish governor to recover the weapons of all deceased soldiers, taking care to see that the Indians received no additional arms (Manucy, 1947: 82).

Region also suffered by English attacks until the survivors finally concentrated around St. Augustine.

SEMINOLE TRADITION

Our knowledge of Seminole occupation in the Northern St. Johns Area is so limited that any discussion of the tradition would have to be based on material from other parts of the state. Summary remarks on the tradition have been briefly made in another paper (Goggin, MS*a*).

It is probable that both aspects of the tradition will be found to have been present on the St. Johns. In the earliest aspect the Seminole were an intensive agricultural group concentrated in large towns and exhibiting a general Southeastern culture. The second aspect represents their adaption to a semi-tropical environment, a shifting from town grouping to matrilocal camps, with a declining emphasis on agriculture. The first aspect is clearly represented in some of the earlier towns in the region; the second aspect is perhaps that of the later occupants, those of Philips Town in 1869, for example.

GENERAL DISCUSSION

HISTORICAL RECONSTRUCTION

THE Northern St. Johns Area was populated at least four thousand years ago; how much before cannot be ascertained, but perhaps even several thousand years earlier. The earliest inhabitants were physically much like the Indians of the sixteenth century, although it is possible that they were dolichocephalic in contradistinction to the later broad-headed natives. At least the only skull from the Mt. Taylor horizon is long-headed (Wyman, 1875: 64–5).[1]

By Mt. Taylor times the area seems to have been densely populated. At this time the culture appears to have been a manifestation of a broader Florida development, especially strong in Central Florida.

Connection must have been maintained also with other Archaic centers in the Southeast. From one of them, the area received the concept of making fiber-tempered pottery.

Exactly what Archaic region inspired pottery development in Florida is uncertain. In many respects the local ware appears closest to that from the Georgia coast but the scarcity of identifiable Georgia specimens militates against active contacts between the two areas, although the idea may have initially gone from Georgia to Florida. Only a single specimen of decorated Georgia fiber-tempered pottery has been found in the St. Johns area, at Ponte Vedra Beach (U.C.A.L.), and only two other sherds of the same Stallings Punctated are known from elsewhere in Florida. One was found at Prairie Creek Midden near Gainesville (Goggin and Rouse, 1948) and the other at Cedar Keys (M.A.I. 10/4732).[2] Another difference between the pottery of the Northern St. Johns and the Georgia Coast is the use of incised decoration in the former and linear punctates in the latter although the basic designs are similar.

The other known nearby Archaic manifestation is the Lauderdale Focus of northern Alabama. This is more distant from the Northern St. Johns, and similarities appear to be less important. However, steatite vessels are very characteristic of the Alabama

[1] Physical anthropology, as such, has not been particularly considered in this paper. Although some skeletal specimens are available, they cannot be in general correlated with specific cultural horizons. The first description of crania from here was made by Allen (1896) but both Wyman and Moore had previously made comments on platycnemia (Wyman, 1875; Moore, 1894a).

More recently Ales Hrdlička has summarized a series of cranial measurements for Southeastern Indians including specimens in our area from the St. Johns River, Amelia Island, St. Augustine, Anastasia Island, Crescent Beach, New Smyrna, and Ormond (Hrdlička, 1940: 324–5, 360–1).

[2] I am not considering here plain fiber-tempered pottery. Willey (1949b) feels that plain Georgia and Florida material cannot be distinguished. On the other hand it seems to me that the distinctive surface treatment of the Georgia ware sets it apart from Florida specimens. A few plain sherds from Murphy Island Midden A (U.F.A.L.) are the only ones similar to Georgia fiber-tempered ware which have been seen in Florida. In further conversations with Gordon Willey (December, 1948), he has pointed out that there are probably two types of surface treatment in Georgia fiber-tempered pottery, although this is not brought out in the scant literature on that region.

Recent discoveries of a plain, coarse, heavily sand- and fiber-tempered ware in the upper levels of the Suwannee Site (Su 2, Suwannee County) to the west introduce a new form into our consideration. This ware is unlike anything else in Florida and may have moved down from south central Georgia.

culture as they are in Florida, while they do not appear to be present in Stalling Island (Fairbanks, 1942: 228–9). This is an important feature because steatite does not naturally occur in Florida and so all the large vessels from the Orange Period, and perhaps earlier, must have been imported. The evidence then, although not conclusive, favors a dual relationship between the Archaic of Florida and that of Northern Alabama and the Georgia coast. The actual source, though, of the Florida culture is not easy to ascertain. But it is probable that all the Southeastern Archaic peoples were more or less closely related culturally and possibly linguistically.

Language is not a trait which can be determined from archeological remains, but the local situation allows us some reflection. This is the unique position of the Timucua language centered, with one exception, on the Atlantic Coast and surrounded by Muskhogean languages.[3] It has all the appearances of being a remnant language with its back to the sea, surrounded but not submerged by the wave of Muskhogean languages. The little island of Tawasa language in Central Alabama (Swanton, 1929) suggests a once wider distribution for Timucuan speech. Since Timucuan was spoken in the Northern St. Johns by a group which culturally goes back into Archaic times it is not impossible that the language also goes back to Archaic times. Thus sixteenth-century Timucuan was perhaps the lineal descendent of a language possibly widely spoken by earlier Archaic peoples.

Correlation of archeology and linguistics is at the very best highly tentative. Working with data from the Gulf Coast, Willey (1949b: 518) suggests a contrary relation between the Archaic horizon language and those spoken by the historic Calusa, Ais, and Tekesta. He further suggests that Timucuan may have been introduced on a Santa Rosa-Swift Creek (St. Johns Ia, late) time level (Willey 1949b: 579). However, as far as the Northern St. Johns Area is concerned the suggestion previously made seems far more probable.

Details of the change from the Orange Period and Archaic Tradition to St. Johns I Period and the St. Johns Tradition are not available. Enough, however, is known to suggest that it was not a basic change in culture sufficient to indicate a change in peoples. The shift in pottery from fiber-tempered ware to chalky ware can be demonstrated, although the details of the loss of decoration are not known.

Much desired information could be obtained if a site with a sequence from Orange through the St. Johns I periods could be located, since all excavated have a gap between Orange and St. Johns II or a mixed picture for that time. This gap may have been caused by a substantial part of the population migrating to the coast to take advantage of new shell-fish resources created by the rising sea level. Nevertheless, large segments of the population remained on the St. Johns to construct the many burial mounds of this time.

Where the new concepts of St. Johns I came from is unknown, but it is most likely from the Florida Gulf Coast. Beginning at this time a cult of the dead appeared involving burial in mounds and the offering of artifacts—a great contrast to the indiscriminate

[3] In Swanton's (1946, Table I) newest classification of the Muskhogean stock, Natchez, Timucua, and Muskhogean are all equivalent divisions. When "Muskhogean" is used here, it is with a meaning equivalent to this second use, not in its broadest sense.

midden burial of earlier times. It is very possible, but again there is no evidence, that agriculture came in at the beginning of this period; at least it seems probable that it came in during the period.

Certain cultural aspects of St. Johns I times can be postulated. One is the change in artistic values from surface decoration, exemplified by the pottery and bone incision of previous time, to form, at least in ceramics. With few exceptions all pottery of the period is either plain or red painted. Incision, punctation, and stamping are rare, although these people were aware of the extensive ceramic developments being made on the west coast and received trade wares from these areas. Some of the west coast techniques were briefly tried early in the period, simple stamping, linear check stamping, and cord marking being applied to local chalky ware. These innovations, however, seem to have had only a very brief life span.

Meanwhile the plain chalky wares were made in a variety of eccentric and effigy forms, as well as less ornate shapes, in contrast to the simple flat-bottomed bowl of the previous period. With this interest in form it is perhaps no accident that one trait was widely accepted from the west coast: the use of three or four legs on the base of a vessel. These legs fit in a pattern where the values tend towards form rather than surface decoration.

Beginning in St. Johns I times and continuing until historic times we have abundant evidence that widespread trade connections existed with other parts of Florida and eastern United States. Early, that is during St. Johns I, there appear to have been considerable Hopewellian influences here. These presumably filtered through the even more strongly Hopewell-influenced peoples of the Gulf Coast (Santa Rosa-Swift Creek). In both St. Johns I and II times, connections throughout Florida, especially with the Gulf Coast, are indicated by trade wares.

Check-stamped pottery was introduced in the St. Johns II horizon. This again is an influence from outside, a manifestation of a broad Southeastern spread of the trait. In any case, on this time level check stamping spreads as far as Louisiana (Willey, 1945: 243). In other respects the culture shows no major changes although variances in occurrence and frequency of minor artifacts continue.

Even in this period widespread trade and cultural affiliations were maintained with far off areas. Temple mounds now appear, inspired no doubt by their importance to the west and north. Unusual ceremonial objects such as copper "long nosed god" maskettes, similar to examples from Tennessee, Louisiana, and Wisconsin, occur, as well as the renowned copper plate from Mt. Royal, which closely resembles one from the Spiro Mound in Oklahoma. Cahokia-type arrow points presumably came from Illinois.

Considering the strong influences from other areas, as represented by a wide variety of exotic artifacts throughout the St. Johns periods, it is surprising that the basic culture was so little affected. Somehow the St. Johns Tradition was so resistant to, or so little interested in, these new ideas that they made little headway. Traits were simply encisted in the tradition and then abandoned. Temple mounds, although adopted, never became widespread. The archeological literature is full of site after site, each of which is distinguished by unusual foreign trade material found nowhere else in the area.

In return for many traits and artifacts received from other Florida regions, the Northern St. Johns gave its distinctive ceramic innovation, chalky ware, both plain and check-stamped. This spread westward across Central Florida and throughout the Central Gulf Coast. To the south, it was important well into the northern part of the Glades Area, being present on the east coast all the way down the Keys, although chalky ware is rare south of the Caloosahatchee River on the Gulf coast.

Oklawaha Plain has very close typological relationships with similar folded rim pottery techniques of the Central Gulf Coast in Weeden Island I times. It is very possible that this is a result of influence from the St. Johns to the west.

More important in some ways is the influence the St. Johns copper work had on the historic metal work of the Indian River and Glades areas. It is uncertain where the copper work of the St. Johns was made. In any case the material was imported; perhaps the specimens were too. But the forms and embossed decoration clearly were the prototypes of Indian River and Glades ornaments.

With the coming of Europeans and the establishment of St. Augustine and the Spanish missions, the St. Johns Tradition was modified into the Spanish-Indian Tradition. Unfortunately before this could become well integrated the culture bearers themselves, the Eastern Timucua, were exterminated by northern Indians and the English.

The final Indian occupation, the Seminole Tradition, has very little continuity, if any, with the preceding cultural tradition. It is basically an expression of the general historic, European, modified Southeastern pattern, although in one sense the Oklawaha-band does bridge the gap between them and the St. Johns Tradition. This Seminole band apparently was a Yamassee group; earlier refugee Yamassees were affiliated with the Timucua in the eighteenth century.

PROBLEMS

This archeological survey, although it organizes much material, nevertheless, raises numerous questions. It is not easy to say which is most important, but certainly one point which is desirable is the location and extensive excavation of a midden site giving a good continuity from the Orange Period into St. Johns I. Details of this change are of great interest, especially the manner in which St. Johns Incised pottery died out— abruptly or gradually. Also it is significant to determine whether any direct or indirect evidence suggesting the introduction of agriculture can be obtained. It is probable that such a sequence can be obtained at many sites, but one which appears to be especially valuable for such an excavation is the Tick Island Midden.

Fully as important a problem, and perhaps even more so, is to explore the cultural content of the Mt. Taylor Period. No adequate excavations have yet been made in any site of this culture and our picture is pieced together from many fragments. Only by a detailed knowledge of this culture can we determine its relation to other preceramic cultures in Florida, and in addition find the hearth where it first developed.

The unclassified complex characterized by bannerstones, here considered under St. Johns I times, is an enigma. Further work is very desirable to place this complex, but it will not be easy to locate a site or sites to give us the necessary information.

Although Clarence B. Moore examined most of the sand mounds in the region, a careful search should be made for others to be excavated in accordance with modern techniques. It would be valuable to dig a site of the kind which appeared on analysis here to range from St. Johns I into St. Johns II times. Were these mounds used at different times intrusively, were they added to from time to time, or is there an actual presence together of traits from both horizons?

Within St. Johns II times there was probably considerably more change than can now be recognized. More detailed stratigraphic analysis of this horizon will probably prove profitable. Such preliminary work as was done by John W. Griffin in coastal Volusia County suggests the potentialities of more detailed work.

Approaching the historic time level our problems become more numerous. With good ethnographic accounts of palisaded towns available, the archeologist should endeavor to locate and excavate such a town to round out our meager cultural summary of the time. More work in sites of the Spanish-Indian horizon will illustrate how cultural change works in the region. And finally an excavated Seminole site would greatly supplement brief ethnographic accounts on the eighteenth century time level.

Turning to more specialized aspects many other problems arise. A more detailed knowledge of physical anthropology tied into the cultural framework would be helpful.

Ecological problems, too, deserve greater attention and will probably pay rich dividends. As a starting point the fluctuation in varieties and size of some of the fresh-water gastropods should be analyzed in connection with other stratigraphic work.

In no case should the reader feel that the last word has been said on St. Johns archeology. There is still a great need for more excavation but it should be done with the hope of solving specific problems, rather than picking a site convenient to a pleasant resort or one next to a highway.

SUMMARY

Data from 432 archeological sites have been analyzed and a synthesis has been given in this paper. This study reveals a long continuity of culture in the Northern St. Johns Region beginning before the time of Christ and extending until the eighteenth century, when the first demonstrable interlopers, the Seminoles, appeared to supplant the earlier natives.

The first horizon, the Mt. Taylor Period, is a non-ceramic culture, whose bearers dwelled mainly along rivers depending on the abundant animal life of the streams and marshes for subsistence.

In the succeeding horizon, the Orange Period, the first pottery makes its appearance, a fiber-tempered ware related to similar pottery of this time level throughout the Southeast. Despite this new trait, though, the over-all cultural picture appears to be little changed and the subsistence pattern is identical. Near the end of the period St. Johns Plain and St. Johns Incised became the basic pottery, the latter carrying on designs from Orange Incised pottery.

St. Johns I is distinguished by more significant changes than marked the previous horizon. Here for the first time appears an elaborate cult of the dead with burial mounds and funeral furniture. It is very likely, too, that agriculture now appeared. Nevertheless, the natives still depended greatly on wild food products and one of the major population shifts of the region took place during this horizon, when large segments of the inhabitants moved to the coast to utilize new shell-fish resources resulting apparently from a rising sea level. Ceramics at this time declined in importance, plain chalky ware (St. Johns Plain) being the dominant form. The lack of interest in surface decoration was compensated for to some extent by an exuberance of form.

St. Johns II is merely a continuance of the previous period, ceramically distinguished by the introduction of check-stamped pottery. In other respects the periods differ only in minor details. In historic times, the mid-sixteenth century, this culture can be identified with the Eastern Timucua Indians. Under Spanish influence the Indian culture was somewhat modified. However, English influence was even more significant—in the eighteenth century, English and English sponsored raids exterminated the Timucua and their culture.

The final Indian inhabitants of the area were the Seminole. No excavations have yet been made in their sites and ethnological data for the period of their residence here are too scarce to give us any detailed picture of their culture.

Our study has indicated quite conclusively that this area in all its cultural content is a part of the broader Southeastern culture pattern. In many ways the relations holding between this area and Eastern United States are unique. Many exotic archeological specimens found here occur elsewhere in Louisiana, Arkansas, Oklahoma, Illinois, and Wisconsin. Trade in raw materials must have been widespread.

Copper, presumably from the Great Lakes, was important in many periods. Also present are mica, rock crystal, and galena from the Appalachians. Even more impressive as articles of trade are the remains of steatite vessels imported from somewhere outside the state, probably Alabama. These weighed many pounds and were no easy transportation problem.

APPENDIX A: SITES

ALL the known sites in the area are listed, together with the period of their occupation (when known), their nature, general location, references in the literature, and references to museum specimens from each particular site.

The thoroughness of site coverage varies. It is certainly most complete along the St. Johns River and secondly along the coast, while very poor in between. Most of the major sites along the river are probably represented as a result of the detailed work of Jeffries Wyman and Clarence B. Moore, but it is quite possible that in other sections many more will be found, as well as smaller ones along the St. Johns itself. Unfortunately the detailed site survey of Volusia County, made by the Florida Park Service, Archeological Survey, was not available for study. Considering all factors, it is estimated that the number of sites given here probably represents less than one-half of all in the region.

Period of occupation is indicated by designations in parenthesis immediately following the site name. The abbreviations used are as follows:

Mt. T.	Mt. Taylor
Or.	Orange
St. J. I	St. Johns I
St. J. II	St. Johns II
S. A.	St. Augustine
Sem.	Seminole

As used in this list the term "mound" refers to a sand mound, in most cases used for burials but not necessarily so. Midden sites may be either large refuse deposits or thin layers more commonly called village sites.

Location is first noted by county, indicated before the site name by a county abbreviation, together with a number designating the site within the county.[1] The following abbreviations are used:

Cn	Charlton
Wr	Ware
Na	Nassau
Du	Duval
Cl	Clay
SJ	St. Johns
Pu	Putnam
Fl	Flagler
Mr	Marion
Vo	Volusia
Se	Seminole
La	Lake

[1] Abbreviations used are those of the University of Florida-Florida State University state-wide recording system. This interlocks in abbreviations and numbers with the other major published site lists (Rouse, 1951; Willey, 1949b). The Georgia abbreviations unfortunately are unique to this paper; previous county designations used by the National Park Service (Ocmulgee National Monument) duplicate Florida abbreviations and this was not realized until too late to change the Florida forms.

With the exception of the first four sites in Georgia (Charlton and Ware counties) all sites are in Florida. The sites are arranged in order from north to south along each major physiographic line within a subarea. Thus, for example, in subarea I sites are listed the whole length of the coast first, then along the St. Johns River. Distances when given are approximate. For further information the reader is urged to consult maps in Moore (1894b, 1895c, 1922a) and Wyman (1875) as well as the map in this paper (Fig. 9) and various navigation charts of the coast and river.

As far as possible all references in the literature are given for each site. In any case the major ones are listed. The coverage of museum collections is not as thorough. Pottery is probably fairly well represented, but many of the more common artifacts, such as stone celts and stone points, are not.

Site locations on the accompanying map (Fig. 9) are not all that can be desired. It was impossible under existing conditions, and beyond the scope of this paper, to precisely pinpoint each site in the field. The locations given on this map are of two types. When the site number is given with an adjacent dot the location is believed to be fairly close and placed on the basis of actual field study, or through published source material. When only a number is given the location is somewhat more generalized and when no number is shown on the map only the county is known.

Undoubtedly local experts will find errors in the map. I only hope they understand the circumstances; if not, then I willingly allow them the thrill of finding a mistake.

SUBAREA I

Cn 1. Red Ant Mound, Floyds Island, Okefenokee Swamp. St. J. II. (Y.P.M. 21574.)

Cn 2. Whooping Crane Mound, Floyds Island, Okefenokee Swamp. St. J. Ia, late. (Y.P.M. 21577.)

Cn 3. Buzzard Mound, Floyds Island, Okefenokee Swamp. St. J. Ib. (Y.P.M. 21575.)

Wr 1. Mound on Bug-a-boo Island, Okefenokee Swamp. St. J. Ib. (Y.P.M. 21579–80.)

Na 1. Petree Farm. St. J. II (?). Location and type of site unknown. (Fort Clinch State Monument Museum.)

Na 2. Lighthouse Midden, one mile east of Fernandina, Amelia Island. (Moore, 1922c: 55; R.S.P.F. 38990.)

Na 3. Lighthouse Mound, one mile east of Fernandina, Amelia Island. (Moore, 1922c: 55–68; C.M.N.H. 49628; R.S.P.F. 38987.)

Na 4. Fernandina Cemetery, Amelia Island, midden (?). S. A. (Simpson Collection.)

Na 5. Fernandina, midden. St. J. II. (Brinton, 1872: 356; H.P.M. 74–26/12763–6.)

Na 6. Amelia Island Mound. (Mitchell, 1875.)

Na 7. Mound northeast of Suarez Bluff, Amelia Island. (Moore, 1922c: 53–5.)

Na 8. Mound south of Suarez Bluff, Amelia Island. (Moore, 1922c: 52–3.)

Na 9. Harrisons Mound, Amelia Island. (Moore, 1922c: 51–2.)

Na 10. Fort San Carlos, Fernandina. Or., S. A. (Anon., 1951.)

Du 1. Mound A, south end of Talbot Island. (Moore, 1922c: 50.)

Du 2. Mound B, south end of Talbot Island. (Moore, 1922c: 50.)

Du 52. Black Hammock Island Midden, north end.

Du 3. Sawpit Mound, ten miles north of the St. Johns River, west of Fort George Island. (Moore, 1922c: 50.)

Du 4. Fort George Island Sand Mound. (Mayberry, 1878: 306.)

Du 5. Fort George Island Midden. Or., St. J. II. (J. Bartram, 1942: 48, 76; Le Baron, 1884: 771; Mayberry, 1878: 305–6; Small, 1923a: 20–1; H.P.M. 81–1–23/187–8,–192.)

Du 53. Unnamed site, Fort George Island. St. J. II, S. A. (U.F.A.L.)

SJ 1. Ponte Vedra Beach. Or., St. J. II, S. A. (U.C.A.L.; U.M.M.A.; F.S.M. 76405–10; U.S.N.M. 379171.)

SJ 14. Palm Valley, midden. S. A. (U.F.A.L.)

SJ 36. Mabry site, sand mound and midden area. St. J. II. (U.F.A.L.)

SJ 37. Jones Mound. (U.F.A.L.)

SJ 38. Jenks Landing, midden. St. J. IIc or S. A. (U.F.A.L.)

SJ 2. San Diego Mound, twelve miles north of St. Augustine, on the west bank of North River. (Douglass, 1885: 81.)

SJ 32. Shellbluff Landing, North River, midden. Or., St. J. II, S. A. (F.S.P.S.; U.F.A.L.)

SJ 3. Wrights Landing, North River, midden. Or., St. J. II, S. A. (Thompson and Ryman Collection; U.F.A.L.)

SJ 33. South of Wrights Landing, North River, midden. Or., St. J. II, S. A. (F.S.P.S.; U.F.A.L.)

SJ 4. Sanchez Mound, eight miles north of St. Augustine.[2] (Douglass, 1882: 586, 1885: 147; U.F.A.L.)

SJ 5. Mound about eight miles north of St. Augustine. (U.S.N.M. 31927–9.)

SJ 6. Shell field about eight miles north of St. Augustine. (U.S.N.M. 31927–9.)[3]

SJ 7. Shell midden near St. Augustine. St. J. II. (U.S.N.M. 148874–6, 148888, 148901.)

SJ 8. Diego and Jenks Mounds, near St. Augustine. St. J. II. (U.S.N.M. 31737–40, 46, 90–91.)

SJ 39. Florida Deaf and Blind School, St. Augustine, midden. St. J. II. (U.F.A.L.)

SJ 40. Fort Moosa, midden. St. J. II, S. A., English, American Territorial. (U.F.A.L., Castillo de San Marcos National Monument Collection.)

SJ 31. "Fountain of Youth" site, midden, cemetery. Or., St. J. I, St. J. II, S. A. (Seaberg, MS; U.F.A.L.)

SJ 34. Nuestra Señora de la Leche Mission. S. A. (U.F.A.L.)

SJ 9. Moat, Castillo de San Marcos, St. Augustine. S. A. (Jordan, 1886; Castillo de San Marcos National Monument Museum.)

SJ 10. St. Augustine, midden. St. J. II, S. A. (St. Augustine Historical Society Collections; U.S.N.M. 148891; H.P.M. 94–26/12751–4; U.F.A.L.)

SJ 10a. St. Francis Barracks, St. Augustine. S. A. (U.F.A.L.)

SJ 11. Fitzpatrick Mound, near St. Augustine. St. J. II, S. A. (Webb, 1894; U.S.N.M. 148911, 148926.)

SJ 12. Anastasia Island, (midden ?, exact location unknown). St. J. II, S. A. (Webb, 1894; M.P.M.; U.S.N.M. 148933; M.A.I. 5/2967.)

SJ 13. Coontie Island, west side of Anastasia Island. (Thompson and Ryman Collection; U.F.A.L.)

SJ 41. Young Ave. site, Anastasia Island, midden. St. J. II. (U.F.A.L.)

SJ 45. Old Spanish Chimney, midden. American Territorial. (U.F.A.L.)

SJ 42. Weff site, midden. St. J. II. (U.F.A.L.)

[2] This is probably the mound at the north end of the Wrights Landing site. SJ 5 may also be this or another reported nearby but not visited.

[3] This may be Wrights Landing, SJ 3.

SJ 43. Crescent Beach Bridge, midden. Or., St. J. II, S. A. (U.F.A.L.)

SJ 44. Fort Matanzas, midden. S. A., English, American Territorial. (Fort Matanzas National Monument Collection.)

Du 6. Midden (?), mouth of St. Johns River. St. J. I, St. J. II. (U.S. N.M. 169534, 289513–14.)

Du 7. St. Johns Bluff Mound. (Moore, 1894*b*: 205.)

Du 8. St. Johns Bluff Midden. Or., St. J. I (?), St. J. II, S. A. (Wyman, 1868*a*: 460–2; H.P.M. 74-26/12711–16.)

Du 9. Fulton Mound, one-half mile southwest of Fulton. (Moore, 1894*b*: 205.)

Du 10. Johnson Mound, one-half mile north of St. Charles Creek, northeast of New Berlin. St. J. Ib. (Moore, 1895*c*: 450–2.)

Du 11. Gilbert Mound, one-quarter mile southeast of Shields Mound. St. J. Ia, early. (Moore, 1895*c*: 468–70; M.A.I. 17/3492, 3838–9, 4501.)

Du 12. Shields Mound, near Newcastle, on south bank of St. Johns River at Mill Cove. St. J. IIa. (Moore, 1894*b*: 204–5, 1895*c*: 452–68; U.S.N.M. 28080–6; M.A.I. 17/513–8, 2335, 3404, 3847, 3484–6, 3488; D.P.M.; R.O.M. HH 77.)

Du 13. Monroe Mound, one-quarter mile southeast of Grant Mound. St. J. Ia, late to Ib. (Moore, 1895*c*: 470–2; J. B. Griffin, 1946: 49, 70; M.A.I. 17/3491, 3834.)

Du 14. Grant Mound, on south bank of St. Johns River, two miles west of Mill Cove. St. J. IIa. (Moore, 1894*b*: 200–4, 1895*c*: 473–88; J. B. Griffin, 1946: 77, 88; M.A.I. 17/621–2, 1216, 1218, 1233, 1813, 2315, 2317, 3481–2, 3496, 3513–19, 3192, 4512; M.A.I. 18/267–8, 283–5, 287–9, 291, 294–9, 301, 303, 305; H.P.M. 96–23–10/49621–2; R.S.P.F. 18576, 18592 (?); D.P.M.; F.S.P.S. Du 2.) Material from around the mound suggests a much longer occupation—St. J. I to St. J. IIb.

Du 15. Low Mound A, south of Grant Mound. St. J. Ib. (Moore, 1895*c*: 488–9; M.A.I. 18/302.)

Du 16. Low Mound B, south of Grant Mound. (Moore, 1895*c*: 489.)

Du 17. Low Mound C, south of Grant Mound. (Moore, 1895*c*: 489.)

Du 18. Low Mound D, south of Grant Mound. (Moore, 1895*c*: 489–90.)

Du 19. Low Mound E, south of Grant Mound. St. J. Ib. (Moore, 1895*c*: 490–4; M.A.I. 17/3825, 3828, 4511, 4513, 4517; R.S.P.F. 27965, 27968.) In addition there are specimens from this group in general (M.A.I. 17/3826, 3842–3; R.S.P.F. 27968).

Du 20. Broward Mound, north shore St. Johns River, one-quarter mile northwest from Cedar Landing. St. J. Ia, late. (Moore, 1895*c*: 495–6; M.A.I. 17/4510.)

Du 21. Horseshoe Landing, Mound A, south shore St. Johns River near Newcastle. St. J. Ia, late. (Moore, 1895*c*: 494–5.)

Du 22. Horseshoe Landing, other mounds. (Moore, 1895*c*: 495.)

Du 23. Brutus Mound, one-quarter mile south of Horseshoe Landing Mounds. (Moore, 1895*c*: 495.)

Du 24. Denton Mound, south bank, St. Johns River, one-half mile east of Chaseville. St. J. Ib. (Moore, 1895*c*: 500–1; M.A.I. 17/3829.)

Du 25. Reddie Point Mound A, south bank of St. Johns River. St. J. Ia, late to Ib. (Moore, 1895*c*: 497–8; M.A.I. 18/312; R.S.P.F. uncataloged.)

Du 26. Reddie Point Mound B. (Moore, 1895*c*: 498.)

Du 27. Daniels Landing Mound, west shore St. Johns River, above Trout Creek, one-quarter mile north of landing. (Moore, 1895*c*: 498.)

Du 28. Chaseville Mound A, east bank, St. Johns River. (Moore, 1895*c*: 501–2.)

Du 29. Chaseville Mound B. (Moore, 1895c: 502.)

Du 30. Low Mound A, Alicia, east bank St. Johns River. (Moore, 1895c: 498–9.)

Du 31. Low Mound B, Alicia. St. J. Ib. (Moore, 1895c: 499–500; M.A.I. 17/3832; R.S.P.F. 27967, uncataloged.) Undesignated material from Alicia includes M.A.I. 17/2344, 3489, 3831.

Du 32. Floral Bluff Mound, St. J. I (?). (Moore, 1895c: 502; M.A.I. 17/3835.)

Du 33. Arlington Mound. St. J. I, very late (?). (Moore, 1922a: 9–16; M.A.I. 17/3833; R.S.P.F. uncataloged.)

Du 34. Jacksonville, midden (?). St. J. II. (U.S.N.M. 28342.)

Du 35. Low Mound A, South Jacksonville. (Moore, 1922a: 17.)

Du 36. Low Mound B, South Jacksonville. St. J. Ib. (Moore, 1922a: 17–18.)

Du 37. Point La Vista Mound. St. J. II. (Moore, 1922a: 18–22.)

Du 38. Low Mound A near Point La Vista, one mile south of Point La Vista. St. J. I?. (Moore, 1922a: 22–4.)

Du 39. Low Mound B near Point La Vista. St. J. I. (Moore, 1922a: 24–6; M.A.I. 17/2340, 3490.)

Du 40. Low Mound C near Point La Vista. St. J. Ib. (Moore, 1922a: 26–8; M.A.I. 18/346.)

Du 41. Clay Bluff, midden, west bank St. Johns River above Jacksonville. Or. (Personal communication, Floyd Newman.)

Du 42. Mulberry Grove Mound, west bank St. Johns River, about ten miles south of Jacksonville. (Moore, 1922a: 28–32; M.A.I. 17/3836–7, 3862.)

Du 43. Large Mound at Beauclerc. St. J. Ib. (Moore, 1894b: 197–200; M.A.I. 17/3401, 3493–5; W.F.I.S. 15066; H.P.M. 49619.)

Du 44. Small mound at Beauclerc. (Moore, 1894b: 196.)

Du 45. Beauclerc, midden (?). St. J. II. (F.S.M. 82474–6.)

Cl 1. Orange Park Mound A. (Moore, 1894b: 196.)

Cl 2. Orange Park Mound B. (Moore, 1894b: 196.)

Cl 3. Peoria Mound, near Doctors Lake. St. J. II. (Moore, 1894b: 195–6, 1922a: 32–4; M.A.I. 17/95.)

Du 46. Mound two miles east of Mandarin in T. 3 S., R. 26 E. (Le Baron, 1884: 771.)

Du 47. Mound two miles east of Mandarin in T. 4 S., R. 26 E. (Le Baron, 1884: 771.)

Du 48. Mandarin Point Mound A. St. J. II (?). (Moore, 1894b: 194.)

Du 49. Mandarin Point Mound B. St. J. II (?). (Moore, 1894b: 194; M.A.I. 17/3823.)

Du 50. Mandarin Point Mound C. St. J. II (?). (Moore, 1894b: 194–5; H.P.M. 94–12–10/ 49618). Undesignated material from these mounds includes M.A.I. 17/3824.

Du 51. Julington Creek Mound, near Tar Landing. (Moore, 1894b: 192–4; Allen, 1896: 371–2; M.A.I. 17/2267.)

SJ 15. Mound A near Fruit Cove, east bank St. Johns River, south of Julington Creek. (Moore, 1894b: 191.)

SJ 16. Mound B near Fruit Creek, 400 yards east of Mound A. (Moore, 1894b: 191–2.)

Cl 4. Flemings Island Mound, between Black Creek and Hibernia on west bank St. Johns River. (Moore, 1894b: 191.)

SJ 17–20. Four mounds one mile south of Switzerland. (Moore, 1894b: 191.)

Cl 5. Magnolia Mound. (Moore, 1894b: 191.)

SJ 21. Orangedale Mound, 200 yards from St. Johns River. (Moore, 1894b: 189–90; R.S.P.F. 18591.)

Cl 6. Mound near Peters Creek, five miles northwest of Green Cove Springs. (Moore, 1894b: 190–1; R.S.P.F. 40361.)

Cl 7. Geiger Mound, west bank St. Johns River, 3.5 miles south of Green Cove Springs. (Moore, 1894b: 190.)

Cl 10. Fort San Francisco de Pupo. Or., S. A. (Goggin, 1951; U.F.A.L.)

Cl 8. Bayard Point Mound, 0.5 mile inland from St. Johns River. S. A. (?) or Sem. (Moore, 1894b: 188–9; M A.I. 17/3006, 3014–5.)

SJ 22. Harris Mound, 3 miles north of Picolata. (Moore, 1894b: 186–8; R.S.P.F. 40386.)

SJ 23. Usina Mound, 0.5 mile south of Picolata. (Moore, 1894b: 185; Le Baron, 1884: 771.)

SJ 24. Mound near St. Augustine Road, 6.5 miles east of Picolata. (Moore, 1894b: 186.)

Cl 9. Mound near Clarks Creek, west of the St. Johns River. (Moore, 1894b: 186.)

SJ 25. Racey Point Mound. St. J. Ia, early to b. (Moore, 1894b: 181–5; J. B. Griffin, 1946: 49; M.A.I. 17/2264, 3598–3603, 18/357; R.S.P.F. 39270, 39320.)

SJ 27. Coco Mound, exact location uncertain. St. J. II. (A.M.N.H. D 109.)

SUBAREA II

SJ 26. Deep Creek Mound. (Moore, 1894b: 181; C.M.N.H. 49613.)

Pu 1. Whetstone Point, midden, east bank St. Johns, 9 miles north of Palatka. (Moore, 1892c: 917.)

Pu 2. Rice Creek Mound, 5 miles north of Palatka. (Moore, 1894b: 181.)

Pu 3. Forresters Point, midden, east bank St. Johns River north of Palatka. (Wyman, 1875: 44; Moore, 1894b: 131.)

Pu 4. Shell midden two miles north of Palatka. Mt. T., Or., St. J. II. (Calkins, 1878: 226–7; Le Baron, 1884: 772; Moore, 1893: 8–10; H.P.M. 19990; W.F.I.S. 15049.)

Pu 5. East Palatka Midden. (Le Baron, 1884: 772; Moore, 1894b: 131.)

Pu 6. East Palatka Mound. St. J. II?. (Moore, 1894b: 178–80; H.P.M. uncataloged; R.S.P.F. 39202.)

Pu 7. Shell midden nine miles east of Palatka. (Le Baron, 1884: 772.)

Pu 8. Palatka Midden. Or., St. J. II. (Wyman, 1875: 42–3; Calkins, 1878: 227; Le Baron, 1884: 772; H.P.M. 74-26/12735.)

Pu 66. Shell midden 200 yards north of Rollestown. St. J. II. (U.F.A.L.)

Pu 64. Rollestown (Charlotia), midden. Mt. T., Or., St. J. I, St. J. II, S. A. (J. Bartram, 1942: 37, 46, 69; Federal Writers Project, 1940: 355; U.F.A.L.)

Pu 65. Rolles Mound, Rollestown.

Pu 67. Midden in swamp opposite Rollestown.

Pu 9. St. Johns Landing Mound 1. St. J. Ib. (Le Baron, 1884: 773; Moore, 1894b: 174; R.S.P.F. 39204; M.A.I. 17/3874.)

Pu 10. St. Johns Landing Mound 2. (Moore, 1894b: 174–5.)

Pu 11. St. Johns Landing Mound 3. (Moore, 1894b: 175.)

Pu 12. St. Johns Landing Mound 4. (Moore, 1894b: 175.)

Pu 13. Browns Landing Mound, 0.5 mile from river, 5 miles south of Palatka. (Moore, 1894b: 174.)

Pu 14. Dunns Creek Mound. St. J. IIa, IIc, intrusive. (Lente, 1877; Moore, 1894a: 7–15; M.A.I. 17/4980–1; H.P.M. 93–13–N/49579, 49580, 49588, 49590, 49591, 49594, 49595, 49600–49604; R.S.P.F. 39203, 39333; U.M.M.A. 254, 257; U.F.A.L.)

Pu 15. Pomona, midden (?). St. J. II. (H.P.M. 81-30/24853–4.)

Pu 16. Mound near Crescent City. St. J. II. (F.S.M. 60504.)

Pu 17. Bear Island, midden, Crescent Lake. (Le Baron, 1884: 773; J. Bartram, 1942: 45, 75.)

Pu 18. Murphy Island Midden A. Or. (J. Bartram, 1942: 37; Wyman, 1875: 42; H.P.M. 74-26/12745; M.A.I. 17/2281; U.F.A.L.)

Pu 19. Murphy Island Midden B. St. J. II. (U.F.A.L.)

Pu 20. North Mound on Murphy Island. St. J. Ia, late, IIc, intrusive. (J. Bartram, 1942: 37, 70; Moore, 1894a: 15, 1895b: 503–15; H.P.M. 96–23–10/49620; C.M.N.H. 49627; M.A.I. 17/57–9, 3393, 3395, 3575, 3578, 3587; R.O.M. HH 72–4; U.F.A.L.)

Pu 21. South Mound on Murphy Island. St. J. IIa. (Moore, 1895b: 515–16; U.F.A.L.)

Pu 63. Murphy Island Midden C, on east side of island.

Pu 22. Buffalo Bluff,[4] midden. St. J. Ia, II. (Wyman, 1875: 42; Le Baron, 1884: 773; Y.P.M. 5450; W.F.I.S. 15154; U.F.A.L.)

Pu 58. Cedar Hammock, midden in swamp about three-quarters mile north of Stokes Landing.

Pu 59. Stokes Island, midden. St. J. II. (U.F.A.L.)

Pu 23. Spaldings Lower Store, Stokes Landing. Or., St. J. Ia, II, S. A., Sem. (J. Bartram, 1942: 37, 45, 70, 75; W. Bartram, 1943: 182 ff.; Goggin, 1949b; U.F.A.L.)

Pu 24. Stokes Landing Midden. St. J. II. (J. Bartram, 1942: 70; U.F.A.L.)

Pu 60. Trout Island, midden.

Pu 25. Barrentines, midden, on Trout Creek. (Moore, 1892c: 917.)

Pu 26. Midden one-half mile north of Horse Landing, shell ridge in swamp. Or. (Moore 1892c: 917; W.F.I.S. 15044.)

Pu 27. Horse Landing,[5] midden. Mt. T., St. J. II. (Wyman, 1868a, 1875: 41–2; Moore, 1894b: 131; H.P.M. 74–26/12624–5.)

Pu 61. Site north of Camp Branch, midden.

Pu 62. Possum Bluff, midden.

Pu 28. Midden one-half mile north of Nashua, east bank St. Johns River. (Le Baron, 1884: 773; U.F.A.L.)

Pu 29. Nashua, midden. (Le Baron, 1884: 773.)

Pu 30. Midden, one-quarter mile west of St. Johns River opposite Nashua. (Le Baron, 1884: 773.)

Pu 31. Midden one mile north of Welaka, east bank St. Johns River. (Moore, 1892c: 917.)

Pu 32. Welaka, midden. (Wyman, 1875: 40.)

Pu 33. Midden, west bank St. Johns River, one-half mile north of mouth of Oklawaha River and one-half mile from St. Johns River. (Le Baron, 1884: 773.)

Pu 34. Mount Hope, midden, Beecher Point, east bank of St. Johns River, south of Welaka. St. J. II. (Wyman, 1875: 40; J. Bartram, 1942: 38, 70; W. Bartram, 1943: 150, 185; F.S.M. 82625–90.)

Pu 35. Mount Royal, mound and/or midden. Or. (?), St. J. IIb. (J. Bartram, 1875, 1942: 38, 45, 70, 74–5; W. Bartram, 1853, 1940: 101–2, 1943: 150, 185 ff.; Brinton, 1859: 168–9; Wyman, 1875; Moore, 1894b: 130–46, 1895a: 16–35; Holmes, 1894: 117–20; Waring and Holder, 1945; J. B. Griffin, 1946: 77; Waring, 1948: 154; M.A.I. 17/1453, 2111, 3561–2, 3565, 3844, 3885–8, 3900, 3906–11, 4977; H.P.M. 94–12–10/49611, 49613, 49615–17; U.F.A.L.)

---

[4] A short distance below here was a site noted by Le Baron (1884: 773) at the home of Mr. White. Measuring from this point Le Baron locates a number of sites, but since the present location of White's place is uncertain these sites are not recorded.

[5] Presumably the present Horse Landing on the west side of the river is the one noted by both Wyman and Moore. However, they locate it on the east side of the river, Moore placing it approximately across from the present site. But Wyman (1875) places it on his map many miles to the north not far from Palatka. This is probably a definite mistake. Still more confusing is the Horse Landing on Dunns Creek, site of the mound.

Pu 35a. Mount Royal, midden. St. J. IIb, IIc (also English plantation site and early nineteenth century American occupation). (U.F.A.L.)

Pu 36. Small mound near Mount Royal. (Moore, 1894a: 35.)

Pu 37. Norwalk Landing Midden. St. J. II. (Letter of A. J. Waring to I. Rouse, 7/4/44.)

Pu 38. Norwalk Landing Mound. St. J. I (?). (Moore, 1894a: 15–16; R.S.P.F. 39233.)

Pu 39. Fort Gates, midden. St. J. II. (Wyman, 1875: 40; Le Baron, 1884: 773; U.F.A.L.)

Pu 40. Rocky Point, midden. Or. (W. Bartram, 1940: 151–2; Wyman, 1875: 40; M.A.I. 17/363–5; H.P.M. uncataloged.)

Pu 41. Shell midden due west of Hog Island. (Le Baron, 1884: 774.)

Pu 42. Louis' Place, mound, 1.5 miles west of Hog Island, 200 feet from river road. (U.S.N.M. 378311.)

Pu 43. Drayton Island, midden, east shore of island. St. J. II. (J. Bartram, 1942: 45, 70; Wyman, 1868a: 462; H.P.M. 19988, 74–26/12744.)

Pu 44–5. Two mounds near Georgetown. (Le Baron, 1884: 774.)

Pu 46–7. Two middens near Georgetown. (Le Baron, 1884: 774; Moore, 1894b: 131.) One of these may be the "shell heap opposite Drayton Island, Lake George." Or. (H.P.M. uncataloged.)

Mr 1. Midden 1, Salt Spring Run, north bank, 0.25 mile from Lake George. St. J. II. (Abshire et al., 1935: 7; U.S.N.M. 378332; U.F.A.L.)

Mr 2. Midden 2 ("Main Shell Heap"), Salt Spring Run, about 5 miles from springs and 0.5 mile from Lake George. Mt. T., Or., St. J. II. (J. Bartram, 1942: 44, 74; Moore, 1893: 10, 1894c: 22; Abshire et al., 1935: 2–6; U.S.N.M. 378319–31, 378414–18; U.F.A.L.)

Mr 3. Midden 3, Salt Spring Run, Ozmores Hammock. St. J. II. (Abshire et al., 1935: 4; U.S.N.M. 378318; U.F.A.L.)

Mr 4. Midden 4, Salt Spring Run, near spring. Or., St. J. II. (U.S.N.M. 378315–7; U.F.A.L.)

La 1. Mouth of Silver Glen Run, midden. (J. Bartram, 1942: 44, 74; Le Baron, 1884: 774.)

La 2. Silver Glen Spring, midden. Or., St. J. II. (J. Bartram, 1942: 44, 74; Wyman, 1875: 38–40; U.S.N.M. 378333–49, 378404–13; Y.P.M. 5454; H.P.M. 74–26/12566–8; M.A.I. 17/1764; Sweett Collection; U.F.A.L.; collection in store at spring.)

La 3. Mound A near Silver Glen Spring. (Moore, 1894b: 176.)

La 4. Mound B near Silver Glen Spring. (Moore, 1894b: 176–7.)

La 5. Juniper Creek Midden, about 2 miles from Lake George (1.5 miles according to Moore) on south side of creek. St. J. II (?). (Wyman, 1875: 38; Le Baron, 1884: 774; Moore, 1894b: 177; Abshire et al., 1935: 27–8.)

La 6. Juniper Creek Mound. St. J. I (?). (Moore, 1894b: 177; R.S.P.F. 39283.)

Vo 1. Several small "mounds" near Seville. (Le Baron, 1884: 774.)

Vo 2. Volusia Bar, midden (?). St. J. II. (H.P.M. 79–23/18230–1.)

Vo 3. Ropes Island, midden, right bank St. Johns River at entrance to Lake George, apparently the present Zinder Point. St. J. I (?), St. J. II. (J. Bartram, 1942: 38–9, 44, 71, 74; Wyman, 1875: 38; Le Baron, 1884: 774; H.P.M. 74–26/12718–9.)

Vo 4. Hitchens Creek Midden A, on north or east bank at short distance above mouth. Mt. T., Or. (Moore, 1893: 11; W.F.I.S. 15101.)

Vo 5. Hitchens Creek Mound. St. J. II (?). (Moore, 1894a: 35–6, 1894b: 148; Allen, 1896: 372; R.S.P.F. 40375.)

Vo 6. Hitchens Creek Midden B, further upstream and on the opposite bank from midden A. (Moore, 1894b: 131.)

La 7. Shell bluff near mouth of Blue Creek, south of Volusia Bar. (Moore, 1892c: 917.)

Vo 7. Large shell heap in swamp near Morrisons Creek. Mt. T. (Moore, 1893: 11–12; H.P.M. uncataloged.)

Vo 8–9. Two shell fields near Morrisons Creek. (Moore, 1892c: 917, 1894b: 131.)

Vo 10. Morrisons Creek Mound. (Moore, 1894b: 131.)

La 8. Duval's Midden. (Moore, 1892c: 917, 1894a: 36.)

La 9. Mound A near Duval's, Blue Creek. St. J. II. (Moore, 1894a: 36–7.)

La 10. Mound B near Duval's, Blue Creek. St. J. II. (Moore, 1894a: 37, 1894b: 146–8; W.F.I.S. 15047; M.A.I. 17/2290, 2292, 3960–1; H.P.M. 92–5–10/49526; R.S.P.F. 39328.)

La 11. Mound in Pine Woods near Duval's, 2 miles west of landing. St. J. II. (Moore, 1894a: 37–42, 120–1; M.A.I. 17/359, 1171; C.M. 17785.)

La 12–15. Four mounds in swamp, 1.25 miles below Astor. St. J. I. (Abshire et al., 1935: 1; U.S.N.M. 378453–4.)

La 16. Shell midden one mile below Astor. Mt. T. (Moore, 1894c: 22.)

Vo 11. Shell midden below Volusia. (Wyman, 1875: 38.)

Vo 12. Shell midden along river bank, Volusia. St. J. II. (J. Bartram, 1942: 44, 74; Wyman, 1868a, 1875: 38; U.S.N.M. 378355–6; W.F.I.S. 15083.)

Vo 13. Dillards Grove, midden, short distance inland at Volusia. (Wyman, 1875: 38; M.A.I. 17/509–10; W.F.I.S. 15056.)

Vo 14–18. Five low mounds near Volusia. St. J. I. (Moore, 1894a: 42–4; U.S.N.M. 149554; H.P.M. 92–5–10/49501–2; M.A.I. 17/3947.)

La 17. Astor (Fort Butler) Midden. Or., St. J. II. (Wyman, 1868a, 1875: 38; H.P.M. 74–26/12747.)

La 18. Spaldings Upper Store, Astor. Sem. (J. Bartram, 1942: 39, 43, 71, 74; W. Bartram, 1943: 151.)

La 19. Astor Mound, 0.25 mile back of Astor. (Moore, 1894b: 177.)

La 20. Midden near Manhatten Landing. (Moore, 1894b: 133; U.S.N.M. 378353–4; U.P.M. 12711.)

La 21. Midden above Manhatten Landing. Mt. T. (Wyman, 1875: 37–8; Moore, 1893: 115.)

Vo 19. Mt. Taylor, midden. Mt. T (Moore, 1893: 12–13, 113–15, 1898; M.A.I. 17/335, 1184, 1557, 2245.)

Vo 20. Shell mound near Mt. Taylor; this is second of two mounds between Lake Dexter and Volusia. (Wyman, 1875: 44.)

Vo 21. Birds Island, midden. St. J. II. (Wyman, 1875: 37; Moore, 1893: 115; H.P.M. 74–26/12561–2; M.A.I. 17/2249; W.F.I.S. 15111.)

La 22. Midden opposite Bluffton. (Moore, 1893: 115–16.)

La 23. Mound opposite Bluffton. (Moore, 1894a: 48.)

Vo 22. Bluffton Midden (Orange Bluff). Or., St. J. I (?), St. J. II. (J. Bartram, 1942: 39, 71; Wyman, 1875: 37; Le Baron, 1884: 774; Moore, 1894a: 44–8; H.P.M. 74–26/12576–9, 12709, 91–5–10/49560, 49562; W.F.I.S. 15154; M.A.I. 17/1176, 1808, 18/316; F.S.M. 36678; U.F.A.L.)

Vo 23. Bluffton Mound. (Moore, 1894a: 44–8.)

Vo 24. Tick Island Midden. Or., St. J. Ia to Ib, St. J. II (?). (Moore, 1893: 605–14; M.A.I. 18/313; U.S.N.M. 149551; W.F.I.S. 15119, 15124; [midden?] U.S.N.M. 272331.)

Vo 25. Tick Island Mound. St. J. Ia, early; intrusive burials, St. J. IIc (?). (Moore, 1894a: 128–43, 1892b: 568–79, 1894a: 48–63, 1894b: 148–58; J. B. Griffin, 1945b, 1946: 47; M.A.I. 17/2169–77, 2201–4, 3933–9; H.P.M. uncataloged, 92–5–101/49650–75.)

Vo 26–8. Three other shell middens on Tick Island. (Moore, 1894b: 131.) Material (U.S.N.M.

272332) from "Ropes Island, Lake Woodruff, mouth of Spring Garden Creek," may be from one of these sites or the main one on Tick Island.

Vo 29. Lake Woodruff. Or., St. J. II. May be shell heap on Spring Garden Creek, east of Lake Woodruff. (Moore, 1892c: 918; U.S.N.M. 317037.)

Vo 30. De Leon Springs, dredged from springs. Or., St. J. II. (F.S.M. 26145–64; U.S.N.M. 149553.)

Vo 31. De Leon Springs Mound. (Moore, 1894a: 63–4.)

La 24. Bartrams Mound (Little Orange Mound), midden. St. J. II. (J. Bartram, 1942: 39, 71; W. Bartram, 1943: 151, 186; Wyman, 1875: 35–6; Le Baron, 1884: 774; H.P.M. 74–26/ 12700–8; M.A.I. 18/348.) Specimens from an unspecified site on Lake Dexter probably came from here (M.A.I. 17/1460).

La 25. Old Ford Mound, north side of Alexanders Creek 2 miles from spring. St. J. Ia. (Abshire et al., 1935; U.S.N.M. 378352.)

La 26. Mound one mile from Alexander Springs, on north side of creek. Or. (?). (Abshire et al., 1935: 28; U.S.N.M. 378351.)

La 27. Alexander Springs, midden (?). (U.S.N.M. 378350.) This should not be confused with Wyman's (1875: 33) Alexander Mound on Spring Garden Creek.

La 28. Mosquito Grove, midden. Or., St. J. II. (J. Bartram, 1942: 39, 71; W. Bartram, 1943: 152, 186; Moore, 1892c: 918; Abshire et al., 1935: 28; H.P.M. uncataloged.)

La 29. St. Francis (Old Town), midden. Mt. T., Or., St. J. II. (J. Bartram, 1942: 39, 71; W. Bartram, 1943: 153, 162, 186, 191; Wyman, 1875: 33–5; Moore, 1894c: 21; J. B. Griffin, 1946: 47; H.P.M. 74–26/12431, 12435–41, 12453–4, 12460–1, 92–7–10/49573–5; W.F.I.S. 4306; C.M. 20407.)

La 30. Small midden on edge of swamp and in rear of St. Francis. (Wyman, 1875: 35.)

La 31. Second midden above St. Francis on small lagoon (St. Francis Dead River?). (Wyman, 1875: 33; Moore, 1894b: 131.)

La 32. Osceola Midden (Crows Bluff). Mt. T. (Wyman, 1875: 32–3; Moore, 1892c: 916; U.F.A.L.)

Vo 32. Mound one mile north of bridge at Crows Bluff (east side of river?). St. J. II. (U.M. M.A. 2220.)

Vo 33. Bryson's Midden, east bank St. Johns River, 0.5 mile below Hawkinsville. (Wyman, 1875: 31–2; Moore, 1894c: 22; W.F.I.S. 15148.)

La 33. Pacataligo, midden, 0.12 mile below Bryson's Midden, west bank St. Johns River. (Wyman, 1875: 32.)

La 34. Hawkinsville Midden. Or., St. J. I. (W. Bartram, 1943: 153, 187; Wyman, 1868a: 403, 1875: 31; H.P.M. 74–26/12598–601, 12605, 12603, uncataloged; U.S.N.M. 149552; W.F.I.S. 15147.)

La 35. Shell field in second lagoon south of Hawkinsville, St. Johns River. (Moore, 1892c: 918; W.F.I.S. 15092.)

Vo 34. Ziegler Mound near Deland. Or., St. J. II. (U.S.N.M. 351547.)

Vo 35. Thursby Midden. (Wyman, 1875: 29; Moore, 1894a: 64.)

Vo 36. Thursby Mound. St. J. I (?), St. J. IIa, b, c. (Wyman, 1875: 29; Moore, 1894a: 64–82, 1894b: 158–67; M.A.I. 17/2981, 3929, 4505, 4507, 18/314; H.P.M. 94–12–10/49530–41, 49566–7; R.S.P.F. 39217, 39332, 39335, 40388; C.M. 17781, 17946; F.S.U. 528, formerly M.A.I. 17/2200.)

Vo 37. Midden A, Lake Beresford, the northernmost of two on the southeastern shore of the lake. (Wyman, 1875: 26.)

Vo 38. Midden B, Lake Beresford, south of the previous site. (Wyman, 1875: 26; H.P.M. 74–26/12580–7.)

Vo 39. Starks Grove Mound, on Lake Beresford. St. J. II. (W. Bartram, 1943: 154, 187; Moore, 1894a: 82.)

La 36. Northernmost midden, Huntoon Creek. Mt. T., St. J. I. This is the site reported by Wyman (1875: 26) to be northwest of Huntoon Creek and the lagoon—apparently the present Huntoon Dead River. (Wyman, 1875: 26–7; H.P.M. 12556–8.)

La 37. Middle midden, Huntoon Creek. According to Wyman (1875: 26) this is a small site where Huntoon Creek (present Snake Creek) enters the lagoon (present Huntoon Dead Creek).

La 38. Southern midden, Huntoon Creek. This is on Huntoon Creek (present Snake Creek), 0.25 mile above previous site.

La 39. Huntoon Island Midden, large site at northern end of island opposite Thursby Mound. Or., St. J. I (?), St. J. II. (Wyman, 1875: 26–8; Le Baron, 1884: 774; Moore, 1894a: 82; H.P.M. 74–26/12425, 12531–9; W.F.I.S. 15122; U.M.M.A. 2219; M.A.I. 18/347; Sweett Collection.) Specimens from "Site 3, Huntoon Island" may be from here (U.S.N.M. 351542).

La 40–1. Two mounds adjacent to Huntoon Island Midden. (Wyman, 1875: 28; Moore, 1894a: 82.)

Vo 40. Palmetto Shell Midden, 0.5 mile below the midden in woods near Blue Spring. (Wyman, 1875: 25–6.)

Vo 41. Midden in woods near Blue Springs. St. J. I (?). (Wyman, 1875: 25; H.P.M. 74–26/12498–502.)

Vo 42. Blue Springs Midden A, right bank of creek at outlet. Or., St. J. II. (Wyman, 1875: 24; Le Baron, 1884: 774; H.P.M. 74–26/12468–70, 12500.) Other material from unspecified localities at Blue Springs includes: W.F.I.S. 15100; H.P.M. 74–26/12465–6, 12502.

Vo 43. Blue Springs Midden B, left bank of creek at outlet. (Wyman, 1875: 24; Le Baron, 1884: 774.)

Vo 44. Midden one mile above Blue Spring (Bartram's Mount Joy?), east bank St. Johns River. Mt. T. (J. Bartram, 1942: 40, 43, 71, 73; Wyman, 1875: 21–2.)

Vo 45. Barkers Landing, midden, east bank, St. Johns River, 2 miles north of the mouth of Wekiva River. (Le Baron, 1884: 774–5.)

Vo 46–7. Two middens on east bank of St. Johns near the mouth of Wekiva River. (Le Baron, 1884: 775.)

Vo 48. Fort Florida Midden. (Wyman, 1875: 21; Moore, 1894a: 83.)

Vo 49. Fort Florida Mound. St. J. IIc, intrusive (?). (Wyman, 1875: 21.)

Vo 50. Mound near Fort Florida. St. J. II. (Moore, 1894a: 83.)

Se 25. Wekiva Shell Field A, right bank Wekiva River between 6 and 7 miles above the St. Johns. St. J. II. (Wyman, 1875: 22; H.P.M. 74–26/12694–5.)

Se 26. Wekiva Shell Field B, located a short distance below previous site. (Wyman, 1875: 22.)

La 42. Mound near Blackwater. St. J. II. (F.S.M. 76482–501.)

Vo 51. Thrashers Shell Pit, about 3 miles below outlet of Lake Munroe, Sec. 7, T. 19 S., R. 30 E. (Le Baron, 1884: 775; Simpson Collection.)

Vo 52. Mound near Railroad Bridge, north of Lake Munroe. (Moore, 1894a: 83.)

Vo 53. Lake Munroe Outlet Midden, north shore of lake at outlet. St. J. II. (Wyman, 1875: 21; U.S.N.M. 62132–41.) The following site names are probably synonyms for this site: Woodruff Pasture site (Simpson Collection) and shell mound, north shore, Lake Munroe, two miles west of Sanford (F.S.M. 75025–34).

Vo 54. Du Barry Creek Midden, on creek which enters Lake Munroe west of Enterprise. (Wyman, 1875: 20–1; Simpson Collection.)

Vo 55. Enterprise Midden. Or., St. J. II, St. J. IIc. (Wyman, 1868a: 399–401, 1875: 19–20;

Le Baron, 1884: 775; Dall, 1885; Thomas, 1894: 328–32; H.P.M. 74–26/12404–16; Y.P.M. 5449; U.S.N.M. 31938, 62112–28.)

Vo 56. Mound near Enterprise. (A.M.N.H. Terry, 2400–1.)

Vo 57. Stone Island (Doctors or Rock Island), midden. (J. Bartram, 1942: 41, 72; Haven, 1856: 86–7; Nott and Gliddon, 1860; Pourtales, 1868; Lyell, 1863; Wyman, 1875: 18–19; Dall, 1887; Hrdlička, 1907: 19; H.P.M. uncataloged.)

Se 1. Site three miles west of Sanford (Mellonville). (U.S.N.M. 6148, 62150.)

Se 2. Sanford (Mellonville). St. J. II. (U.S.N.M. 62137, 62142–5, 62147.)

Se 3. Buzzards Roost Midden, left bank St. Johns River just above Lake Munroe. (Wyman, 1875: 18.)

Se 4. Ginns Grove Mound (Speers or Spears Landing). St. J. Ib, IIc, intrusive. (Brinton, 1859: 170; Wyman, 1875: 15, 45; Le Baron, 1884: 775; Moore, 1894a: 84–8, 1894b: 167; M.A.I. 17/280–1, 297.)

Se 5. Ginns Grove Midden A. Mt. T. (Moore, 1894c: 21.)

Se 6. Ginns Grove Midden B. Or., St. J. Ia, St. J. II. (Wyman, 1875: 15, 45; Le Baron, 1884: 775; Moore, 1894a: 84–8; H.P.M. 74–26/12736, 84–3/31426–9; U.M.M.A. 246–128; U.S.N.M. 65151–8; W.F.I.S. 15152; M.A.I. 17/1837, 2314.)

Vo 58. Thornhill Lake Mound 1. Unclassified complex, St. J. I (?). (Moore, 1894a: 88–9, 1894b: 167–73; M.A.I. 17/2181–4, 17/2191, 2193, 17/535 ?.)

Vo 59. Thornhill Lake Mound 2. Unclassified complex, St. J. I. (?). (Moore, 1894b: 172; M.A.I. 17/2178–80.)

Vo 60. Thornhill Lake Midden. St. J. II. (Moore, 1892c: 918, 1894a: 88.) Perhaps this site is Wyman's two mounds below Black Hammock (Wyman, 1875: 44; H.P.M. 74–26/12648–9).

Se 7. Bird Island, Lake Jessup. (J. Bartram, 1942: 43, 73; Moore, 1894b: 131; W.F.I.S. 15111.)

Se 8. Shore of Lake Jessup, midden (?). St. J. II. (Y.P.M. 5452.)

Vo 61. Lemon Bluff, midden. St. J. II. (J. Bartram, 1942: 41, 72; Le Baron, 1884: 776; F.S.M. 62892–4; Simpson Collection A 3395.)

Se 9. Black Hammock Midden. Or., St. J. I (?), St. J. II. (Wyman, 1868a: 398–9, 1875: 17–18; Moore, 1894a: 88; H.P.M. 74–26/12633–47; W.F.I.S. 15093.) The site on west bank of St. Johns above Lake Jessup is probably this midden (Y.P.M. 5451).

Se 10. Black Hammock Mound. (Moore, 1894a: 88.)

Se 11. Huntingdon's, midden. Or. (Moore, 1894b: 211; Holmes, 1894: 114.)

Vo 62. Watsons Landing, midden. Or., St. J. II. (Wyman, 1868a: 462; H.P.M. 67–1/2898, 74-26/12651–3, 12655–8.)

Se 12. Cooks Ferry Midden (King Phillips Town). Or., St. J. I (?), St. J. IIc, Sem. (Brinton, 1859: 171; Wyman, 1868a: 397–8, 1875: 16–17; Moore, 1894a: 89; H.P.M. 74–26/12666–73, 12676, uncataloged; M.A.I. 18/279; F.S.M. 62880–3; U.F.A.L.)

Se 13. Cooks Ferry Mound. Or. (?), St. J. II, IIc, intrusive (?). (J. Bartram, 1942: 41, 42, 71, 73; Le Baron, 1884: 776; Moore, 1894a: 89–91; W.F.I.S. 15106; H.P.M. 74-26/12681–4; H.P.M. 49552–4.)

SUBAREA III

SJ 28. Midden (?) near Fort Matanzas. S. A. (Webb, 1894.)

SJ 29. Matanzas Bar, midden (?). (Webb, 1894.)

SJ 30. Moses Creek Mound, 12 miles south of St. Augustine. (Douglass, 1885: 80–1.)

SJ 46. Summer Haven site. Or. (St. Augustine Reconstruction Project Collection; F.S.P.S.)

Fl 2. Duponts Mound, 25 miles south of St. Augustine on South Matanzas River. St. J. IIc. (Douglass, 1885: 76–7; M.P.M.)

SJ 35. Pellicer Mound, north side of Pellicer Creek.

Fl 3. Rhotan Midden, on Pellicer Creek, opposite Dupont mound. (Douglass, 1885: 77–8.)

Fl 4. Rhotan Mound, adjacent to Rhotan Midden. (Douglass, 1885: 77–8.)

Fl 5. Bon Terra Farm. (Connery, 1932; E. B. Howard, 1940.)

Fl 6. Marineland Midden. S. J. II. This is probably Webb's (1894) midden 2 miles below Matanzas Inlet. (Webb, 1894; Brower, 1906: 332; Lamme, 1941; Y.P.M. 142478–82, uncataloged; C.M. 40, 78.2.)

Fl 1. Mound three miles north of Bulow Forks, on east side of Old Kings Road. (Douglass, 1885: 81.)

Vo 63. Tomoka River Midden, north side of creek at mouth. (Small, 1929: 18.)

Vo 64. Halifax River 1, midden, 0.6 mile south of bridge at Bulow. (Small, 1929: 18.)[6]

Vo 65. Halifax River 2, midden, extends from 1.3 to 1.4 miles south of bridge. (Small, 1929: 18.)

Vo 66. Halifax River 3, midden, extends from 1.5 to 1.7 miles south of bridge. (Small, 1929: 18.)

Vo 67. Halifax River 4, midden, at 2.1 miles south of bridge. (Small, 1929: 18.)

Vo 68. Halifax River 5, midden, at 2.3 miles south of bridge. (Small, 1929: 18.)

Vo 69. Halifax River 6, midden, at 2.7 miles south of bridge. (Small, 1929: 18–19.)

Vo 70. Halifax River 7, midden, extends from 3.3 to 3.4 miles south of bridge. (Small, 1929: 19.)

Vo 71. Halifax River 8, midden, extends from 4.5 to 4.7 miles south of the bridge. (Small, 1929: 19.)

Vo 72. Halifax River 9, midden, at 5.7 miles south of bridge. (Small, 1929: 19.)

Vo 73. Halifax River 10, midden, at 6.3 miles south of bridge. (Small, 1929: 19.)

Vo 74. Halifax River 11, midden, extends between 6.5 to 6.7 miles south of bridge. (Small, 1929: 19.)

Vo 75. Ormond Beach Mound, east bank Halifax River, one mile south of bridge in city of Ormond Beach. St. J. II. (Stirling, 1935: 388–9.) This is probably Small's (1929: 19) mound 9.6 miles south of bridge and Le Baron's (1884: 780) mound on the farm of Andrew Bostrom.

Vo 76. Ormond Beach Midden, underlies previous site. (Stirling, 1935: 388.) Probably the same as Small's (1929: 19) midden 9.6 miles south of bridge.

Vo 77. Mound at Smiths place about a mile south of Bostrom's. (Le Baron, 1884: 780.)

Vo 78. Mt. Oswald Mound, east bank of Tomoka River 2 miles from mouth. Unclassified complex, St. J. I (?). (Douglass, 1882, 1883, 1885: 82.)

Vo 79–80. Two small mounds near Mt. Oswald. (Douglass, 1882: 100, 109.)

Vo 81. Mt. Oswald Midden. (Douglass, 1882: 108.)

Vo 82. Nocoroco (F.S.P.S. no. V44), midden, mouth of Tomoka River, south bank. St. J. IIc. (J. W. Griffin, 1948a; Griffin and Smith, 1949.)

Vo 83. Cotten site (Hernandez site), midden. Or., St. J. II. (Douglass, 1882: 108; Hay, 1902; Blatchley, 1902; Hitchcock, 1902; Lucas, 1903; J. W. Griffin, 1948a.)

Vo 84. Mound two and one-half miles west of Daytona. (Douglass, 1885: 141.)

Vo 85. Veseys Place (Butler's no. 21, Small's Two House Mound ?), midden, south of east end of Port Orange bridge. St. J. II. (Butler, 1917: 106; Small, 1929: 21; U.M.M.A. 2873.)

---

[6] Small does not make it clear if this bridge is the one at Bulow but it appears to be from his data. Furthermore, although he does not state that these sites are along the ocean side of the lagoon, it does seem from his description that they are on that side.

Vo 86. Castle Midden, 1.2 miles south of "Two House Mound." (Small, 1929: 21–2.)

Vo 87. Small midden 0.8 mile south of Castle Midden. (Small, 1929: 22.)

Vo 88. Small midden, 1.1 miles south of Castle Midden. (Small, 1929: 22.)

Vo 89. Wilbur midden (Butler's no. 19, Small's site 1.6 miles south of Castle Midden?). (Butler, 1917: 106.)

Vo 90. Green Mound, midden. St. J. II. (Butler, 1917: 106; Small, 1924, Pl. 285; Small, 1929: 22, 109; J. W. Griffin, 1948a, 1948b; Y.P.M. 142514–18.)

Vo 91. Rhodes site (Butler's no. 17, Babcock Place), midden, about one mile north of Mosquito Inlet in Ponce Park. St. J. II. (Butler, 1917: 106; Small, 1929: 22; U.S.N.M. 97141.)

Vo 92. Iona Park Mound, midden (?), near Mosquito Inlet. St. J. II. (U.S.N.M. 92037.)

Vo 93. Midden, 1.2 miles south of Port Orange, west bank Halifax River. (Small, 1929: 23.)

Vo 94. Midden, 2 miles south of Port Orange. (Small, 1929: 23.)

Vo 95. Bill Allen Mound, midden. St. J. II. (Butler, 1917: 106; Nelson, 1918: 91; Small, 1929: 23; Sweett and Marsden, 1925: 19; F.S.M. 24165–7; U.M.M.A. 2390, 2874; Sweett Collection, 110, 242.)

Vo 96. Midden, 1.5 miles south of Bill Allen Mound. (Small, 1929: 23.)

Vo 97. Midden, 0.1 mile south of previous. (Small, 1929: 23.)

Vo 98. Midden, 0.6 mile south of previous. (Small, 1929: 23.)

Vo 99. Spruce Creek Mound, southwest bank of creek, 6 miles above mouth. St. J. IIc, intrusive (?). (Douglass, 1885; H.P.M. 78–15/14167–70; U.S.N.M. 10988–11003.)

Vo 100. Nordman's Mound (Black Hammock, Butler's no. 16, Small's site 2.5 miles south of Bill Allen Mound ?), midden. St. J. IIc. (Harrison, 1878: 305; Le Baron, 1884: 780; Butler, 1917: 106; Small, 1929: 23; U.S.N.M.; F.S.M. 28070–8.)

Vo 101. Rock House Mound (Butler's no. 15, Small's site 3.3 miles from Bill Allen Mound ?), midden, west bank Halifax River opposite Mosquito Inlet. Or., St. J. II. (Douglass, 1885: 143; Brower, 1906: 333; Butler, 1917: 106; Small, 1929: 23; Sweett and Marsden, 1925: 19, 35; Sweett Collection; U.M.M.A.) Material from Halifax Inlet (H.P.M. 78–48–10/15376–7) is probably from this site.

Vo 102. Stone House Mound, 0.5 mile west of Rock House Midden. (Douglass, 1885: 143–4; Moore, 1922b: 39–41; Butler, 1917: 106.)

Vo 103. Riverside Park Mound (Butler's no. 14, Small's site 1.2 miles below his previous one ?), midden, west bank of Halifax River, north edge of New Smyrna. St. J. II. (Butler, 1917: 106; Sweett and Marsden, 1925: 19; Small, 1929: 23; U.M.M.A. 2394, 2875; Sweett Collection.)

Vo 104. New Smyrna "Early Man" site, location unknown. (Gidley, 1929: 491, 493.)

Vo 105. Old Fort Mound (Old Turnbull Mound, Butler's no. 11, Small's site 0.3 mile south of his previous one ?), midden on Halifax River in the middle of New Smyrna. St. J. II. (Le Baron, 1884: 780; Brower, 1906: 333; Butler, 1917: 104; U.M.M.A. 2393; Sweett and Marsden, 1925: 19, 25–6; University of New Mexico, Anthropology Department, Pottery Laboratory; Sweett Collection.)

Vo 106. Dummitts Place (Mt. Pleasant, Old Dimmitts Place, Butler's no. 13), midden. St. J. II, IIc. (Brinton, 1872: 357; Le Baron, 1884: 780; Butler, 1917: 104; U.M.M.A 2257; U.S.N.M. 99340.)

Vo 107. Dummitts Mound, back of the midden. (Butler, 1917: 104.)

Vo 108. Browns Mound (Butler's no. 12, Small's site 2.6 miles south of Coronado), midden. (Butler, 1917: 104; Small, 1929: 24.)

Vo 109. Turtle Mound, midden. St. J. II. (Brinton, 1872: 357; Le Baron, 1884: 781; Douglass, 1885: 80; Brower, 1906: 333; Butler, 1917: 104; Sweett and Marsden, 1925: 14–16; Y.P.M. 142488–97; M.P.M. 24497/6857; Sweett Collection; U.F.A.L.)

Vo 110. Pumpkin Point, midden, across from Bissett's Midden on east bank of Halifax River. (Le Baron, 1884: 781.)

Vo 111. Turtle Mound Burial Mound. (Butler, 1917: 104.)

Vo 112. Castle Windy, midden. (Butler, 1917: 106.)

Vo 113. South Canal site (Hamilton Place, Butler's no. 10), midden, south part of New Smyrna near Halifax River. Or., St. J. II. (Le Baron, 1884: 780; Butler, 1917: 104; U.M.M.A. 2258; Sweett Collection.)

Vo 114. Sand mounds north of South Canal site. (Butler, 1917: 104.)

Vo 115. Vaux Place (Butler's no. 9), midden, south of New Smyrna. (Butler, 1917: 104.)

Vo 116–117. Two sand mounds near the Vaux Place. (Butler, 1917: 104.) One may be Le Baron's (1884: 780) Fox Mound.

Vo 118. Packwood Place (Butler's no. 8, Lockwood Place), midden. (Le Baron, 1884: 780; Butler, 1917: 104.)

Vo 119. Cedar Creek Midden, opposite Packwood Place in the mangroves. (Le Baron, 1884: 780.)

Vo 120. Brickhouse Cove Mound (Butler's no. 7), midden. (Le Baron, 1884: 780–1; Butler, 1917: 104.)

Vo 121. Bissett's Midden (Butler's no. 5). (Le Baron, 1884: 781; Butler, 1917: 104.)

Vo 122. Bissett's Mound. (Douglass, 1885: 79–80; Butler, 1917: 104.)

Vo 123. Grovey Allen Mound (Live Oak Hill, Butler's no. 4), midden. (Le Baron, 1884: 781; Butler, 1917: 104.)

Vo 124. Snyders Mound (Lowd Place, Butler's no. 3), midden. (Butler, 1917: 104.)

Vo 125. Oak Hill Midden. Mt. T., St. J. I, St. J. II. (Le Baron, 1884: 781; Douglass, 1885: 79; Brower, 1906: 333; Butler, 1917: 104; Nelson, 1918; J. W. Griffin, 1948a; U.M.M.A. 2392; A.M.N.H. 20.1/217–227.)

Vo 126–7. Two small middens near Oak Hill. (Butler, 1917: 104.)

Vo 128. Sam's Midden, 0.5 mile south of Oak Hill. (Le Baron, 1884: 782.)

Vo 129. Scobey Place (Butler's no. 1a), midden. (Butler, 1917: 104.) Perhaps this is Swift's site (midden and mound) noted by Le Baron (1884: 782).

Vo 130. Ross Hammock midden (Butler's no. 1). (Le Barron, 1884: 782; Douglass, 1885: 78–9, 80; Butler, 1917: 104.)

Vo 131. Ross Hammock Mound. (Le Baron, 1884: 782; Douglass, 1885: 78–9, 80; Butler, 1917: 104.)

Vo 132. Butler Campbell's mound, 2.5 miles north of Haulover Canal. (Le Baron, 1884: 782.)

Vo 133. Mill Island, midden (?), unlocated site. (Sweett Collection.)

SUBAREA IV

Pu 48. Mound near Bear Island. (Moore, 1894b: 175.)

Pu 49. East of Davenport, midden (?), about 0.12 mile on Davenport Landing Branch. (U.S.N.M. 378358.)

Pu 50. Davenport Mound. St. J. II (?). (Moore, 1894b: 175–6; R.S.P.F. 39327.)

Pu 51. Davenport Landing, midden (?). St. J. II. (U.S.N.M. 378357.)

Mr 5. Cedar Landing 2, midden, about 0.25 to 0.5 mile down from Cedar Landing. (Watkins, MSa.)

Pu 52. Putnam County 52, midden, north bank Oklawaha River, downstream from Cedar Landing. (Watkins, MSa.)

Mr 6. Cedar Landing 1, midden. (Watkins, MSa.)

Mr 7. Cedar Landing 3, midden, about 300 yards upstream from landing. (Watkins, MSa.)

Mr 8. Watkins Camp Mound, near Cedar Landing. (Watkins, MSa.)

Pu 53. Mound A, Ditch Creek, mound near landing. (Moore, 1895c: 519.)

Pu 54. Mound B, Ditch Creek, mound north of landing. (Moore, 1895c: 520.)

Pu 55. Health Aid Springs Mound. (Watkins, MSa.)

Pu 56. Brooks Landing. Sem. (U.S.N.M. 378359.)

Pu 57. Orange Springs Ferry Road Mound, about 0.5 to 1 mile from Oklawaha River. (Watkins, MSa.)

Mr 9. Cotton Patch Landing, midden, 3 miles south of Orange Ferry. St. J. II. (Abshire et al., 1935: 19–20; U.S.N.M. 278360–2, 378419.)

Mr 10. Tobacco Patch Landing, midden, 14 miles below Eureka on Oklawaha River. St. J. II. (Abshire et al., 1935: 29.)

Mr 11. Indian Bluff Mound. (Moore, 1895c: 519.)

Mr 12. Eureka Log Landing, midden. St. J. I (?). (U.S.N.M. 378363–5.)

Mr 13. Sunday Bluff Midden. Or., St. J. II. (U.S.N.M. 378373–6.)

Mr 14. Old Site, Eaton Creek, midden, 0.25 mile south of Eureka road. Or., St. J. II. (Abshire et al., 1935: 10–12, 22–3; U.S.N.M. 378383–5, 378422.)

Mr 15. Eaton Creek, 1.5 miles above Scrub Lake. (U.S.N.M. 378421.)

Mr 16. Eaton Creek, 1.25 miles above Scrub Lake, midden. Or. (U.S.N.M. 378379–80.)

Mr 17. Eaton Creek, 0.5 mile above Scrub Lake. (U.S.N.M. 378381–2.)

Mr 18. Eaton Creek Sand Mound, one mile below Eaton Lake. (Abshire et al., 1935: 15–16; U.S.N.M. 378377–8.)

Mr 19–25. Seven mounds at Palmetto Landing. No. 7 (Mr 25) may be St. J. I (?). (Moore, 1895c: 520–1.)

Mr 26. Old Stroud Place (Site 1), midden. Or., St. J. II. (Abshire et al., 1935; U.S.N.M. 378368–72.)

Mr 27. Priest Landing, Stroud Creek (Site 2), midden. Or., St. J. II (?). (Abshire et al., 1935; U.S.N.M. 378366–7, 378420.)

Mr 28. Jones Midden, Stroud Creek (Site 3). (Abshire et al., 1935.)

Mr 29. Site 4, Stroud Creek, midden. (Abshire et al., 1935.)

Mr 30. Gores Landing, midden. (Watkins, MSa.)

Mr 31. Gores Landing Mound, 100 yards upstream from landing. (Watkins, MSa.)

Mr 44. Shell midden, east bank Oklawaha River, about 4 miles downstream from Connor. St. J. II. (U.F.A.L.)

Mr 32. Delks Landing Mound. (Moore, 1895c: 519.)

Mr 33. Mound near Silver Springs, 1 mile east of springs. St. J. Ia to Ib. (Moore, 1895c: 521–5; M.A.I. 18/358–9.)

Mr 53. Midden, Silver Spring Run. (U.S.N.M. 378349.)

Mr 34. Electra Landing Mound. (Moore, 1895c: 519.)

Mr 35. Lake Weir Landing Mound. (Moore, 1895c: 519.)

Mr 36–8. Three mounds at Moss Bluff. (Moore, 1895c: 519.)

Mr 39. Gamble Mound. St. J. I (?). (Moore, 1895c: 525–8.)

Mr 40. Kauffman Island, Lake Kerr, midden. Mt. T., Or., St. J. II, S. A. (Abshire et al., 1935: 8–9; Watkins, MSb; U.S.N.M. 378392–7; U.F.A.L.)

Mr 41. Shore and bottom of Lake Kerr, midden. St. J. II. (U.S.N.M. 378389–91.)

Mr 42. Southeast shore, Lake Kerr (Morgan Old Field), midden. St. J. II. (U.S.N.M. 378387–8.)

Mr 43. Sand Mound near Lacota, 10 miles southwest of Salt Springs. (Abshire et al., 1935: 30–1.)

APPENDIX B: TYPES OF ARTIFACTS

THE artifact assemblage for the Northern St. Johns area is extensive, particularly so because of the large number of unique ceremonial and ornamental objects found in St. Johns I and II times. In view of such a large series of objects it will be necessary to limit their discussion in two ways. First, we will consider mainly those which are specifically mentioned in the text as being attributable to a given culture or horizon. Second, these artifacts will only be briefly discussed—in some ways it would be perhaps better to call this an artifact glossary rather than an exhaustive consideration.

In another paper (Goggin, MSb) a detailed analysis has been made of Glades Area artifacts. In that study it was decided to abandon the conventional archeological categories of materials and use instead categories based on function. These are, to be sure, somewhat subjective and dependent on the writer's interpretation but despite this objection it is still a classification closer to culture than the old "materials" categories. The inevitable "ceremonial objects" section is included to handle many objects appearing to be in that category, while a "miscellaneous" section encompasses specimens which do not fit well in any of the other categories.

Two departures have been made from consistency in this classification. First, pottery is considered separately and distinct from other vessels. This is because ceramics have a two-fold interest to the archeologist, both as cultural objects and as chronological markers. Second, European objects and European derived objects (those made from European material) are grouped together instead of being distributed in the various functional categories. It is thought that the historical significance of this group outweighs other factors.

More detailed discussions of Florida artifacts, including most of the types occuring here, will be found: for the Indian River area, in Rouse (1951) and Ferguson (1951); for the Glades Area, in Goggin and Sommer (1949), Willey (1949a), and Goggin (MSb); and for the various regions bordering the Gulf of Mexico in Willey (1949b).

POTTERY

Pottery types will be considered in general chronological order and arranged in series wherever possible. The form used in describing Southeastern pottery is not followed here—most of these types have been described elsewhere. They are merely briefly identified and discussed. Exceptions are Stokes Brushed and St. Johns Cob Marked, new forms first described here.

ORANGE SERIES

Orange Plain. This is the basic fiber-tempered ware of the region, defined by James B. Griffin (1945b: 220). In its typical form fiber was the only tempering material, which on firing burnt out leaving a characteristic honeycombed appearance. However, the later forms of the ware often have quartz sand as an added aplastic, and some examples tend towards chalky ware (St. Johns series) in texture.

The surface is often well smoothed, but normally has a vermicular appearance due to fiber strand holes. The interior sometimes exhibits pronounced tooling marks. The rim is usually simple and straight sided with a rounded or slightly flattened lip. A lug is rarely found on the rim; it is an outward rounded extension of the lip (Pl. 1, c and E). The base is normally flat and unmarked but a few sherds show impressions of twined and plaited textiles (Pl. 1, B and D).

This pottery most commonly is found in sites on the St. Johns River above Palatka, but occurs sporadically on the coast. Its temporal position is the Orange Period. The type has been described and discussed in detail by J. B. Griffin (1945b), Rouse (1951), Ferguson (1951), and Sears and Griffin (1950).

Orange Incised. This is the incised variety of Orange Plain defined by James B. Griffin (1945b: 219–20). In ware characteristics, vessel form, and surface finish, it is similar to Orange Plain except for incised decoration.

Incision was made by a sharp or rounded tool on a fairly wet surface producing either narrow or wide cuts with a ridge of clay pushed up along the sides. Punctations and ticks were occasionally added. Designs are normally rectilinear and are characterized by extensive hatching arranged in a number of patterns, e.g., nested chevrons, nested squares or diamonds, hatched oblique lines in a band, or triangular area with oblique hatching (J. B. Griffin, 1945b: 219; Ferguson, 1951).

The range of the type is identical with Orange Plain, as is its chronological position, the Orange Period. Further detailed discussions can be found in James B. Griffin (1945b), Rouse (1951), Ferguson (1951), Sears and Griffin (1950), with illustrations in Wyman (1875, Pl. 5: 4 and 5), Moore, (1893: 608–10, 616–20 and Fig. 1; 1894b, Fig. 78) and Holmes (1894: 10–11, 13–14, 21–2, Fig. 1, A and B; 1903, Pl. 84, A, B, D–F, and H, and Fig. 87, A, B, and D).

Tick Island Incised. This is another fiber-tempered type defined by James B. Griffin (1945b: 222). In ware, vessel form, and surface decoration it is similar to the two previously described forms.

Its distinction lies in the nature of the designs. They are often curvilinear, and usually the incised zones are replaced by punctate-filled areas (J. B. Griffin, 1945b, Fig. 1, D to I).

This is a minority type in the St. Johns valley, found at only six sites: Mt. Royal, Silver Glen Spring Midden, Bluffton, Tick Island, Enterprise, and Black Hammock. Even at these sites it is not as numerous as Orange Incised.

Temporally, this type fits in the Orange Period but its exact position within that horizon is not certain. James B. Griffin (1945b: 222) suggests that this type may be later than Orange Incised, but other data tend to negate this hypothesis. It is stratigraphically clear that St. Johns Incised follows Orange Incised, perpetuating the same decorative elements on a different paste. If Tick Island Incised were later than Orange Incised, St. Johns Incised should carry on the Tick Island decorative tradition but it does not. However, the strong similarities between Tick Island Incised and certain Weeden Island styles have yet to be explained. This type has been figured by Wyman (1875, Pl. 5: 3, Pl. 6: 3), Moore (1893: 607, 609) and Holmes, (1894, Figs. 1, c, and 9, 12; 1903, Pl. 84, c, Fig. 87, c, Fig. 58).

No Series

Stallings Punctated. This is a fiber-tempered type of coastal Georgia (James B. Griffin, 1943). In many respects the paste is similar to the Orange Series, but the surface generally has a smoother finish with fewer fiber strand marks. Decoration is made by linear punctating forming simple rectilinear designs.

For some unknown reason this ware is very rare in the Northern St. Johns Area, only a single example being found at Ponte Vedra (Pl. 1, A; U.C.A.L.) and but two others elsewhere in the state. Presumably it is coeval with the Orange Period in time. Examples from Georgia are illustrated by Claflin (1931) and Fairbanks (1942), while South Carolina forms are described by James B. Griffin (1943).

St. Johns Series

The St. John series includes a variety of differently decorated pottery types, all on a distinct chalky paste. This ware, which has been characterized as Florida's contribution to ceramic art (Stirling, 1936: 352), was first noted by Holmes (1894: 111–12), who applied the term chalky ware. This paste is not found elsewhere than Florida in the Southeast, although surprisingly similar wares are found in Venezuela (G. D. Howard, 1943: 22) and in Gulf Coast Mexico (specimens in A.M.N.H. collected by Gordon Ekholm), where they appear to be related to the Fine Orange ware.[1]

In Florida this ware is widely distributed throughout the peninsular portion of the state, but the focus of concentration seems to be this region. To the south, in the Glades Area, this ware was previously described as the Biscayne ware or series with several types which are closely similar to or identical with the parallel types of the St. Johns series. The paste as described under St. Johns Plain is the same with few exceptions for all the types included in the series.

The types named to date (December, 1950) do not include all those potentially eligible for definition. Numerous incised and other forms may prove to be important enough to warrant such definition. Among these are the fine simple-stamped (Pl. 1, H to J), linear check-stamped (Pl. 1, F), and cord-marked (Pl. 1, G), examples which appear to have had only a brief span of existence in St. Johns Ia, early, times.

A characteristic of certain types, especially St. Johns Plain, Dunns Creek Red, and St. Johns Red on Buff was the practice of preparing vessels especially for mortuary purposes. Instead of making a basal perforation or "kill hole" in these before deposition in the mound, they were constructed with a basal perforation, which was usually as well finished as the mouth of the vessel.

The pottery types included in this series comprise all the chalky ware types believed to be endemic to this region. Other chalky ware types characteristic of other areas, and included in other series, are not considered here but are discussed under their own series. These include Little Manatee Shell Stamped and Little Manatee Zoned Stamped of the Little Manatee series, Sarasota Incised of the Englewood pattern complex, and Papy's Bayou Punctated of the Papy's Bayou series.

Animal, plant, human, and unclassified effigies. These unusual figures made of

---

[1] A detailed discussion of chalky wares in Florida and elsewhere will be found in Goggin (MS*b*).

chalky ware have attracted considerable attention. They can be roughly divided into two groups—those which occur sporadically, usually as isolated specimens, and those found in groups. These are very general categories and are only tentative until more detailed study is made.

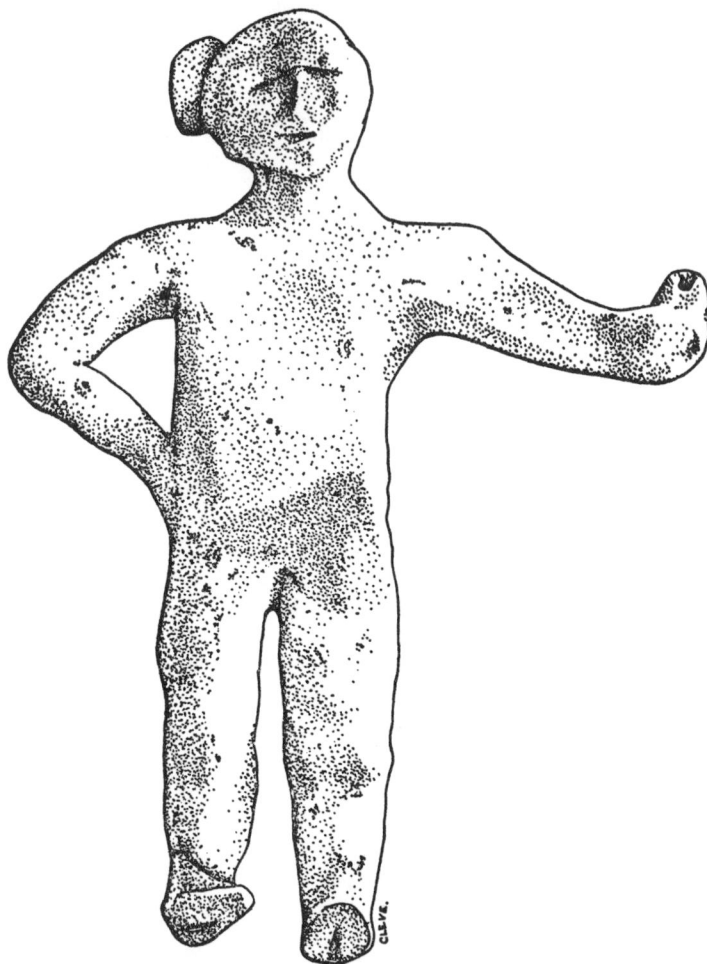

FIG. 4. Human Figure of Chalky Pottery Ware, Kauffman Island.

The first group includes such specimens as the duck effigy from Tick Island Mound (Pl. 3, F) and the quadruped animal effigy from the Mound in Pine Woods near Duval's (Moore, 1894a, Pl. 24: 3). This class of effigy is not distinctive enough to serve as a time marker, examples being found in both St. Johns I and II periods.

The human effigy from Kauffman Island (Fig. 4) probably also belongs in this group. This specimen, unfortunately not dateable, is notable for its occipital hair knot, a late trait often present in the Southern Cult art.

The second group of effigies includes a wide variety of forms from Thursby Mound. Identifiable animal effigies include birds, mammals, fish, and turtles. Plants include acorns and ears of corn. In addition, many eccentric vessel forms as well as gourd and boat vessels occur. This group, which dates from St. Johns II times, is not matched by anything else in the region. These objects have often been considered as typical of the region; their single occurrence indicates their unusual nature. In contrast to the first group they are smaller and much cruder in execution.

St. Johns Plain. This plain chalky ware type was defined by James B. Griffin (1945b: 220). With a wide range in time and space it is logical that the type should exhibit considerable variation in many aspects. Most of these can be noted, although quantitative studies of the differences have yet to be made.

Vessels appear to have been coiled, many of the coils being poorly joined with subsequent breakage along that line. The paste is typically temperless with a soft chalky texture so that the ware can be recognized by feel alone. Some of the earlier examples contained fiber temper and apparently represent an evolution from late Orange Plain forms. Other inclusions are rarely a few small shell fragments, probably accidental, and small red to brown colored inclusions of the same texture as the remainder of the paste.[2] They are suggestive of ocher or crushed sherds, but no analysis has been made.[3] Slender spicules, perhaps from sponges, are also rarely included in the paste. Of more importance is an increasing amount of sand sometimes found in examples of this type from late St. Johns II sites. Often it is in such quantity that the sherds merge into a grit-tempered series.

In general the paste is soft enough to be scratched by a fingernail, but some later examples, from St. Johns II times, are very hard and ring with a clear, sharp sound when tapped.

The surface is generally poorly smoothed, although such an impression may be deceptive because the softness of the ware leads to rapid weathering. Well finished and smoothed examples may be found in both the soft and hard paste. Early examples, from the Orange Period, sometimes tend to be rather thick and crudely finished.

The vessels are not decorated by any surface treatment although certain vessels with sculpturing, modeling, and appendages are included in this category. Where to draw the line between St. Johns Plain and effigy forms is not clear. Certain of the latter groups will be discussed here.

Bowls are the most common vessel form. They are usually large, very commonly with straight outsloping sides although examples with constricted mouth are not uncommon (Pl. 3, E). Small necked, pear-shaped jars (Pl. 3, H) may be an early form; at least the form appears more often in St. Johns I sites, but jars with constricted necks and flaring orifices (Pl. 4, J) occur later in St. Johns II times. In both of the St. Johns

---

[2] Similar inclusions are found in Venezuela chalky ware material (G. D. Howard, 1943: 22).

[3] Since this was first written J. W. Griffin and Smith (1949: 349) have established the provisional type Tomoka Plain to include the material with reddish inclusions. It seems to this writer that such a type has doubtful validity. It has no distinct geographical or temporal range, merely occurring as a variant of St. Johns Plain in all parts of the peninsula. Further, the inclusions range in quantity from a single one in large sherds to numerous inclusions in the same size specimen.

periods small vessels of unusual shape and variable rims, flanged or pointed, for example, occur (Pl. 4, A, B, and D). Gourd forms are not uncommon and are perhaps most abundant in St. Johns I Period.

During this same horizon basal supports or feet were in style. These generally numbered four, but a few tripod vessels, and one which can only be described as a bipod, are known. Feet varied greatly in form from those which appear to be mere pinching-up of the surface (Pl. 3, G) to well modeled supports (Pl. 3, A).

The boat vessel with square cut end lugs is noteworthy in that it appears in greatest frequency in the Southeast in this area, where it ranges from St. Johns I into St. Johns II times (Pl. 2, B).[4] Eccentric forms not considered elsewhere include flanged earthenware tubes (Pl. 5, E; Moore, 1894b, Pl. 18: 3), spool-shaped objects (Moore, 1894a, Pl. 8: 4; 1894b, Pl. 28: 1), and four-legged miniature stools (?) (Moore, 1894b, Pl. 27: 1 and 2).

St. Johns Plain is found in all parts of the region as well as in much of peninsular Florida. It ranges in time from the last phase of the Orange Period well into historic times, or the St. Augustine Period. Numerous examples are illustrated by Moore (1894a, 1894b, 1895a, 1895c) and by Wyman (1875, Pl. 5: 2 and 6).

St. Johns Incised. This type, defined by J. B. Griffin (1945b: 220–1), is a continuation of Orange Incised decorative motifs applied to chalky ware. Paste descriptions previously given for early St. Johns Plain hold true for this type, while the decoration and perhaps vessel forms are very close to Orange Incised.

This type is not rare but occurs with few exceptions only in the St. Johns Valley above Palatka. It is used as the diagnostic marker of the late division of the Orange Period. St. Johns Incised is discussed by J. B. Griffin (1945b, Fig. 1, S–T), Rouse (1951), and Ferguson (1951).

Dunns Creek Red. An unpublished description of this type was first prepared by James B. Griffin and later, with his permission, published in Goggin (1948a). This type is essentially nothing more than St. Johns Plain, with red paint covering either the interior or exterior or both.

Vessel forms seem somewhat more limited in variety with large bowls as the predominant form, but other shapes such as "wash basins" (Moore, 1894b, Pl. 26: 1), gourd vessels (Moore, 1895a, Pl. 84: 2), bottles (Moore, 1895a, Pl. 78), and flanged tubes (Moore, 1894b, Pl. 18: 4) occur.

Dunns Creek Red has almost as general a distribution in the area as St. Johns Plain, but appears to be more common in certain sections of the St. Johns Valley. Temporally it ranges from St. Johns I to II periods, but is most common in the former horizon, where it is often the predominant ware in burial mounds.

The references to Clarence B. Moore, cited above include the most important illustrations of the type, but note can also be taken of Holmes (1903: 125).

St. Johns Red on Buff. This type defined in Goggin (1948a) is not easily recognizable. Its broad-lined simple geometric design in red paint on a buff or tan colored back-

[4] This type of vessel may have been more common in wood in the Glades Area (Goggin, MSb). The distinctive crescent-shaped lug motif occurs there on the wooden vessels.

ground is easily weathered and in extreme cases it cannot be distinguished from St. Johns Plain.

Vessel forms are usually large bowls (Pls. 3, c and 5, h; Moore, 1894a, Pls. 13 and 14; Holmes, 1903, Pl. 99), but vase forms have been found (Moore, 1894a, Pl. 12; Holmes, 1903, Pl. 100).

The time range of the type may include both St. Johns I and II periods, but it is most typical of the former horizon. It is probable that the type is widespread throughout most of the region but when found is often so weathered that it cannot be distinguished from Dunns Creek Red. W. H. Holmes has briefly noted this painted ware (Holmes, 1903: 125).

Oklawaha Plain. This is another recently described type (Goggin, 1948a), distinguished from St. Johns Plain by its broad folded rim, often decorated with cut-out geometrical designs. This folded rim technique is probably related to a similar although less extreme development, found in various Weeden Island types.

All known vessels are large globular bowls with slightly constricted mouths (Pl. 3, d). Designs cut in the rim fold are triangles, rectangles, other geometric patterns, and combinations of these. Examples with the usual broad folded lip but not cutout, can also be included in the type.

This form of pottery occurs sporadically throughout most of the St. Johns and Oklawaha river basins. Data for its temporal range are not detailed but at the present it can be said to be limited to St. Johns Ia, early, times. It may perhaps have extended somewhat later.

Clarence B. Moore illustrates several vessels of this type (Moore, 1894a, Pl. 15: 3; 1894b, Pl. 27: 3; 1895a, Pl. 71: 1).

Oklawaha Incised. This poorly known type, represented by only a few examples, has been described in Goggin (1948a). It is characterized by bold simple geometric and curvilinear designs, crudely executed with broad incisions, often 7 to 8 mm. in width. Vessels appear to be medium sized bowls and jars.

The type occurs sporadically in the middle and lower St. Johns and Oklawaha valleys and perhaps elsewhere in the area. It also appears in Central Florida and in the Lake section directly south of that area. It dates from St. Johns Ia, early.

No good examples of this type have been illustrated. Those illustrated by Moore are not typical (Moore, 1894b, Pl. 30: 4; 1895a, Pls. 121: 3 and 122: 1).

St. Johns Punctated. This is again a type represented by only a few examples (Goggin, 1948a). The rim is decorated by a single incised line and one to three lines of well-spaced punctations. Several lines of punctations are also found without an incised line (Pl. 2, d). In one example, triple lines of punctations formed a crude series of arcades on the body proper. Vessel form, based on one complete specimen, is a deep bowl or jar.

St. Johns Punctated is sporadically found throughout the area both on the coast and along the St. Johns. It apparently dates from St. Johns II times, and perhaps earlier.

St. Johns Check Stamped. This is one of the most important and widely distributed types found in Florida, having been recognized as a distinct form for many years, although it has only recently been defined by James B. Griffin (1945b: 220). Like St. Johns Plain, the paste of this type varies from soft examples to the very hard forms found in some sites along the coast.

Decoration was formed by check stamping, usually over the whole vessel surface (Pl. 5, D). Execution may be neat carefully applied impressions, ranging to careless, overlapping, and blurred imprints. Check size is also not consistent. Many of the interior sites have small neat checks while numerous, apparently very late sites, usually coastal, have large, crude checks. There is a suggestion of temporal difference here as well as a geographical one.[5] Occasional combinations of simple incision with check-stamping are rare.

The most common vessel form is the large bowl, often with straight out-flaring sides. Other bowl forms occur (Moore, 1894b, Pl. 19: 2), as well as various eccentric vessels, including bowls with conoidal bottoms.

The range of the form includes every part of the area as well as most of northern Florida, while its parallel type Biscayne Check Stamped is found in much of the Glades Area. This type is not found earlier than St. Johns II being characteristic of that period and occurring in gradually diminishing quantity in the St. Augustine horizon.

Examples have been illustrated by Wyman (1875, Pl. 6: 2 and 3), Moore (1894b, Pl. 19: 2), Nelson (1918, Fig. 7), Ferguson (1951), and Rouse (1951).

St. Johns Cob Marked (new type).

Paste: Similar in all details to St. Johns Plain.
Surface Finish: Similar in all details to St. Johns Plain.
Decoration:
    Technique: The surface is patted with a corn cob.
    Design: No pattern is apparent, in some cases it is only lightly and/or sparsely marked. In other cases it is heavily marked and may be applied many times giving a very thorough coverage to the surface.
    Distribution: Apparently applied to most of the vessel.
Form: Similar to St. Johns Plain bowl forms.
Usual Range of Type: Sporadically throughout most of the area.
Chronological Position of Type: St. Johns II, probably IIb and IIc.

St. Johns Simple Stamped. This is a typical chalky ware form recently described by Griffin and Smith (1949: 346–7). It is characterized by broad parallel, or

---

[5] J. W. Griffin (1949a) notes a chronological sequence of check sizes in this type ranging from large to small and back to large again. At Nocoroco (Griffin and Smith, 1949: 352–53) excavated material which they equated with the late large check development, while the historic surface material with small checks was dismissed as evidence of an earlier occupation now washed away.

It is quite probable, though, that the small check material on the surface of Nocoroco represents a valid development at that time. In North Central Florida, and along the St. Johns River, historic St. Johns Check Stamped is more typically marked with small-sized checks than large. With this evidence and accepting the Griffin chronology mentioned above, we have from early to late a large, small, large, small sequence of check sizes.

slightly crossed, simple stamping. At Nocoroco it is dated in St. Johns IIb or IIc times.[6] It is widely distributed but nowhere common.

St. Johns Scored. Griffin and Smith (1949: 348) have also defined this type of chalky ware. It is marked by shallow straight to wavy or curved scoring marks. It is often difficult to separate from the previous type. Like the latter, it dates from St. Johns IIb or IIc times and is widely but only occasionally found.

Miscellaneous. Various examples of chalky ware pottery are not common enough to be called types, yet they should be noted. Unclassified punctated (Pl. 2, c) and/or incised specimens are widespread (Pl. 4, c).

One form of incised and punctated pottery is common along the Atlantic Coast. It is decorated with curvilinear areas of crude irregular punctations framed with poorly executed incisions or punctated lines (Griffin and Smith, 1949, Fig. F). In some respects it seems to be a local copy of Gulf Coast forms. Its chronological position is not positively known but it appears to be late, probably St. Johns IIb.

DEPTFORD SERIES

Deptford Simple Stamped. This type, best known from the Georgia Coast and Northwest Florida Gulf Coast, rarely occurs here (Caldwell and Waring, 1939a; Willey and Woodbury, 1942: 240). Vessels are coiled, with a buff-colored, sand-tempered paste.

The surface is impressed with groups of short, parallel bars. Not enough is known of the type's occurrence in this area to define vessel forms; elsewhere vessels often have conoidal bottoms.

Occurrences of single sherds have been noted at Tick Island Midden and Mt. Royal (probably midden), while other examples are known from Rollestown midden and Spaldings Lower Store. Unclassified simple-stamped gritty ware from Enterprise, Ropes Island, Silver Glen Springs, and Bartram Mound may be identical with or related to this type. The type probably dates in St. Johns Ia, early times. Examples from elsewhere are illustrated by Willey and Woodbury (1942, Fig. 1, G and H).

Deptford Bold Check Stamped. This is another type most characteristic of Georgia and Northwest Florida (Caldwell and Waring, 1939c; Willey and Woodbury, 1942: 240; Willey, 1949b: 357–8). In paste and vessel form it is similar to other types in the series. The surface is distinguished by large check stamping with heavy lands.

In this region the type is represented by numerous sherds from the "Fountain of Youth" site, a single specimen from Horseshoe Landing, a questionable sherd from Tick Island (probably the midden), and material from Rollestown. They probably date in St. Johns Ia, early times. Willey and Woodbury (1942, Fig. 1, c) and Willey (1949b, Pl. 13, A–C) illustrate this type on the Gulf Coast.

Deptford Linear Check Stamped. Like other types of the series, this one is not typical of the region, but is more often found in Georgia and on the Northwest Florida Gulf Coast (Caldwell and Waring, 1939b; Willey, 1949b: 354–6).

---

[6] This type should not be used as a period marker because of its close similarity to an unnamed (Speers Simple Stamped, J. B. Griffin manuscript notes) simple-stamped form of St. Johns Ia, early times.

One example from our region (Pl. 3, B) is a small tetrapod vessel with linear check stamping. It dates from St. Johns Ia, early and was found in the mound near Silver Springs. Sherds have been seen from Grant Mound, and some came from the deeper levels of Spaldings Lower Store (Pl. 5, c).

The Silver Springs vessel has also been illustrated by Moore (1895c, Pl. 85: 1). Other examples are in Willey and Woodbury (1942, Fig. 1, A and B) and Willey (1949b, Pl. 12).

Unnamed cord-marked type. Associated with Deptford material is an unnamed cord-marked ware. Joseph Caldwell (personal communication) plans to name this Deptford Cord Marked. It is characterized by medium-sized cord impressions on a sand-tempered ware. Occurrences have been noted at the mouth of the St. Johns River and in the bottom levels of Spaldings Lower Store.

Santa Rosa-Swift Creek Pottery Complex

Franklin Plain. This type of Willey's (1949b: 392–3) is characteristic of the North-west Gulf Coast. In paste and vessel form it is similar to the Deptford types but has no decoration.

A single questionable example of this type is a tetrapod jar from the Northernmost Mound on Murphy Island. Other plain gritty ware from Spaldings Lower Store and Rollestown is probably of this type. It dates from St. Johns Ia, late.

Swift Creek Complicated Stamped. This widely distributed type occurs in some quantity in our region, although it is not common. It is best known from Georgia (Jennings and Fairbanks, 1939a) and the Northwest Florida Gulf Coast (Willey and Woodbury, 1942). The paste is similar to Franklin Plain, a thin, hard, sand-tempered ware, sometimes with mica inclusions.

Two varieties are distinguished (Willey, 1949b: 378–83), an early form characterized by over-all stamping with a simple or notched rim, and a late variety. This latter form (Willey, 1949b: 429–35) is distinguished by stamping confined to a band on the upper body and rim as well as a folded lip of the Weeden Island style. Both forms occur in the Northern St. Johns Area.

This type occurs throughout the whole region but is most numerous on the lower St. Johns River. The early variety is found in St. Johns Ia, late and Ib sites, while the late variety occurs in St. Johns Ib sites.

Examples of the early variety from the area are illustrated by Moore (1895a, Figs. 4 and 44), as are late variety examples (Moore, 1895a, Pls. 80, 81: 1 and 2). An intermediate (?) form is also illustrated (Moore, 1895a, Pl. 77).

Weeden Island Series

Weeden Island Plain. This important form of the Gulf Coast (Willey and Woodbury, 1942; Willey, 1949b: 409–11) occurs sporadically in the Northern St. Johns Area. The paste of this type is similar to Franklin Plain and Swift Creek Complicated Stamped, although the surface is usually better finished. This similarity in ware characteristics makes the identification of body sherds difficult, so as a rule only rim sherds and whole vessels are classified.

Rims are usually modified, ranging from a plain fold, or a simulated fold made by an incised line, to heavy collars (Moore, 1895a, Pl. 81: 3). Vessels are most commonly simple bowls with slightly incurved rims, but many unique forms occur (Willey, 1949b). Multiple compartment vessels are of this last type. They range from three-compartment examples, like one from Monroe Mound (Pl. 3, 1), to more complex, five-compartment vessels as, for example, the one from Low Mound C near Point La Vista (Moore, 1922a, Pls. 1 and 2). Collared rims may have simple incisions.

Weeden Island Plain is found throughout the region but is most common in the lower St. Johns Valley. Its presence on Floyds Island in the Okefenokee Swamp is not far from the northeasternmost recorded occurrence at Ft. Frederica on St. Simons Island. The temporal range is St. Johns Ib and IIa.

Examples from the West Coast are illustrated by Willey (1949b); those from the lower St. Johns are in Moore (1895a, Pls. 72: 1 and 81: 3).

Weeden Island Incised. This well-known pottery type has a paste similar to Weeden Island Plain (Willey and Woodbury, 1942; Willey, 1945, 1949b: 411–19). The upper body surface and rims of vessels are decorated by an elaborate negative design formed of hatchure (Moore, 1895a, Pl. 82) or punctation enclosed by incised lines (Pl. 4, 1). Terminal pits are used as a design element. Applique bird heads are often combined with the incision (Moore, 1895a, Pl. 84: 1). Vessel forms are usually bowls, but a variety of eccentric shapes and zoomorphic forms appear.

The type is found throughout the region. It dates from St. Johns Ib and IIa periods. Examples are illustrated by Moore (1894a, Pl. 2: 1–3; 1895a, Pls. 75: 4, 77, and 78: 1).

Weeden Island Punctated. This type is similar to the previous in most respects (Willey, 1945, 1949b: 419–22), except that the decoration is completely formed by punctation. It is not as commonly found as Weeden Island Incised, but its temporal and geographical range is similar. A sherd is illustrated by Moore (1894a, Pl. 2: 4).

Weeden Island Zoned Red. This is another type closely similar to Weeden Island Incised (Willey, 1945, 1949b: 422). The use of red paint to set off incised areas distinguishes this type. In paste, design, and vessel form it is otherwise similar to Weeden Island Incised.

This type is not so common in the Northern St. Johns Area, but appears sporadically throughout the St. Johns Valley in St. Johns Ib and IIa times. It is, perhaps, more characteristic of the earlier horizon. Examples are illustrated by Moore (1894b, Pl. 15: 4 and 5).

Wakulla Check Stamped. This all-important type of the Gulf Coast (Willey and Woodbury, 1942; Willey, 1945; 1949b: 437–8) is very rare in our region. This is understandable because it parallels a local form. In paste, general bowl forms, and rim modifications it is like others in the series. The rim, and usually the whole body, is covered with neatly applied small check stamping.

This type occurs throughout the area, but is not common. It dates from St. Johns IIa times. No examples from this area have been illustrated but Gulf Coast forms are in Moore (1902, Figs. 52 and 91; 1903c, Figs. 137 and 139) and Willey (1949b, Fig. 53, Pl. 40, A–F).

Tucker Ridge Pinched. This type is similar to others of the Weeden Island series in paste and rim fold (Willey and Woodbury, 1942; Willey, 1945, 1949b: 428–9). It is characterized by a band of pinched-up decoration on the rim. Vessel forms are either bowls or jars.

Few examples of the type are known in the region but it can be expected to occur in most parts of the area. It ranges in time from St. Johns Ib to IIa. A sherd from Low Mound E, south of Grant Mound is illustrated by Moore (1895a, Fig. 45).

Carrabelle Punctated. This is another form typical of the Weeden Island series in paste and rim modifications (Willey, 1949b: 425). The type is distinguished by a rim band containing neat rows of punctations. These may be triangular, hollow, round, or eccentrically shaped. Jars are perhaps the most typical vessel form.

Examples have been found on both the coast and in St. Johns Valley, but it is a rare form. It dates from St. Johns Ib and IIa times. No examples from this area have been illustrated, but specimens from the Gulf Coast may be seen in Moore (1901, Figs. 66, 72; 1903c, Fig. 14).

Thomas Simple Stamped. Similar to other types of this series in paste and rim modification (Willey, 1949b: 438–40), this type is characterized by small, palmate simple stamping scattered over the body of the vessel.

Examples have been found on the Atlantic Coast. It probably dates from St. Johns IIa times, although it may occur earlier in St. Johns Ib.

No Series

Sarasota Incised. This is the third of the Tampa Bay area types (Willey, 1949b: 474) to be found in some quantity in the Northern St. Johns Area. The typical form has a chalky ware paste, but the same decoration rarely appears on a gritty paste. This design most commonly consists of a series of pendant triangular flags on the vessel rim. They are outlined by incision and the interior is filled with round punctations or more commonly with short incised dashes. Connected triangles and diamonds filled with punctates also occur.

The type occurs throughout the whole area in sites of St. Johns II times. Examples have been illustrated by Moore (1894a, Pl. 7: 2), Rouse (1951), and Willey (1949b, Pl. 48, G–H).

St. Petersburg Incised. Although not grouped in any series this form belongs in the Weeden Island complex, and is most commonly found on the Central Gulf Coast (Willey, 1949b: 442). The ware is sand-tempered and decorated by a series of parallel incised lines on the vessel rim.

This is a rare type in the area, a single sherd being found at Mount Royal (M.A.I. 17/4977). It dates from St. Johns II times. The type is illustrated by Willey (1949b, Pl. 46, F).

Gainesville Linear Punctated. This is another trade ware, characteristic of Central Florida (Goggin, 1948a). The paste may be either a fine grit-tempered form or a chalky ware. Decoration consists of neat rows of linear punctations either radiating from the vessel bottom or encircling the rim.

A single example of this has been seen from Grant Mound. It presumably dates from St. Johns II times. Examples have been illustrated in Goggin (1948a, Fig. 1, F–H).

Prairie Cord Marked. Another trade form from Central Florida, this type was first defined by Goggin (1948a). It is a sand-tempered ware, the surface of which is impressed with fine- to medium-sized cords.

A few possible examples of this form occur on the northern coast and lower St. Johns Valley. It dates from St. Johns II times. Examples of the type are illustrated in Goggin (1948a, Fig. 1, D and E).

Savannah Fine Cord Marked. A form characteristic of the Georgia coast (Caldwell and Waring, 1939d), this is decorated with fine cord impressions usually neatly placed in a crosshatched pattern. The paste is often sand- or clay-tempered, as is the case with those found in Florida.

The type is best known from Mt. Royal, where it was first reported by Waring (1948: 154), at Du 53, the "Fountain of Youth" site, on Amelia Island (F.S.P.S.), and elsewhere. It probably dates from St. Johns IIb. Examples are shown in Caldwell and Waring (1939d) and Caldwell and McCann (1941, Figs. 16 and 17; Pl. 16).

Alachua Cob Marked. This Central Florida type occurs at only one site, Mr 44, on the Oklawaha River. In a small sample it is proportionately important. The paste is hard and sand-tempered and the surface is covered with corn cob impressions (Goggin, 1948a, Fig. 1, A–C). It dates from St. Johns IIb times.

PAPYS BAYOU SERIES

Papys Bayou Punctated. This type (Willey, 1949b: 443) is similar to Weeden Island Punctated in all respects except that the ware is chalky—similar to the St. Johns series. A few examples of this type have been found in St. Johns IIa sites.

LITTLE MANATEE SERIES

Little Manatee Zone Stamped. The presence of this type in some quantity in the area is of interest as it is a Weeden Island II form, described from the Tampa Bay area (Willey, 1949b: 443–4). The type is found on a chalky ware paste with decorations formed by neat stamping impressed by a toothed tool, which is placed in geometric zones bordered by incised lines.

The form is found sporadically throughout the area in St. Johns II sites. Along the coast, this and other forms of the same series are often the only decorated pottery forms in addition to check-stamped ware.

Little Manatee Shell Stamped. Like the previous types, this is also a Tampa Bay area form (Willey, 1949b: 444). However, it occurs on the St. Johns in some numbers, being found even more commonly than the previous zone-stamped variety. This is similar in all respects to the former type except that the stamped impressions are made with the toothed portion of a shell (Pls. 2, A; 4, E, G, and H).

The range covers both the St. Johns River and coast, dating from St. Johns II times.

PASCO SERIES

Pasco Plain. Sherds of this limestone-tempered ware come from the deeper levels of Spaldings Lower Store. Its time range is probably St. Johns I and II (Goggin, 1948*a*).

Pasco Check Stamped. This type of limestone-tempered ware is also known from Spaldings Lower Store. The variety found there is that with small checks (Goggin, 1948*a*). Its time range is presumably St. Johns II.

FORT WALTON SERIES

Fort Walton Incised. This is another trade ware from the Northwest Florida Coast (Willey and Woodbury, 1942; Willey, 1949*b*: 460–2). It has a grit-tempered paste. The rim bears an incised and punctated geometric, anthropomorphic, or zoomorphic design.

The type is not common in our area but a few sherds are found in the larger river and coastal sites. Strictly speaking, most of these finds are not Fort Walton Incised but rather appear to be local manufactures on chalky paste copying Fort Walton styles. They date from St. Johns IIb.

Illustration of the typical West Coast forms may be found in Willey and Woodbury (1942), Willey (1949*b*), and in various papers by Clarence B. Moore (see Willey, 1949*b*, for reference to these).

SAN MARCOS SERIES

San Marcos Stamped. This distinctive type has only recently been defined by Hale G. Smith (1948); examples are also illustrated by Rouse (1951). The ware is usually sand tempered. In the St. Augustine area it may be sand or limestone-tempered or a combination of the two. Rarely shell is included. Decoration consists of paddle (?) stamped impressions of check, simple, crossed-simple, or complicated patterns (Pl. 5, G). The designs are bold, sometimes badly smeared, and often crude. Further modifications include a folded lip, at times marked by reed punctations.

Vessel forms are usually large, deep, rounded-base jars, with a constricted area below a slightly flaring rim. The Spanish "soup plate" shape is not uncommon. Occasionally, the Spanish type of ring foot base is found on some vessels. The insides of most vessels are well smoothed and may be painted red. Rarely red and white paint are used on the same vessel.

The resemblance between this type and Caldwell's King George Malleated has been pointed out by Smith (1948: 315). This similarity can be further emphasized; in fact, except for vessel shapes found only in Georgia it is doubtful whether or not the two can be distinguished apart.

The type is abundant in late seventeenth century sites on the St. Johns River, near St. Augustine, and northwards along the coast. Smith (1948: 314) has noted a post-1686 date for simple and crossed-simple stamping with the other methods of decoration reaching their peak of popularity before that time. To some extent our work corroborates this, but some anomalies yet remain to be explained. Westward it occurs in Central Florida and near Tallahassee. Examples have been illustrated by Webb (1894, Pl. 80) and Smith (1948).

San Marcos Plain and San Marcos Red. Plain ware forms of this series are less common than the stamped. They are distinguished by the presence or absence of red paint on one or both surfaces.

Miscellaneous. Deep, broad line incision is sometimes found by itself or in combination with stamping. It is relatively rare. This form is close to incised ware at Fort King Georgia, Georgia.

HALIFAX SERIES

This new series is known from the Nocoroco study of J. W. Griffin and Hale Smith (1949). The material is a heavily sand-tempered ware with varying surface decoration; types are Halifax Plain, Halifax Check Stamped, Halifax Scored, and Halifax Simple Stamped.[7]

The material has been dated in early historic times by the describers, i.e., St. Johns IIc. The range is unknown, being reported only from Nocoroco.

MISCELLANEOUS TYPES, VARIOUS SERIES

Jefferson Complicated Stamped A. This is another type recently defined by Smith (1948), a form most characteristic of northwest Florida. The paste is grit-tempered, while the surface is decorated with stamped impressions of concentric squares or diamonds.

Sherds from Kauffman Island (Watkins, MS*b*) can perhaps be attributed to this type. Presumably they date, as do those from elsewhere, from the seventeenth and eighteenth centuries. Examples have been illustrated by Smith (1948).

Lamar Complicated Stamped. This Georgia type (Jennings and Fairbanks, 1939*b*) occurs occasionally in the Northern St. Johns Area in association with San Marcos Stamped. It is basically a sand-tempered ware decorated with complicated-stamp impressions. A folded lip marked with reed impressions is very characteristic.

All specimens reported are from the moat at Castillo de San Marcos or from excavations in St. Augustine. The type apparently dates, in this area at least, in the seventeenth and eighteenth centuries, the St. Augustine Period. Examples are illustrated in Jennings and Fairbanks (1939*b*).

Moundville Black Filmed. A single sherd of this type has been classified from the area by James B. Griffin (manuscript notes). The type is characteristic of Central Alabama. The surface is well smoothed and black in color. Shell tempering is usually present.

The specimen, from Thursby Mound, is a large duck effigy head sherd (formerly M.A.I. 17/2220, now F.S.U. 528). The eye is triangular in form and the usual shell tempering is present (this is not the specimen illustrated in Moore, 1894*b*, Fig. 34). The type dates from St. Johns II times.

Point Washington Incised. This West Florida type (Willey, 1949*b*: 463) is represented by an example from the Davenport Mound (R.S.P.F. 39327). It is a late form dating in Fort Walton times on the West Coast or St. Johns IIb here.

---

[7] The similarities between this series and the Deptford are remarkable, even including the use of podal supports in the Halifax material.

UNNAMED SERIES

In the course of this study a new series of sherd-tempered pottery was recognized. Inasmuch as it is most common on Amelia Island, which is now the subject of a detailed study by other archeologists, the types will not be defined here, only a general statement being presented.

Small to large chunky pieces of crushed potsherds are included in a sandy paste. Method of vessel construction is not clear but probably is coiling. Surface finish may be well compacted.

Plain sherds are most common but various surface texturing techniques were practiced. Cob marking was most common but fabric impressing, simple stamping, complicated stamping, and check stamping were practiced.

This material dates from St. Johns II and perhaps later. It extends as far south as Mt. Royal and the Yonge Avenue site, Anastasia Island. To the northwards it becomes more abundant, reaching a point of highest frequency on Amelia Island.

SEMINOLE SERIES

Stokes Brushed (Pl. 12, L to P).

Paste:

> Method of manufacture: Coiled ?
> Tempering: Coarse sand and/or crushed quartz. Some fine mica added to paste or in clay.
> Texture: Coarse; laminated and contorted.
> Hardness: Interior, 3.5–5.5, average 4.2; exterior, 3.5–4.5, average 4.
> Color: Surface ranges from black through light brown to grey. Firing clouds are present

Surface Finish:

> Modifications: Interior, smoothed, rarely brushed. Exterior, uneven and brushed. Heavy tempering particles protrude.
> Filming: Absent.

Decoration:

> Technique: Usually wiped or brushed with a bundle of flat fibers, perhaps grass.
> Design: The brushing is apparently random, crossing in every direction.
> Distribution: The brushing was applied to most of the vessel. Pinched punctates may be placed below the lip.

Form:

> Rim: Slightly constricted neck, flaring rim.
> Lip: Rounded.
> Body: Large bowl or jar?
> Base: No data.
> Thickness: Body, 6–9 mm.
> Appendages: None.

Usual Range of Type: Found in the area only at Spaldings Lower Store (Stokes Landing). A related form occurs at Manatee Springs and Pine Bluff on the Suwannee River; it is uncertain whether the type is locally made or imported from the northwest.

Chronological Position of Type: Seminole Period; at Spaldings Lower Store, 1763-83 A.D.

Unclassified plain. Sherds of a well made, hard, thin, ware were found at Spaldings Lower Store (Pl. 12, J). The paste contains a heavy proportion of fine mica and the surface is well smoothed.

Unclassified incised. One small sherd of the above-described paste from Spaldings Lower Store has an incised design on the rim (Pl. 12, K). It is similar in some respects to Ocmulgee Fields Incised.

EUROPEAN WARES

Spanish olive jar. Fragments of this typical wheel-turned pottery occur throughout the area, being found in St. Augustine period sites, and earlier in St. Johns IIc sites. These are large jars of hard sand-tempered pottery often with a white slip. They may have a thin green interior and/or exterior glaze, often weathered away.

These vessels served as general shipping and storage containers. Examples are illustrated by Holmes (1903, Fig. 59).

Majolica. This pottery is characterized by a soft paste and hard tin-enameled or glazed surface. It may be decorated with a variety of colors—blue, yellow, green, or black—on a white or cream ground. The type is a basic Mediterranean and Near Eastern form. Apparently, Florida material came from both Spain and Mexico.

A preliminary study of this material (Goggin, 1950b) indicates at least two seventeenth-century concentrations of types. The earliest, previous to 1650, is characterized by Fig Springs Polychrome, Ichtucknee Blue on Blue, and several other forms. The later complex, post-1675, is marked by Puebla Polychrome, Abo Polychrome, and other types.

Majolica occurs sporadically in most Spanish contact sites in small quantities. It may be used as a marker, the first group of types being St. Johns IIc in time while the second is associated with the San Marcos series and is thus of the St. Augustine Period.

Miscellaneous types. At Spaldings Lower Store a variety of eighteenth-century non-Indian ceramic forms are found, including English creamware china, salt-glazed ware, scratched blue salt-glazed ware, brown and yellow glazed "slipware" pottery (American Colonial or English), Delft ware, and other forms. These are in a Colonial context, although it is not improbable that they were sometimes traded to the Seminole. Very much the same complex appeared at Mt. Royal, and examples of various of the above types come from many sites near St. Augustine (SJ 3, SJ 33, SJ 40, SJ 9, SJ 10, SJ 44) and Nocoroco (Griffin and Smith, 1949). A slightly earlier group of similar forms came from Fort Pupo. A full discussion of these types will be included in the final report on Spaldings Lower Store.

Early American occupation, 1820–40's, is often ceramically marked by blue or green "feather edge" chinaware, flower painted chinaware, and printed Staffordshire chinaware. Such material is everywhere common but is only found in association with Seminole material at Middleburg. However, it should be associated with late Seminole occupation elsewhere in the area.

ORIENTAL WARES

Chinese and Japanese porcelains are not uncommon in Indian sites in the state but they have been found here only in an English Colonial context at Fort Pupo, Spaldings Lower Store, Mt. Royal, and near St. Augustine (SJ 3, SJ 9, SJ 40). The several varieties present have not been identified, but they are presumably of the late eighteenth century.

Underglaze blue decorations are most common, but overglaze enamels in a number of colors are sometimes found. The variety of forms in a large collection, such as from Spaldings Lower Store, is extensive.

OTHER ARTIFACTS

VESSELS

In this region shell was not extensively used in the making of vessels and the variety of forms is limited, although Busycon dippers are common. Wooden vessels were undoubtedly used, but none have been found.

Busycon dipper. This common artifact was made by removing the interior whorls of a *Busycon perversa* shell. The type is found throughout the area occurring in quantity at some sites. Those deposited in burial mounds were often "killed" by basal perforation.

This form extends from St. Johns I into historic times, and perhaps earlier.

Busycon cup. A cup-like vessel was made from the outer whorl of a Busycon shell. It is similar to a dipper but has lower sides and no handle (Pl. 6, M).

The few specimens known in the area include those from "Site 3," Huntoon Island (U.S.N.M. 351542), Rock House Mound (Sweett-Wilson Collection), and Silver Glen Springs (U.S.N.M. 378412). The type's temporal position is not known. To the south specimens are found in the Indian River Area (Rouse, 1951) and it is a common form in the Glades area, where it dates from Glades III times.

Busycon saucer. This shallow receptacle is a disk cut from the outer whorl of the Busycon shell. A common form to the south, only a single specimen is known here from the Cotten site (John W. Griffin, MS). It apparently dates in the Orange Period.

Steatite vessels. Sporadic occurrences of steatite vessel sherds indicate the presence of these vessels here. In context they appear at the Cotten site (J. W. Griffin, MS) and at the "Fountain of Youth" site (Seaberg, MS).

One whole vessel comes from Putnam County (Bushnell, 1940, Pl. 10: 1). Some rim fragments found have incised designs on the lip similar to those from South Indian Field (Ferguson, 1951).

Specimens datable are from the Orange Period. Perhaps others will be found from Mt. Taylor (?) times. It is not impossible, too, that a few heirlooms continued in use in later periods. Steatite sherds picked up on the older sites probably furnished the later Indians with raw material for various ornaments.

CUTTING AND PICKING TOOLS

Busycon pick X. This is a distinctive whole shell tool, characteristic of this area. It is made from the right-handed shell, *Busycon carica.* Modifications consist of a ground beak, often beveled following the curve of the shell, producing a gouge blade, and a hole pierced in the top of the shoulder a short distance behind the aperture.

The manner of hafting these picks is not certain, but if they were used like an adze or ax they could have been hafted with a bent branch type of handle passing through the hole (Moore, 1921, Fig. 8–9).

Another method of hafting could have been placing the tool on the end of a handle, with the long axis a continuation of and parallel to the handle. This would be similar to a digging stick or a palstave. Neither appreciable wear nor any other clue is available to indicate whether either or both of these methods, or another still unknown, was used.

The great bulk of the specimens came from sites of St. Johns I or II periods. Both Moore (1893: 720–1) and Wyman (1875: 58) note their absence from the Mt. Taylor and Orange periods. However, two questionable examples from the latter period are now known, one from Kauffman Island (Watkins, MS*b*) and the other from the Cotten site (John W. Griffin, MS).

Strombus celt. A practical cutting tool was made from the heavy lip of the pink conch, *Strombus gigas.* It is celt-like in form with a square to rounded blade and a tapering poll. Specimens range from approximately 7 to 16 cm. in length (Wyman, 1875, Pl. 8: 1).

The origin of these celts is of some interest since the *Strombus gigas* does not now live in the area and apparently did not during Indian occupation. It was necessary, then, for either the finished celts or the raw shell to be brought up from extreme southeastern Florida in the Glades Area, where the mollusc lives.

Specimens are common in shell mounds throughout the whole area. They appear in the Orange Period and continue into St. Johns II times. In view of the fact that they are probably imports from the south, their absence in Mt. Taylor times is perhaps understandable, because there is scant evidence for peoples in the Glades Area at that time.

Busycon celt. Thin curved celts made from sections of Busycon shell are occasionally found. They differ from the gouge in being made from a section of shell taken further towards the shoulder; thus they lack the sharp curved blade and the beak poll.

The geographic range is sporadic and wide, while the time distribution is not known. Several specimens were found in the Thrasher Shell Pit (Simpson collection, A3380, A3382). The form is most typical of the Gulf Coast.

Stone celts. Stone celts made of hard local limestones and foreign igneous or metamorphic rocks occur in some numbers in the area. Presumably they are trade items. Their forms and size vary (Pl. 6, E–G, K, L, O, P) and an occasional one is similar in form to the petaloid celts of the West Indies (Pl. 6, H).

Specimens occur in all parts of the area but seem to be most common in the north. None are known from either the Mt. Taylor or Orange periods, but they occur in St. Johns I and II and in the St. Augustine (?) periods.

Busycon gouge. Triangular sections from the bottom of the outer whorl of a Busycon shell were used for gouges. The broad blade was sharpened on a pronounced bevel forming a curved adze-like gouge blade. The poll was formed by the twisted beak of the shell (Pl. 6, A–D).

The geographical range of the type is the whole area and its temporal range is as broad. They first appear in Mt. Taylor levels continuing into St. Johns II times. The horizon of greatest frequency is not known. This artifact is most typical of this and the neighboring Indian River areas (Rouse, 1951).

Columella chisel. The heavy columellae of the *Fasciolaria gigantea* shell were carefully trimmed, sometimes ground flat on one side and sharpened at one end (Wyman, 1875, Pl. 6: 5). Specimens occur sporadically in the area, although they are more typical of the Florida Gulf Coast. The temporal position in the Northern St. Johns Area is not known.

Stone chisel. Moore uses this term for narrow chisel-like celts found in St. Johns I and II sand mounds (Pl. 10, D).

Perforated shark tooth. Shark's teeth, perforated for attachment, were used as knives or perhaps set in clubs as at Key Marco in the Glades Area (Cushing, 1897: 370–1). A single perforation is most typical but one example is known with a double perforation (Moore, 1894*b*, Fig. 40). These specimens are nowhere common but occur along the river in St. Johns I and II sites.

Flint celts. Flint or chipped stone celts are reported by Moore in a number of sites. There is no information as to whether any received supplementary grinding (Pl. 6, Q).

Specimens date from St. Johns I and II times, a time level equivalent in general to their presence elsewhere in the south.

Flint blades. Flint blades, usable for either cutting or scraping, are found sporadically but widely. Less selective collecting will probably reveal more.

Forms are not standardized. Oval types occur (Wyman, 1875, Pl. 2: 1) and more tapering forms slightly suggestive of a *coup-de-poing* (Wyman, 1875, Pl. 2: 2). This latter type is somewhat similar to types from Central Florida.

Wyman (1875, Pl. 2: 3 and 4) also figures slender blades of a willow-leaf form as does Moore (1895*a*, Fig. 17). A square blade (Wyman, 1875, Pl. 2: 7) may be one of the earliest specimens in the area, dating from well back in Mt. Taylor times. A larger, more finely worked specimen comes from Beauclerc and dates later (Moore, 1894*b*, Fig. 68). A specimen from the midden one-half mile north of Nashua (Pl. 6, N) may be a blade or scraper.

A large oval specimen is illustrated from the midden three miles north of Palatka (Moore, 1893, Fig. 2). Judging from the description, one side is the smooth original flake surface, while the other has been modified by secondary chipping. This probably dates from the Mt. Taylor Period. Similar forms occur in Central Florida on a pre-ceramic horizon. Another form similar to early Central Florida types is a retouched flake found near the base of Cooks Ferry Mound (Moore, 1894*a*, Fig. 106).

HAMMERING AND POUNDING TOOLS

Flint hammerstone. These are small pieces of flint, probably cores in many cases, which were used as pounding tools. Generally they are of a size to fit comfortably in the hand and show considerable wear from percussion.

Specimens are present in all parts of the area. They occur as early as the Mt. Taylor Period and continued in use through St. Johns II times.

Stone celt-hammer. Celts dulled through use were used as a hammer, the blade being beaten to a rounded surface. A specimen comes from Tick Island Mound (Pl. 6, J).

Pebble hammers. This is a name given by Moore to a type of artifact found rather commonly by him in sand mounds. Presumably they are natural pebbles showing percussion wear. They occur along the St. Johns River and probably elsewhere. Their temporal range is the St. Johns I and II periods.

PIERCING TOOLS

Bone awl: cylindrical shaft variety. This type of awl is a simple cylindrical piece of bone smoothed and sharpened to a point. They occur sporadically through the area. The time range is not known.

Bone awl: splinter variety. This awl form is a small piece of dense bone, with an end or corner ground to a sharp point.

This is the commonest and most widespread form of awl found through the area. They are first noted from the Mt. Taylor Period and are found up through St. Johns II times.

Bone awl: ulna variety. A single specimen, apparently of this form comes from the Shields Mound (Pl. 8, L).

Bone needle. A possible bone needle was found by Moore in the Tick Island Sand Mound. Although fragmentary (Moore, 1894a, Fig. 31) it appears to have had a long slit perforating the base.

This is the only specimen known. It dates from St. Johns Ia, early.

GRINDING, SCRAPING, AND SMOOTHING TOOLS

Omitted from consideration here are various flint blades mentioned in a previous section. Many of these may have served as scraping tools rather than cutting blades.

Thin grinding stone. Flat sections of sandy limestone or coquina were used as grinding or sharpening stones. Specimens are usually only 1 to 2 cm. in thickness and no more than 12 cm. in either other dimension. They show no working other than wear resulting from use.

The range of this form is universal throughout the area. They occur from the Mt. Taylor period into historic times.

Stone hone. These are thin slabs of sandy limestone or coquina similar to grinding stones. However, they show one or more deep grooves in the surface as a result of abrasion from a pointed implement.

The type is found through the area, although of sporadic occurrence. The earliest examples reported were found in St. Johns Ia, late, sites and others occur in later sites.

Stemmed flint scraper. A single stemmed chipped flint scraper, a type often called a "blunt," has been reported (Moore, 1893, Fig. 1). It has a short stem and a wide rounded blade. This specimen probably dates from Mt. Taylor times.

Shell scraper. Undescribed shell scrapers are reported from a St. Johns II site.

WEAPONS

Small bone point. These are slender bi-pointed sections of bone ranging from 3 to 6 cm. in length, and usually less than 10 mm. in diameter.

The type is not uncommon throughout the area, but has not been stratigraphically placed. It occurs throughout the state, and in most of Eastern United States, and is usually early when dated.

Short bone point. These are similar to the small points except for their slightly larger size and proportionately greater massiveness. They range up to 10 cm. in length.

Specimens are found sporadically in much of the area and apparently date from as early as the Mt. Taylor or Orange periods. Their latest occurrence is not known but they probably range into St. Johns II times.

Long bone point. These are slender, usually less than 1 cm. in diameter and 6 to 14 cm. in length. They are sporadically found, some dating as early as Mt. Taylor times.

Socketed bone point. This form of point is made of a hollow animal bone, usually mammal. The articular end is removed and the shaft is cut diagonally—this end forming the point. The other end was simply slipped on the weapon shaft.

Like other bone points this is sporadically but widely found. Specimens date from St. Johns II times but undoubtedly they were used much earlier, probably at least by Orange times.

Extra large socketed bone point. Large hollow bones were made into points in a manner similar to the preparation of small points. They range from 24 to 30 cm. in length. One, made from a human femur, has three perforations in the base (Moore, 1894a, Fig. 25). Others are made from deer bone (Nelson, 1918: 90; Sweett-Wilson Collection).

Occasional specimens are found over this area. These forms date from as early as St. Johns Ia, early (Tick Island Mound, human femur example), but probably were made both earlier and later.

Socketed antler point. These are made of deer antler tines, cut a suitable length, usually 7 to 12 cm. The tip is sharpened and the base hollowed to hold a shaft.

This form is not common, but occurs in many parts of the region. It may occur as early as Mt. Taylor or Orange times.

Flint points. Considering that flint is practically absent in the region the number and variety of chipped flint points is astonishing. A broad variety from a single site is shown by Moore (1895a, Fig. 11). An area-wide series is illustrated in Plate 7.

At the present time it is not yet possible to clearly assign point types to definite time ranges although some tentative conclusions can be given. A single specimen, suggestive of a Suwannee point comes from the area, at Watson's Landing (Pl. 7, R and s).

A channel flake has been removed from one side. It is presumably Mt. Taylor or earlier in date.

Various forms of broad, triangular, stemmed points date, in part, from Mt. Taylor and Orange periods (Pl. 7, J–M). Points of St. Johns Ia times include an eccentric form with serrated sides (Pl. 7, AA) and broad-stemmed slender points (Pl. 7, T and U).

Small triangular points made from thin flakes appear in St. Johns IIb. It is possible (judging from Central Florida data) that square-based, barbed points date from the same time (Pl. 7, Q). Another late form is the basal and side-notched Cahokia type point (Moore, 1894a, Fig. 5).

However, it appears that the time range of many of the points is quite broad and perhaps only the small triangular and the Cahokia type forms can be used as temporal markers.

WEIGHTS

Grooved stone weight. Objects of this type are small stones, only slightly worked, with notches and/or grooves around the short diameter. They are not common but occur sporadically in St. Johns II sites. They undoubtedly occur earlier.

Perforated shells. Certain types of shells pierced below the hinge are known to have been net weights in the Glades Area. Such a use is inferred here. Moore (1894a: 62) reports perforated Arca, Pectunculus, and Pecten shells from Tick Island Mound. Nelson (1918: 90) reports perforated Arca shells at Oak Hill Midden.

Those from Tick Island Mound date from St. Johns Ia, early, while the Oak Hill, specimens were found at the bottom of the site, thus either in the Mt. Taylor or St. Johns I Period, and at the top, in St. Johns II times.

ORNAMENTS

The greater attention paid to this class of objects is really a reflection of available data, not necessarily the proportional importance of ornaments. Various collectors, including Clarence B. Moore, have tended to be more interested in these objects. On the other hand, there is a wide variety of unusual forms found only here and representing casual experimentation not followed up. These forms, combined with various exotic types traded from elsewhere, swell the total picture.

Shell beads. Shell beads are not abundant in the region and in many rich sites only a few occur; yet in some places they are very numerous. Various forms found include disk, tubular, and large forms made from a columella. Shell beads are found in St. Johns Ia, early, sites and later.

Pearl beads. These are not common probably because they are so susceptible to erosion. Those found are misshapen and discolored; yet, modern treasure seekers are inflamed by tales of the early explorers concerning the quantity of pearls among the Indians, and tell of "valuable" pearl treasures remaining to be found in Indian sites. All pearls found are definitely only of archeological interest. Pearl beads are known sporadically from St. Johns II sites.

Red stone bead. Red stone beads made of material variously called jasper or catlinite are found. None personally examined appear to be catlinite—all were harder than steel. Specimens are generally tubular in form.

Occasional specimens occur in late sites, but when any numbers are found they appear in an undefined horizon. This has been previously discussed.

Massive stone beads. These are large tubular and barrel shaped beads, 2 to 5 cm. long. The material is a hard foreign stone.

A number of specimens were found at Coontie Island (Thompson and Ryman Collection). As previously discussed their exact temporal position is not clear.

Steatite bead. Tubular, discoid, and barrel shaped beads of steatite occur. They were probably locally made utilizing old vessel sherds for material.

Their range is widespread in the area although in no place common. The first recorded specimens are from a St. Johns Ia, late, horizon while others occur later in the St. Johns II Period.

Bone beads. Sections of hollow mammal and bird bones are cut into lengths, smoothed and polished forming tubular beads. They occur possibly as early as Mt. Taylor times.

FIG. 5. Incised Shell Object, Dillards Grove.

Circular Busycon gorget. Disk gorgets made from sections of the outer whorl of the Busycon shell occur in the area. They vary greatly in size from a few centimeters to nine or more in diameter. Methods of suspension include a large central or near central hole (Pl. 8, A), two central holes (Pl. 8, B), four central holes (Pl. 8, c) and two holes near the perimeter.

Specimens occur occasionally throughout the region. The earliest may be possible ones from the Mt. Taylor level at Midden 2, Salt Springs Run. Shell disks, dating from St. Johns Ia, early, found at Tick Island Mound, can also be included. Other specimens from the northernmost mound, Murphy Island may be dated from St. Johns Ib, late, or later, if intrusive. No specimens dating from St. Johns II times have been noted.

Pierced shell gorget. A neatly designed and executed cut-out shell gorget was found at Kauffman Island (Abshire *et al.*, 1935: 8–9). It is almost identical with one found by Moore in the Indian River Area (Moore, 1894*a*, Fig. 110).

Incised shell maskette. Incised shell of any kind is uncommon in the region. A small shell representation of a face (Fig. 5) from Dillards Grove (M.A.I. 17/509) is unique.

Elliptical shell ornament. Moore (1894*b*: 152) reports an elliptical ornament of shell, 8.9 cm. long, from the Tick Island Mound.

Stone two-holed gorget. Two forms of two-holed stone bar gorgets are known. The simplest has an expanded middle and tapering ends (Moore, 1894b, Fig. 62) while the other is similar but with expanded ends (Pl. 8, T). This second is made of foreign stone.

These are rare forms, only two being known. The first, from the Harris Mound, has not been dated, while the other comes from the Shields Mound, a site apparently dating mainly from St. Johns IIa, but possibly occupied earlier.

Stone pendants: general. Pendants, either perforated or grooved, are found in a wide variety of forms. In general few types are standardized—the form depending on the conformation of the raw material and the maker's taste. An examination of figures in Moore (1894a, 1894b, 1895a) will indicate this variety. They occur at all periods including and after St. Johns Ia, early.

Stone pendant: plummet variety. This type, widespread throughout Florida, includes a variety of forms. They are essentially plummet or tear-drop shaped forms but also include more cylindrical types, such as long quartz crystals.

A groove was made around the upper end of the object. There is considerable variation in form and neatness of execution. Some are made of local coquina or sandy limestone, others are made of imported foreign material. These pendants occur throughout the area. They appear in the St. Johns Ia, early Period and continue through St. Johns II.

Stone pendant: double grooved variety. A variation on the plummet form are those specimens with another groove or a flange, producing a groove at the bottom. Some are so slender as to be almost columnar with double flanges. They are often finely finished.

These are much less common than the previous form. They first appear in St. Johns Ia, early times and continue into St. Johns II. Specimens are somewhat more common in the earlier period, a temporal distribution similar to that on the Gulf Coast.

Stone pendant: perforated rectangular variety. Thin rectangular, or approximately rectangular, slabs of stone were shaped with slightly tapering ends. Near one end a single perforation was made (Moore, 1894a, Fig. 10; 1895a: 47). The materials used are hard foreign stones. Occasionally small relatively unworked pebbles were perforated to make pendants.

These types are rare. One from Low Mound E, south of Grant Mound, dates from St. Johns Ib; another from Mt. Royal is probably from St. Johns IIa times.

Stone pendant: bannerstone wing variety. Broken wings of the flared wing bannerstone (Type 3) were utilized as pendants. The edge of the central perforation was ground smooth and two holes were drilled at the corners (Pl. 8, D and G).

Two examples were found at Thornhill Lake Mound 1 (Moore, 1894b: 169–70). A third comes from Orange Park, Clay County (U.P.M.). Their temporal position is not known.

Stone pendant: boat-shaped variety. A single boat-shaped pendant was found by Moore (1895a, Fig. 15) in the Shields Mound. Although called "boat shaped" by Moore, actually the form is more like the basketry "wall pocket" of the Southeastern Indians (Goggin, 1939).

Shell pendant: general. An even greater variety and number of shell pendants is found than of stone, although the material limitations, mainly thickness, offered problems to the artisan. An examination of Moore's papers (1894a, 1894b, 1895a) will give some indication of the variety to be found. Their shape is quite variable and they may be grooved or perforated for suspension.

Shell pendant: flat variety. This is one of the most common of all types. It is essentially a section of shell, usually Busycon, grooved or notched for suspension. Specimens are found as early as St. Johns Ia, early, and continue through St. Johns II.

Shell pendant: double grooved columella variety. This pendant usually made from the columella of the *Fasciolaria gigantea*, has a groove and/or a flange at each end. The examples are usually well made.

The type is widespread throughout the state and occurs sporadically over the region. Its temporal range is from St. Johns Ia, early, through St. Johns II.

Shell pendants: imitation tooth variety. Shell replicas of animal canine teeth have been noted at the Shields Mound (Moore, 1895a, Fig. 22). They are realistic imitations, perforated at the base for suspension. The form is widely but sporadically found throughout the state. In this area they have been reported at the Shields Mound, a St. Johns IIa site.

Clay pendants. The variety and form of clay pendants or similar objects seems only limited by the vast imagination of the craftsmen. A wide variety are illustrated by C. B. Moore. This interest in clay ornaments is undoubtedly a side development, stemming from the general artistic interest in form, mainly expressed in effigy figures and odd vessel shapes. The time range is St. Johns I and II periods.

Perforated canine tooth. Large mammal canine teeth were perforated at the base for suspension (Moore, 1895a, Fig. 21). They are not common and date from St. Johns II times.

Shell pin: round head variety. This type of pin made from a shell columella with a round large head (Moore, 1893) is widespread throughout the Southeast. Specimens found here are typical (Moore, 1894b, Figs. 47 and 48). Specimens are generally in late sites (St. Johns II) or are with intrusive burials.

Coral pin. A simple unique coral pin is reported by Moore (1894b, Fig. 31) from the Tick Island Mound.

Bone pins. Bone pins are a very typical artifact of the Southeast and those of Florida are unlike any elsewhere. Many of the recognized Florida varieties are found in the region.

In general these are long, slender sections of deer bone finely worked and polished to a tapering point. Difference in the form of the butt are some of the main criteria to distinguish varieties (see Goggin, MSb and Willey, 1949a for a detailed discussion). Some of the forms found here include the peg-topped variety (Pl. 8, M, Q, and R), simple variety (Pl. 8, O), and expanded head variety (Pl. 8, P). Others are illustrated in Moore's papers.

Although pins are probably earlier, the first definite record we have of them is in the Orange Period. At this time we also get our only sharp evidence of typological correlation with a given horizon. Apparently bone pins with a detailed geometrical design of incised lines bordered by ticks are typical of the horizon (Pl. 8, s). Their presence in the Orange level at the Cotten site cross dates with their presence at this time at South Indian Field. Other pin forms occur throughout the area, persisting into St. Johns II times.

CEREMONIAL OBJECTS

As in most archeological reports, this section tends to be a catch-all category of objects whose function is not surely known. In addition to the usual series of materials, there are included here all prehistoric copper ornaments. These are so unusual that

FIG. 6. Forked Eye Plate, Mt. Royal.

their purpose is not considered to have been necessarily and solely ornamental. Objects such as bannerstones whose function is either utilitarian or utilitarian-ceremonial are not included, but are considered under Miscellaneous along with other objects whose use is debatable but not necessarily ceremonial.

Objects of copper or other metal dated from historic times, either through context or form, are included under European and European-derived materials.[8]

Embossed copper plates, disks, and other ornaments. Copper objects fabricated from native metal were especially abundant in St. Johns II times. These are generally square or rectangular (Pl. 9, M–O, Q–U), but circular specimens are found (Pl. 9, F). The specimens were decorated by means of embossed lines and beading. More elaborate varieties include the forked eye plate from Mt. Royal (Fig. 6; Moore, 1894a, Pl. 1).

[8] This may appear inconsistent but it follows the general artifact pattern laid out in another paper, on the Glades Area (Goggin, MSb). In that paper this division is more reasonable since all worked metal appears to be historic.

Copper crescent. A large crescent-shaped copper object (Pl. 9, G) came from the northernmost mound on Murphy Island. It dates from St. Johns Ia, late, times.

Copper point. An unique copper point (Pl. 9, E) comes from the Monroe Mound. It dates from St. Johns Ia, late.

Copper conjoined tube. This typical Hopewellian artifact is represented by one typical and one variant example (Pl. 9, K) at the northernmost mound on Murphy Island. They date from St. Johns Ia, late, times.

Copper ear spool. Cymbal-shaped copper ear spools or halfs of such spools (Pl. 9, L) are found at northernmost mound, Murphy Island and Monroe Mound. They date in the St. Johns Ia, late Period.

Copper covered stone ear spool. Pulley type stone ear spools or plugs were covered with a thin layer of copper (Pl. 9, H and I). These date from St. Johns II times.

Copper covered wood objects. It was a practice to apply thin sheets of copper to objects of many kinds. It was most prevalent in St. Johns II. Worthy of comment is the covered bi-conical ear plug (Pl. 9, P) from Grant Mound.

Copper covered mammal jaw. A representative example of this artifact (Pl. 9, C) was found at the Tick Island Mound. It dates from St. Johns Ia, early.

Long nosed god maskette. Two examples of this unique object (Pl. 9) came from Grant Mound. As already has been noted, this is a widely dispersed object, yet the specimens are very similar to each other. For general purposes in this paper they have been placed in the St. Johns II Period, the date given to the Grant Mound. However, if Krieger's (Newell and Krieger, 1949: 198) dating for the Gahagan Focus of Louisiana is correct, then by cross-correlation we would have to move the date for the Grant specimens back to St. Johns Ia, late. It is not improbable that this site was one of multiple occupancy.

Spatulate celts. This odd form of artifact here achieves one of its main concentrations, with several examples coming from St. Johns II sites (Pl. 10, B, C, E–H).

Hoe-shaped implement. This is a widely but sporadically spread artifact in the Eastern United States (Moore, 1903b), represented by a single specimen here (Pl. 6, I). It dates from St. Johns II.

Discoidal stone. Discoidal stones are rare in Florida but one is reported from Grant Mound (Moore, 1894b: 203). It is probably of the St. Johns II Period.

EUROPEAN OBJECTS

In this category there are included, with one exception, all objects obtained from European sources, all such modified objects, and all Indian made objects of European materials. The one exception is European pottery, which is included with the Indian pottery because of its significance as a temporal marker.

This material came from varied sources. In the earliest days it was mainly obtained from shipwrecks; later some was obtained through casual trade, especially in mission areas. However, no systematic trade supply was established until English (1763–83) and later American (1821–) times. The Spanish never exploited the trade possibilities.

Miscellaneous iron tools: knives, chisels, axes, awls, and nails. These are all simple steel tools of upmost functional value to the native as a change from their old tools. They are mainly found with intrusive burials in mounds and date from St. Johns IIc times.

Flint and steel (?). This is reported, but not described, from the Bayard Point Mound (Moore, 1894b: 188–9). It dates from the St. Augustine or Seminole Period.

Flint lock guns. These are also reported but not described from the above mentioned Bayard Point Mound.

Powder horn. The remnants of a powder horn came from the Bayard Point Mound. The base was studded with brass tacks.

Musket balls. Fourteen spherical musket balls accompanied a burial in the Bayard Point Mound.

Iron horseshoe. A horseshoe came from the Spruce Creek Mound (U.S.N.M. 10998). Why it was placed there is unknown.

Glass fragments. Glass fragments, very likely those of a mirror, were associated with a burial at the Bayard Point Mound.

FIG. 7. Bone Comb, North Mound on Murphy Island.

Coins. These turn up rarely, the earliest one, from Spruce Creek Mound, dating *circa* 1516. It is a pistareen of Charles and Joana (U.S.N.M. 11003).

Bone comb. Moore (1895b: 513) calls this a "leather comb" but to me it seems more than likely of bone. It is decorated with a running scroll design (Fig. 7). Similar combs have come from Safety Harbor mounds on the west coast (Willey, 1949b, Pls. 58, A, B, 59, A, B).

Hawks bells. These bells, similar to sleigh bells but smaller, are found in historic sites.

Copper cone "tinkler." A conical roll of sheet copper about 4 cm. long from Spaldings Lower Store is undoubtedly a "tinkler" formerly attached to leggings, pouches, or other paraphernalia. Such tinklers are common in Southeastern, and for that matter North American, ethnological collections. Similar archeological specimens attributable to the Seminole came from the Glades Area (Willey, 1949a). Other archeological finds are in a late South Carolina site (Storey, 1941).

European ornaments. A few ornaments made by Europeans have been found. One unusual silver pendant from Cooks Ferry is illustrated by Moore (H.P.M. 49553; Moore, 1894a, Fig. 104) and a small silver bar pendant comes from Dunns Creek Mound (Moore, 1894a, Fig. 1).

Metal disk ornaments. Specimens of this type were made in Florida with metal obtained from shipwrecks or other sources. This type is most common in the Glades Area. Metals used were copper (Pl. 12, A–C, I), silver (Pl. 12, E), and gold (Pl. 12, D).

These ornaments differ considerably from the prehistoric. They are, to begin with, almost invariably round, and most always have a central perforation. The area around this perforation is often countersunk to make room for a wooden button which furnished suspension for the ornament.

Objects of this kind are rare and were probably trade pieces from the south. They date from St. Johns IIc times.

Coin bead. A single gold coin bead, another Glades form, comes from Black Hammock or Nordmans Mound (Harrison, 1878: 305).

Silver earrings. A pair of trade earrings made of silver were found in the Bayard Point Mound (Pl. 12, F). They date from either the St. Augustine or Seminole Period.

Silver brooch. A small silver trade brooch comes from Spaldings Lower Store (Pl. 12, G). It has the twisted heart shape, a favorite design introduced by English traders into North America.

Glass beads. A variety of beads have been found here, of which the most common are probably the small seed type. Others include the rare chevron form, from several sites, and a twisted tubular example (Moore, 1895b: 514). The chevron beads probably date from the sixteenth or seventeenth centuries.

Red pigment. Cinnabar (mercuric sulphide) was found with a burial at Bayard Point Mound. This is a commercial pigment introduced by Europeans.

MISCELLANEOUS

Bannerstones. Artifacts of this type are very rare in Florida so it is of interest to note their quantity here in the area, 27 being found in contrast to 11 known for the remainder of the state. Furthermore, they occur together in numbers in some sites, and in addition, as has been discussed, they occur consistently with certain other types of artifacts.

Materials used in making these include not only local limestones, and sandy limestones, but various kinds of foreign rocks including steatite, diabase, and greenstone. A shaped but only partially drilled specimen, from Midden 2, Salt Springs Run (U.S.-N.M. 378329), suggests that these were not necessarily imports but that some were made locally.

To facilitate our consideration of bannerstones a series of types have been defined. Type 1 (Fig. 8, A) is ovoid in outline, with a central crest on one side and a flat ridge on the other. Type 2 exhibits a range of outlines, varying from rectangular (Fig. 8, B) to ovoid (Fig. 8, C). However, in cross section one side is flat, or only slightly curved, while the other rises gently to a sharp or rounded ridge. The profile of the ridge may be concave. Type 3 includes those forms with thin outflaring wings (Fig. 8, D). Miniature forms of this were made.

Type 4 is oval in outline, flat on one side, and with undifferentiated central section (Fig. 8, E). Type 5 is rectangular or rounded rectangular in outline and often longer, longitudinally, than wide (Fig. 8, F).

One of the first finds of these objects was at Mt. Oswald (Douglass, 1882, 1885: 82).

Three varieties were found including five examples of Type 1 made of diabase, steatite, "ferruginous stone," and fine limestone. Three measured 10.5 cm. by 12.7 cm., with one slightly larger and the other smaller. Type 2 is represented by a single specimen of diabase, measuring 8.6 cm. by 10.1 cm. Two examples of Type 3 were made of greenstone, one measuring 10 cm. by 13.3 cm., the other slightly smaller.

In Thornhill Lake Mound 1, the following specimens were found: Type 3, three specimens (2 miniature, Pl. 11, F to H). Type 5, one specimen (Pl. 11, K) and an undescribed specimen. The Type 3 specimens were made of hard foreign stone, the other of limestone.

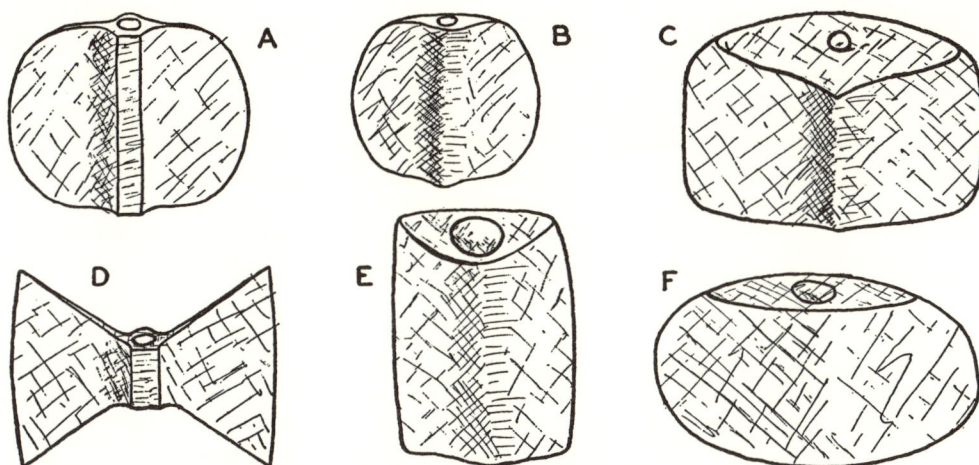

FIG. 8. Bannerstone Types.

Three specimens came from Thornhill Lake Mound 2, all Type 2 (Pl. 11, J, M, and N). Two are of "soft phosphate rock" (limestone) and the other of "soft serpentine."

Three specimens were found in the Shields Mound, one of Type 3 (Moore, 1895a: 461-2), one of Type 2 (Pl. 11, I) and one of Type 4 (Pl. 11, L). Other specimens include one at Dillon's Grove (Type 4, W.F.I.S. 15056), one of shell from the surface at Mt. Taylor (Type 3, variant ?, Moore, 1898), a Type 5 specimen from Stokes Landing Midden (U.F.A.L.), and two specimens (one Type 5) from Midden 2, Salt Springs Run (U.S.N.M. 378329). Three bannerstones from Coontie Island include a variation of Type 1, a Type 4, and a Type 5 specimen (Thompson and Ryman Collection).

The temporal position and general significance of these has been previously discussed (pp. 51-3). Little else can be added.

Pipes. Smoking pipes were made of stone and fired clay in a variety of forms but those of clay are most common. The earliest examples from Tick Island Mound are elbow forms of a gritty paste earthenware. The stem section is very short (Moore, 1894b, Figs. 29 and 30). A somewhat later example from Racey Point is fragmentary

(Moore, 1894b, Fig. 60) but appears similar although the exact length of the stem section cannot be determined. A Murphy Island specimen (Northernmost Mound) made of clay has an effigy adorno on the bowl (Moore, 1895b, Fig. 55).

Later forms from Dunns Creek Mound have stem sections longer than the bowl and include a possible effigy form (Moore, 1894a, Figs. 2 and 3). Specimens of clay and steatite from Shields Mound are square in cross section (Moore, 1895a, Figs. 7 and 16).

Grant Mound specimens occur in a great variety (Pl. 11, A–D). They are mainly of elbow shape but include an odd monitor-shaped one of earthenware (Pl. 11, D). Another unusual trait here is a copper appliqué piece on a pipe bowl (Moore, 1895a, Fig. 28). A single fragmentary tubular pipe of chalky ware from Bluffton Midden has been seen (private collection).

Pipes occur widely and sporadically, mainly as burial offerings. They very clearly seem to make their appearance in St. Johns Ia, early and continue until historic times, where their presence is recorded by historians.

Incised turtle bone. A fragment of turtle carapace from the Cotten site (F.S.P.S.) bears an incised detailed, maze-like geometric design. The piece, dating from the Orange Period, is similar to one of the same date from South Indian Field (Rouse, 1951).

Stone tubes. Simple cylindrical stone tubes are found. Some are made of foreign igneous or metamorphic rock (Moore, 1894a, Fig. 21), while others are formed of local sandstone (Moore, 1894a, Fig. 13). Variations include a tapering double-flanged tube from the northernmost mound on Murphy Island (Moore, 1895b, Fig. 65). These are not common, but they occur from the St. Johns Ia, late into the St. Johns II Period.

Shell tube. A tapering shell tube with a flange at one end (Pl. 8, J) was found at Mt. Taylor. Its age is not known.

Curved clay tube. A single example of this artifact was found at Mt. Royal (Moore, 1894b, Fig. 16). It is a small, U-shaped earthenware tube, square in cross section. It is the only one of its kind and probably dates from St. Johns II times.

Clay wedge. A small wedge-shaped or ax-shaped object of clay came from Mt. Royal (Moore, 1894b, Fig. 17). It is only 5.3 cm. long. It probably dates from St. Johns II times.

Galena. This mineral is of widespread occurrence in the form of small cubes sometimes badly decomposed. Since no deposits of galena exist in Florida it must have been imported, perhaps from Alabama or elsewhere in the Appalachians.

It is found in sand mounds mainly along the river. These sites date from St. Johns Ia, early to St. Johns II times.

Mica. Like the previous mineral, this is an import perhaps from, or near, the same source as the galena. It occurs in thin sheets, often worked or shaped, in burial mounds along the river. They date from St. Johns Ia, early through St. Johns II times.

Hematite. This red mineral is found in the form of powder in burial mounds, sometimes in appreciable quantity. It was probably used as body paint. Its exact source is not known but deposits are found in Florida.

Hematite is noted in sites of St. Johns II times, but undoubtedly was used earlier.

In any case the extensive earlier use of red paint on pottery was probably dependent on an iron oxide.

Pebbles. Clusters of pebbles are reported by Moore in many burial mounds. Their function is not known, but they may have been noise makers in gourd rattles now decayed. They are widely distributed in sites dating from St. Johns Ia, late into St. Johns II times.

Flint chips. These occur throughout many of the refuse sites, presumably as by-products of flint working. Clarence B. Moore notes their presence in many sand mounds, sometimes in pockets or nests. They may have been noise makers in gourd rattles.

Drilled mammal phalange. A perforated mammal phalange may have been an ornament (Wyman, 1868, Fig. 7; 1875, Pl. 4: 5) or else have served some unknown function. It dates from Mt. Taylor times.

Sawed bone. Sections of mammal bone showing sawing occur in most refuse heaps. They have particularly been noted in Mt. Taylor deposits.

Sawed antler fragments. Worked sections of antler showing saw cuts are present in refuse sites, being noted most commonly in the earlier Mt. Taylor levels.

BIBLIOGRAPHY*

ABSHIRE, A. E.; ALDEN L. POTTER; ALLEN R. TAYLOR; CLYDE H. NEIL; WALTER H. ANDERSON; JOHN
I. RUTLEDGE; AND STEVENSON B. JOHNSON
    1935. *Some Further Papers on Aboriginal Man in the Neighborhood of the Ocala National Forest*
        (mimeographed, Civilian Conservation Corps Company 1420, Ocala Camp, Florida, F-5).

ALLEN, HARRISON
    1896. *Crania from the Mounds of the St. Johns River, Florida; a Study made in Connection with
        Crania from Other Parts of North America* (Academy of Natural Sciences, Journal, n.s.,
        vol. 10, pp. 368–448, Philadelphia).

ANONYMOUS
    1680–1700? *Mapa de la Isla de la Florida* (original in Ministry of War, Madrid, 9a - 2ª-a, 10;
        copy in Library of Congress; reproduced in Chatelain, 1941).
    1872. *Objects From the Florida Mounds* (Annual Record of Science and Industry, vol. 2, pp. 332–3,
        New York).
    1873. *Prehistoric Cannibalism in Florida* (Annual Record of Science and Industry, vol. 3, pp.
        281–2, New York).
    1876a. *A Remarkable Discovery in Florida* (Scientific American Supplement, vol. 1, no. 11, p.
        171, March 11, New York).
    1876b. *Prehistoric Antiquities in Florida, U. S.* (Journal of the Anthropological Institute, vol.
        6, pp. 99–100, London).
    1923a. *Tubular Pipe, Illustration* (Arrowpoints, vol. 6, no. 1, p. 14, Montgomery).
    1923b. *Tubular Pipe, Calhoun County* (Arrowpoints, vol. 7, no. 2, p. 20, Montogomery).
    1940. *Walnut Roughened* (Southeastern Archaeological Conference, News Letter, vol. 2, no. 2,
        p. 10, Lexington, Ky.).
    1951. *Notes and News* (American Antiquity, vol. 16, pt. 3, Salt Lake City).

AUDUBON, JOHN JAMES
    1926. *Delineations of American Scenery and Character* (New York).

BAILEY, HAROLD H.
    1925. *The Birds of Florida* (Baltimore).

BARRIENTOS, BARTOLOMÉ
    1902. *Vida y hechos de Pero Menendez de Aviles* (in "Dos Antiguas Relaciones de la Florida,"
        Genaro Garcia, editor, Mexico).

BARTRAM, JOHN
    1875. *Antiquities of Florida* (Smithsonian Institution, Annual Report for 1874, p. 393, Wash-
        ington).
    1942. *Diary of a Journey through the Carolinas, Georgia and Florida* (annotated by Francis Har-
        per, American Philosophical Society, Transactions, n.s., vol. 33, pt. 1, pp. 1–120, Phila-
        delphia).

BARTRAM, WILLIAM
    1853. *Observations on the Creek and Cherokee Indians* (American Ethnological Society, Transac-
        tions, vol. 3, pt. 1, pp. 3–81, New York).
    1940. *The Travels of William Bartram* (New York).
    1943. *Travels in Georgia and Florida, 1773–74, a Report to Dr. John Fothergill* (American Philo-
        sophical Society, Transactions, n.s., vol. 33, pt. 2, pp. 121–242, Philadelphia).

BIDDLE, HENRY J.
    1880. *Correspondence* (in "Summary of Correspondence of the Smithsonian Institution previous

---

* The following bibliography is, in general, limited to materials cited in the text. However, a few
papers specifically on the area but not cited, are also included. With these added, the bibliography
includes all major references to the area.

to Jan. 1, 1880, in Answer to Circular No. 316," p. 442, Smithsonian Institution, Annual Report for 1879, pp. 428–48, Washington).

BLATCHLEY, W. S.
1902. *A Nature Wooing at Ormond by the Sea* (Indianapolis).

BOYD, MARK F.
1939. *Mission Sites in Florida* (Florida Historical Quarterly, vol. 17, pp. 254–80, Tallahassee).
1948. *Enumeration of the Florida Spanish Missions in 1675* (Florida Historical Quarterly, vol. 28, pp. 181–8, St. Augustine).

BRANNON, PETER A.
1926. *Indian Pipe, Dallas County* (Arrowpoints, vol. 12, nos. 4–5, p. 45, Montgomery).
1928. *Jackson County Place Names* (Arrowpoints, vol. 13, no. 1, pp. 9–11, Montgomery).

BRINTON, DANIEL G.
1859. *Notes on the Floridian Peninsula, its Literary History, Indian Tribes and Antiquities* (Philadelphia).
1872. *Artificial Shell Deposits of the United States* (Smithsonian Institution, Annual Report for 1866, pp. 356–8, Washington).
1896. *Crania from Florida* (Science, vol. 4, pp. 717–18, New York).

BROWER, CHARLES DE WOLFE
1906. *The Shell Heaps of Florida* (Records of the Past, vol. 5, no. 11, pp. 331–8, Washington).

BULLEN, RIPLEY P.
1950. *An Archeological Survey of the Chattahoochee River Valley in Florida* (Washington Academy of Sciences, Journal, vol. 40, pp. 101–25, Washington).

BUSHNELL, DAVID I., JR.
1940. *The Use of Soapstone by the Indians of the Eastern United States* (Annual Report of the Smithsonian Institute for 1939, pp. 471–89, Washington).

BUTLER, AMOS W.
1917. *Observations on Some Shellmounds of the Eastern Coast of Florida* (19th International Congress of Americanists, Proceedings, pp. 104–7, Washington).

CABEZA DE VACA, ALVAR NUÑEZ
1907. *The Narrative of Alvar Cabeza de Vaca* (edited by F. W. Hodge, in "Spanish Explorers in the Southern United States, 1528–43," New York).

CALDWELL, JOSEPH R., AND ANTONIO J. WARING
1939a. *Deptford Simple Stamped* (Southeastern Archaeological Conference, News Letter, vol. 1, no. 5, p. 4, Lexington, Ky.).
1939b. *Deptford Linear Check Stamped* (Southeastern Archeological Conference, News Letter, vol. 1, no. 5, pp. 8–9, Lexington, Ky.)
1939c. *Deptford Bold Check Stamped* (Southeastern Archaeological Conference, News Letter, vol. 1, no. 6, Lexington, Ky.).
1939d. *Savannah Fine Cord Marked* (Southeastern Archaeological Conference, News Letter, vol. 1, no. 6, pp. 8–9, Lexington, Ky.).

CALKINS, W. V.
1878. *Some Notes of Personal Investigation Among the Shell Mounds of Florida* (Davenport Academy of Natural Science, Proceedings, vol. 2, pp. 225–9, Davenport, Iowa).

CAMIN, ALFONSO
1944. *El adelantado de la Florida, Pedro Menendez de Aviles* (Mexico).

CARR, A. F.
1940. *A Contribution to the Herpetology of Florida* (University of Florida, Biological Series, Publications, vol. 3, no. 1, Gainesville).

CHATELAIN, VERNE E.
1941. *The Defenses of Spanish Florida, 1565 to 1763* (Carnegie Institution of Washington, Publication no. 511, Washington).

CLAFLIN, WILLIAM H.
  1931. *The Stallings Island Mound, Columbia County, Georgia* (Peabody Museum Papers, vol. 14, no. 1, Cambridge).

CLARKE, S. C.
  1880. *Correspondence* (in "Summary of Correspondence of the Smithsonian Institution previous to Jan. 1, 1880 in Answer to Circular No. 316," pp. 442–3, Smithsonian Institution, Annual Report for 1879, pp. 428–48, Washington).

COHEN, M. M.
  1836. *Notices of Florida and the Campaigns* (New York).

CONNERY, J. H.
  1932. *Recent Find of Mammoth Remains in the Quaternary of Florida together with Arrowheads* (Science, vol. 75, p. 516, New York).

CONNOR, JEANETTE THURBER
  1925. *Colonial Records of Spanish Florida, Volume I, 1570–1577* (Florida State Historical Society, Publication no. 5, vol. 1, Deland).
  1930. *Colonial Records of Spanish Florida, Volume II, 1570–1577* (Florida State Historical Society, Publication no. 5, vol. 2, Deland).

COOKE, WYTHE
  1945. *Geology of Florida* (Florida Geological Survey, Geological Bulletin, no. 29, Tallahassee).

COULTER, E. MERTON (EDITOR)
  1937. *Georgia's Disputed Ruins* (Chapel Hill, North Carolina).

CUSHING, FRANK H.
  1897. *Exploration of Ancient Key Dwellers' Remains on the Gulf Coast of Florida* (American Philosophical Society, Proceedings, vol. 35, pp. 329–448, Philadelphia).

DALL, WILLIAM H.
  1885. *Memorandum on the Mounds at Satsuma and Enterprise, Florida* (American Journal of Archaeology, vol. 1, no. 2, pp. 184–9, Baltimore).
  1887. *Notes on the Geology of Florida* (American Journal of Science, 3rd s., vol. 34, pp. 161–70, New Haven).

DAVIS, T. FREDERICK
  1935. *History of Juan Ponce de Leon's Voyages to Florida* (Florida Historical Quarterly, vol. 14, pp. 8–66, Tallahassee).

DETWILER, J. Y.
  1908. *Origin of Shell Mounds* (Florida Historical Quarterly, vol. 1, pp. 14–17, Tallahassee).

DIAZ DEL CASTILLO, BERNAL
  1927. *The True History of the Conquest of Mexico* (New York).

DICKINSON, JOHNATHAN
  1945. *God's Protecting Providence* (edited by E. W. and C. McL. Andrews, Yale Historical Publications, Manuscripts and Edited Texts, no. 19, New Haven).

DIXON, ROLAND B.
  1913. *Some Aspects of North American Archeology* (American Anthropologist, n.s., vol. 15, pp. 549–77, Lancaster, Pa.).

DOUGLASS, ANDREW E.
  1882. *A Find of Ceremonial Axes in a Florida Mound* (American Antiquarian, vol. 4, pp. 100–9, Chicago).
  1883. *A Find of Ceremonial Weapons in a Florida Mound, with Brief Notice of Other Mounds in that State* (American Association for the Advancement of Science, Proceedings, vol. 31, pp. 585–92, Salem, Mass.).
  1884. *Some Characteristics of the Indian Earth and Shell Mounds of the Atlantic Coast of Florida* (American Association for the Advancement of Science, Proceedings, vol. 33, pp. 599–601, Salem, Mass.).
  1885. *Some Characteristics of the Indian Earth and Shell Mounds on the Atlantic Coast of Florida* (American Antiquarian, vol. 7, pp. 74–82, 140–7, Chicago).

EHRMANN, W. W.
    1940. *The Timucua Indians of Sixteenth Century Florida* (Florida Historical Quarterly, vol. 18, pp. 168–91, Tallahassee).

FAIRBANKS, CHARLES H.
    1942. *The Taxonomic Position of Stallings Island, Georgia* (American Antiquity, vol. 7, pp. 223–31, Menasha).

FAIRBANKS, G. R.
    1871. *History of Florida, 1512–1842* (Philadelphia).

FEDERAL WRITERS PROJECT
    1940. *Florida, a Guide to the Southernmost State* (New York).

FERGUSON, VERA MASIUS
    1951. *Chronology at South Indian Field, Florida* (Yale University Publications in Anthropology, no. 45, New Haven).

FLINT, RICHARD F.
    1947. *Glacial Geology and the Pleistocene Epoch* (New York).

FONTANEDA, DO. DE ESCALANTE
    1944. *Memoir* (translated by Buckingham Smith, Historical Association of Southern Florida, Miscellaneous Publication, no. 1, Miami).

FORD, JAMES A., AND GORDON R. WILLEY
    1941. *An Interpretation of the Prehistory of the Eastern United States* (American Anthropologist, vol. 43, pp. 325–63, Menasha).

GATSCHET, ALBERT S.
    1877. *The Timucua Language* (American Philosophical Society, Proceedings, vol. 16, pp. 626–42, Philadelphia).
    1878. *The Timucua Language* (American Philosophical Society, Proceedings, vol. 17, pp. 490–504, Philadelphia).
    1880. *The Timucua Language* (American Philosophical Society, Proceedings, vol. 18, pp. 465–502, Philadelphia).

GEIGER, MAYNARD
    1937. *The Franciscan Conquest of Florida (1573–1618)* (Studies in Hispanic American History, vol. 1, Catholic University, Washington).
    1940. *Biographical Dictionary of the Franciscans in Spanish Florida and Cuba (1528–1841)* (Franciscan Studies, vol. 21, Paterson, N. J.).

GIDLEY, JAMES W.
    1929. *Ancient Man in Florida: Further Investigations* (Geological Society of America, vol. 40, pp. 491–502, New York).

GLECK, U. F.
    1894. *A Florida Shell Mound* (Indiana Academy of Science, Proceedings, vol. 4, pp. 48–9, Indianapolis).

GOGGIN, JOHN M.
    1939. *Louisiana Choctaw Basketry* (El Palacio, vol. 46, pp. 121–3, Santa Fe).
    1947. *A Preliminary Definition of Archaeological Areas and Periods in Florida* (American Antiquity, vol. 13, pp. 114–27, Menasha).
    1948a. *Some Pottery Types from Central Florida* (Gainesville Anthropological Association, Bulletin no. 1, Gainesville, Florida).
    1948b. *Florida Archeology and Recent Ecological Changes* (Washington Academy of Sciences, Journal, vol. 39, pp. 225–33, Menasha).
    1948c. *A Revised Temporal Chart of Florida Archaeology* (The Florida Anthropologist, vol. 1, pp. 57–60, n.p.).
    1949a. *Cultural Traditions in Florida Prehistory* (in "The Florida Indian and His Neighbors," John W. Griffin, editor, pp. 13–44, Rollins College, Winter Park, Florida).
    1949b. *A Florida Indian Trading Post, Circa 1763–1784* (Southern Indian Studies, vol. 1, pp. 35–8, Chapel Hill, North Carolina).

1950a. *Florida Archaeology—1950* (The Florida Anthropologist, vol. 3, pp. 9–20, Gainesville, Florida).

1950b. *A Preliminary Consideration of Spanish Introduced Majolica in Florida and the Southwest* (University of Florida, Gainesville, Florida).

1951. *Fort Pupo—a Spanish Frontier Outpost* (Florida Historical Quarterly, vol. 30, pp. 139–92, St. Augustine).

MSa. *Culture and Geography in Florida Prehistory* (unpublished Ph.D. dissertation, Yale University, New Haven).

MSb. *Archeology of the Glades Area, Southern Florida* (manuscript, Yale Peabody Museum, New Haven).

MSc. *The "Long Nosed God" Masks* (manuscript).

MSd. *Florida Bannerstones* (manuscript).

MSe. *Culture—Archaeological, Ethnological, and Linguistic—in North Central Florida* (manuscript).

GOGGIN, JOHN M.; MARY E. GODWIN; EARL HESTER; DAVID PRANGE; AND ROBERT SPANGENBERG
  1949. *An Historic Indian Burial, Alachua County, Florida* (The Florida Anthropologist, vol. 2, pp. 10–25, Gainesville).

GOGGIN, JOHN M., AND IRVING ROUSE
  1948. *A West Indian Ax from Florida* (American Antiquity, vol. 13, pp. 323–5, Menasha).

GOGGIN, JOHN M., AND FRANK H. SOMMER
  1949. *Excavations on Upper Matecumbe Key* (Yale University Publications in Anthropology, no. 41, New Haven).

GREENMAN, E. F.
  1938. *Hopewellian Traits in Florida* (American Antiquity, vol. 3, pp. 327–32, Menasha).

GRIFFIN, JAMES B.
  1943. *An Analysis and Interpretation of the Ceramic Remains from Two Sites near Beaufort, South Carolina* (Bureau of American Ethnology, Bulletin, no. 133, pp. 155–68, Washington).

1945a. *The Ceramic Affiliations of the Ohio Valley Adena Culture* (in "The Adena People," by W. S. Webb and C. E. Snow, University of Kentucky, Reports in Anthropology and Archeology, vol. 6, pp. 220–46, Lexington).

1945b. *The Significance of the Fiber-Tempered Pottery of the St. Johns Area in Florida* (Washington Academy of Sciences, Journal, vol. 35, no. 7, pp. 218–23, Menasha).

1946. *Cultural Change and Continuity in Eastern United States Archaeology* (in "Man in Northeastern North America," Papers, Robert S. Peabody Foundation for Archaeology, vol. 3, pp. 37–95, Andover).

GRIFFIN, JOHN W.
  1948a. *Towards Chronology in Coastal Volusia County* (The Florida Anthropologist, vol. 1, pp. 49–56, n.p.).

1948b. *Green Mound—a Chronological Yardstick* (The Florida Naturalist, vol. 22, pp. 1–8).

1949. *The Historic Archaeology of Florida* (in "The Florida Indian and His Neighbors," John W. Griffin, editor, pp. 45–54, Rollins College, Winter Park, Florida).

GRIFFIN, JOHN W., AND HALE G. SMITH
  1949. *Nocoroco, a Timucua Village of 1605, now in Tomoka State Park* (The Florida Historical Quarterly, vol. 27, pp. 340–61, St. Augustine, Florida).

HALDEMAN, S. S.
  1878. *On a Polychrome Bead From Florida* (Smithsonian Institution, Annual Report for 1877, pp. 302–5, Washington).

HALE, E. M.
  1887. *A Prehistoric Amphitheatre in Florida* (American Antiquarian, vol. 9, pp. 207–11, Chicago).

HARPER, ROLAND
  1914. *The Geography and Vegetation of Northern Florida* (Florida Geological Survey. 6th Annual Report, pp. 163–437, Tallahassee).

1921.   *Geography of Central Florida* (Florida Geological Survey, 13th Annual Report, pp. 71–307, Tallahassee).

HARRISON, A. M.

1878.   *Colored Bead dug from a Mound at the Extreme North End of Black Hammock, 3 Miles West of Mosquito Inlet, Eastern Coast of Florida* (Smithsonian Institution, Annual Report for 1877, p. 305, Washington).

HAVEN, SAMUEL F.

1856.   *Archaeology of the United States* (Smithsonian Institution, Contributions to Knowledge, vol. 8, no. 2, Washington).

HAY, O. P.

1902.   *On the Finding of the Bones of the Great Auk* (Plantus impennis) *in Florida* (The Auk, vol. 19, pp. 255–8, Cambridge).

HERRERA, ANTONIO DE

1720.   *Historia general de los hechos de los castellanos en las islas i tierra firme del mar oceano* (5 vols., Madrid).

HITCHCOCK, C. H.

1902.   *The Hernandes Shell-heap, Ormond, Florida* (Science, vol. 16, p. 203, New York).

HOLMES, WILLIAM H.

1883.   *Art in Shell of the Ancient Americans* (Bureau of American Ethnology, Annual Report, no. 2, pp. 179–305, Washington).

1884.   *Illustrated Catalogue of a Portion of the Collections made during the Field Season of 1881* (Bureau of American Ethnology, Annual Report, no. 3, Washington).

1894.   *Earthenware of Florida* (Academy of Natural Sciences, Journal, n.s., vol. 10, pp. 106–28, Philadelphia).

1903.   *Aboriginal Pottery of Eastern United States* (Bureau of American Ethnology, Annual Report no. 20, Washington).

1910.   *Shell-heaps* (in "Handbook of the American Indians," pt. 2, pp. 541–4, Bureau of American Ethnology, Bulletin no. 30, Washington).

1914.   *Areas of American Culture Classification* (American Anthropologist, n.s., vol. 16, pp. 413–46, Lancaster, Pa.).

HOWARD, E. B.

1940.   *Studies bearing upon the Problem of Early Man in Florida* (Carnegie Institution of Washington, Yearbook, vol. 39, pp. 309-12, Washington).

HOWARD, GEORGE D.

1943.   *Excavations at Ronquin, Venezuela* (Yale University Publications in Anthropology, no. 28, New Haven).

HOWELL, ARTHUR H.

1932.   *Florida Bird Life* (New York).

HRDLIČKA, ALES

1907.   *Skeletal Remains Suggesting or Attributed to Early Man in North America* (Bureau of American Ethnology, Bulletin no. 33, Washington).

1940.   *Catalog of Human Crania in the United States National Museum Collections—Indians of the Gulf States* (United States National Museum, Proceedings, vol. 87, pp. 315-464, Washington).

HURT, WESLEY R., AND HERBERT DICK

1946.   *Spanish-American Pottery From New Mexico* (El Palacio, vol. 53, pp. 280–5, 307–12, Santa Fe).

JENNINGS, JESSE D., AND CHARLES H. FAIRBANKS

1939a.   *Swift Creek Complicated Stamped* (Southeastern Archaeological Conference, News Letter, vol. 1, no. 2, Lexington, Ky.).

1939b.   *Lamar Complicated Stamped* (Southeastern Archaeological Conference, News Letter, vol. 1, no. 2, Lexington, Ky.).

1939c. *Ocmulgee Fields Incised* (Southeastern Archaeological Conference, News Letter, vol. 1, no. 2, Lexington, Ky.).

JORDAN, FRANCIS, JR.
1886. *[Letter concerning Indian Pottery embedded in Mortar at Fort San Marcos]* (Report of the Proceedings of the Numismatic and Antiquarian Society of Philadelphia for 1885, pp. 10–11, Philadelphia).

KELLY, ARTHUR R., AND FAY-COOPER COLE
1931. *Rediscovering Illinois* (in "Blue Book of the State of Illinois 1931–1932," pp. 318–41, Springfield).

KIDDER, A. V., AND ANNA O. SHEPARD
1936. *Pottery of Pecos, Vol. II* (Papers of the Phillips Academy Southwestern Expedition, no. 7, New Haven).

KÖPPEN, WLADIMIR
1918. *Klassifikation der Klimate nach Temperatur, Niederschlag und Jahreslauf* (Petermanns Mitteilungen, vol. 64, pp. 193–203, Gotha).

KRIEGER, ALEX D.
1946. *Culture Complexes and Chronology in Northern Texas* (University of Texas Publication no. 4640, Austin).
1947. *The Eastward Extension of Puebloan Datings Towards Cultures of the Mississippi Valley* (American Antiquity, vol. 12, pp. 141–8, Menasha).

LAMME, VERNON
1941. *Archaeological Investigations at Marineland, Florida* (manuscript in Library, Florida Historical Society, Gainesville).

LANNING, JOHN TATE
1935. *The Spanish Missions of Georgia* (Chapel Hill).

LAWSON, EDWARD W.
1946. *The Discovery of Florida and its Discoverer Juan Ponce de Leon* (St. Augustine).

LE BARON, J. FRANCIS
1876. *The Naturalist and Sportsmen in Florida* (Rod and Gun, vol. 9, pp. 21–2, 39, 53–9, 69–70, 83–4, 97–8, 113–15, New York).
1884. *Prehistoric Remains in Florida* (Smithsonian Institution, Annual Report for 1882, pp. 771–90, Washington).

LE MOYNE DE MORGUES, JACQUES
1946. *The Narrative of Jacques Le Moyne de Morgues* (in "The New World," Stefan Lorant, editor, pp. 33–87, New York).

LENTE, FREDERICK D.
1877. *The Mounds of Florida* (reprinted from "Semi-Tropical," March-April, Jacksonville, Florida).

LORANT, STEPHEN (EDITOR)
1946. *The New World* (New York).

LOWERY, WOODBURY
1901. *The Spanish Settlements within the Present Limits of the United States, 1513–1561* (New York).
1905. *Spanish Settlements within the Present Limits of the United States: Florida, 1562–74* (New York).

LUCAS, F. A.
1903. *The Great Auk* (Science, vol. 17, pp. 311–12, New York).

LYELL, CHARLES
1863. *The Geological Evidences of the Antiquity of Man* (London).

MANUCY, ALBERT C.
1947. *Florida in North Carolina Spanish Records, Part II* (Florida Historical Quarterly, vol. 26, pp. 77–91, St. Augustine).

MARTIN, PAUL; GEORGE QUIMBY; AND DONALD COLLIER
  1947. *Indians Before Columbus* (Chicago).
MAYBERRY, S. P.
  1878. *Shell Heaps at the Mouth of St. John's River, Florida* (Smithsonian Institution, Annual Report for 1877, pp. 305–6, Washington).
McGUIRE, J. D.
  1905. *The Explorations of Clarence B. Moore* (American Anthropologist, n.s., vol. 7, p. 368B, Lancaster, Pa.).
MERCER, H. C.
  1895. *Certain Sand Mounds of the St. John's River by Clarence B. Moore* (American Naturalist, vol. 29, pp. 76–81, Philadelphia).
MITCHELL, AUGUSTUS
  1875. *Antiquities of Florida* (Smithsonian Institution, Annual Report for 1874, pp. 390–3, Washington).
MITCHELL, A. J., AND M. R. ENSIGN
  1928. *The Climate of Florida* (University of Florida Agricultural Experiment Station, Bulletin 200, Gainesville).
MOORE, CLARENCE B.
  1892a. *A Burial Mound of Florida* (American Naturalist, vol. 26, pp. 128–43, Philadelphia).
  1892b. *Supplementary Investigation at Tick Island* (American Naturalist, Vol. 26, pp. 568–79, Philadelphia).
  1892c. *Certain Shell Heaps of the St. Johns River, Florida, Hitherto Unexplored* (American Naturalist, vol. 26, pp. 912–22, Philadelphia).
  1892d. *Mounds in Florida* (American Antiquarian, vol. 14, pp. 292–5, Chicago).
  1893. *Certain Shell Heaps of the St. Johns River, Florida, Hitherto Unexplored* (American Naturalist, vol. 27, pp. 8–13, 113–17, 605–24, 709–33, Philadelphia).
  1894a. *Certain Sand Mounds of the St. John's River, Florida, Part I* (Academy of Natural Sciences, Journal, n.s., vol. 10, pp. 5–105, Philadelphia).
  1894b. *Certain Sand Mounds of the St. John's River, Florida, Part II* (Academy of Natural Sciences, Journal, n.s., vol. 10, pp. 129–246, Philadelphia).
  1894c. *Certain Shell Heaps of the St. Johns River, Florida, Hitherto Unexplored* (American Naturalist, vol. 28, pp. 15–26, Philadelphia).
  1894d. *Tobacco Pipes in the Shell Heaps of the St. John's River, Florida* (American Naturalist, vol. 28, pp. 622–3, Philadelphia).
  1895a. *Certain River Mounds of Duval County, Florida* (Academy of Natural Sciences, Journal, n.s., vol. 10, pp. 449–502, Philadelphia).
  1895b. *Two Mounds on Murphy Island, Florida* (Academy of Natural Sciences, Journal, n.s., vol. 10, pp. 503–16, Philadelphia).
  1895c. *Certain Sand Mounds of the Ocklawaha River, Florida* (Academy of Natural Sciences, Journal, n.s., vol. 10, pp. 518–43, Philadelphia).
  1895d. *Archaeology of the St. John's, Florida* (abstracted from Moore's works, The Archaeologist, vol. 3, pp. 1–5, 33–43, 114–18, 149–55, Columbus, Ohio).
  1897. *Certain Aboriginal Mounds of the Georgia Coast* (Academy of Natural Sciences, Journal, n.s., vol. 11, pp. 1–142, Philadelphia).
  1898. *Recent Acquisitions: Shell "Banner Stone" from the St. John's River, Florida* (Academy of Natural Sciences, Journal, n.s., vol. 11, pp. 185–8, Philadelphia).
  1901. *Certain Aboriginal Remains of The Northwest Coast of Florida, Part I* (Academy of Natural Sciences, Journal, n.s., vol. 11, pp. 421–97, Philadelphia).
  1902. *Certain Aboriginal Remains of the Northwest Coast of Florida, Part II* (Academy of Natural Sciences, Journal, n.s., vol. 12, pp. 127–358, Philadelphia).
  1903a. *Sheet-copper from the Mounds is not necessarily of European Origin* (American Anthropologist, vol. 5, pp. 27–49, Lancaster, Pa.).

1903b. *The So-called "Hoe Shaped Implement"* (American Anthropologist, n.s., vol. 5, pp. 498–502, Lancaster, Pa.).

1903c. *Certain Aboriginal Mounds of the Central Florida West Coast* (Academy of Natural Sciences, Journal, n.s., vol. 12, pp. 361–438, Philadelphia).

1913. *Some Aboriginal Sites in Louisiana and Arkansas* (Academy of Natural Sciences, Journal, n.s., vol. 13, pp. 427–56, Philadelphia).

1916. *Some Aboriginal Sites on the Green River, Kentucky* (Academy of Natural Sciences, Journal, n.s., vol. 16, pp. 432–87, Philadelphia).

1921. *Notes on Shell Implements from Florida* (American Anthropologist, vol. 23, pp. 12–18, Lancaster, Pa.).

1922a. *Additional Mounds of Duval and of Clay Counties, Florida* (Indian Notes and Monographs, Museum of the American Indian, Heye Foundation, Miscellaneous Papers, no. 26, pp. 9–34, New York).

1922b. *Mound Investigations on the East Coast of Florida* (Indian Notes and Monographs, Museum of the American Indian, Heye Foundation, Miscellaneous Papers, no. 26, pp. 34–49, New York).

1922c. *Certain Florida Coast Mounds North of the St. Johns River* (Indian Notes and Monographs, Museum of the American Indian, Heye Foundation, Miscellaneous Papers, no. 26, pp. 49–70, New York).

MURDOCK, GEORGE P.

1941. *Ethnographic Bibliography of North America* (Yale Anthropological Studies, vol. 1, New Haven).

NELSON, NELS C.

1918. *Chronology in Florida* (American Museum of Natural History, Anthropological Papers, vol. 22, pt. 2, pp. 75–103, New York).

NEWELL, H. PERRY, AND ALEX D. KRIEGER

1949. *The George C. Davis Site, Cherokee County, Texas* (Memoirs of the Society for American Archeology, no. 5, Menasha).

NOTT, JOSIAH CLARK, AND GEORGE R. GLIDDON

1860. *Types of Mankind* (Philadelphia).

ORÉ, LUIS GERÓNIMO DE

1936. *The Martyrs of Florida, 1513–1616* (Franciscan Studies, no. 18, New York).

PARKMAN, FRANCIS

1880. *Pioneers of France in the New World* (Boston).

PIERCE, JAMES

1825. *Notice of the Agriculture, Scenery, Geology, and Animal, Vegetable, and Mineral Productions of the Floridas and of the Indian Tribes* (American Journal of Science, vol. 9, pp. 119–36, New Haven).

POTTER, ALDEN L., AND ALLEN R. TAYLOR

1937a. *A Summary of our Archeological Work in the Ocala National Forest and Vicinity* (n.p.).

1937b. *A Summary of Reports Dealing with the Archeology of the Ocala National Forest and Vicinity, Florida* (C.C.C. Camp 1420, Ocala, Florida).

[POURTALES, L. F.]

1868. *Antiquity of Man* (American Naturalist, vol. 2, p. 443, Salem).

PUTNAM, FREDERICK WARD

1895. *Review of C. B. Moore's Certain Sand Mounds of the St. John's River, Florida* (Harvard Graduate Magazine, vol. 3, 587–9, Cambridge).

1896. *Review of Certain Sand Mounds of Florida: By Clarence B. Moore* (Science, n.s., vol 3, no. 58, New York).

RIBAUT, JEAN

1927. *The Whole and True Discovery of Terra Florida* (Florida State Historical Society, Publication no. 7, Deland).

ROBERTS, FRANK H. H., JR.
 1940. *Developments in the Problem of the North American Paleo-Indian* (Smithsonian Institution, Miscellaneous Collections, vol. 100, pp. 51–116, Washington).

ROUSE, IRVING
 1942. *Archeology of the Maniabón Hills, Cuba* (Yale University Publications in Anthropology, no. 26, New Haven).
 1949. *The Southeast and the West Indies* (in "The Florida Indian and His Neighbors," John W. Griffin, editor, pp. 117–37, Rollins College, Winter Park, Florida).
 1951. *A Survey of Indian River Archeology, Florida* (Yale University Publications in Anthropology, no. 44, New Haven).

ROUSE, IRVING, AND JOHN M. GOGGIN
 1947. *An Anthropological Bibliography of the Eastern Seaboard* (Eastern States Archeological Federation, Research Publication no. 1, New Haven).

SCHMITT, KARL
 1950. *Two Creek Pottery Vessels From Oklahoma* (The Florida Anthropologist, vol. 3, pp. 3–8, Gainesville, Florida).

SCISCO, LOUIS D.
 1913. *The Track of Ponce de Leon in 1913* (American Geographical Society, Bulletin, vol. 45, no. 10, New York).

SEABERG, LILLIAN
 MS. *Report on the Indian Site at "The Fountain of Youth," St. Augustine* (manuscript in preparation).

SEARS, WILLIAM H.
 1948. *What is the Archaic?* (American Antiquity, vol. 14, pp. 122–4, Menasha).

SEARS, WILLIAM H., AND JAMES B. GRIFFIN
 1950. *Fiber-Tempered Pottery of the Southeast* (in "Prehistoric Pottery of the Eastern United States," no. 6–50, Ann Arbor, Michigan).

SERRANO Y SANZ, M. (EDITOR)
 1913. *Documentos históricos de la Florida y la Luisiana, siglos XVI al XVIII* (Madrid).

SHEA, JOHN GILMARY
 1884–89. *Ancient Florida* (in "Narrative and Critical History of America," Justin Winsor, editor, Boston and New York).
 1886. *The Catholic Church in Colonial Days* (vol. 1, New York).

SHEPARD, JAMES
 1885. *Shell Heaps and Mounds in Florida* (Smithsonian Institution, Annual Report for 1885, pp. 902–6, Washington).

SHERMAN, H. B.
 1936. *A List of Recent Land Mammals of Florida* (Florida Academy of Science, Proceedings, vol. 1, pp. 102–28).

SMALL, JOHN K.
 1920. *Of Grottos and Ancient Dunes* (New York Botanical Garden, Journal, vol. 21, pp. 25–38, 45–54, New York).
 1921. *Historic Trails, by Land and Water* (New York Botancial Garden, Journal, vol. 22, pp. 193–222, New York).
 1923a. *The Land of the Question Mark* (New York Botanical Garden, Journal, vol. 24, pp. 1–23, 25–43, 62–70, New York).
 1923b. *Green Deserts and Dead Gardens* (New York Botanical Garden, Journal, vol. 24, pp. 193–247, New York).
 1924. *The Land Where Spring Meets Autumn* (New York Botanical Garden, Journal, vol. 25, pp. 53–94, New York).
 1925. *Gathering Cacti in the Eastern Coastal Plain* (New York Botanical Garden, Journal, vol. 26, pp. 241–58, 265–85, New York).

1927. *Among Floral Aborigines* (New York Botanical Garden, Journal, vol. 28, pp. 1–20, 25–40, New York).

1929. *From Eden to Sahara, Florida's Tragedy* (Lancaster, Pa.).

SMITH, HALE G.

1948. *Two Historical Archaeological Periods in Florida* (American Antiquity, vol. 13, pp. 313–19, Menasha).

SMITH, MAXWELL

1937. *East Coast Marine Shells* (Ann Arbor).

SOLÍS DE MERÁS, GONZALO

1923. *Pedro Menendez de Aviles* (Florida State Historical Society, Publication no. 3, Deland).

SPARKE, JOHN

1941. *The Voyage made by M. John Hawkins Esquire* ... (in Richard Hakluyt's "Voyages," Everymans Library Edition, vol. 7, pp. 6–53, London and New York).

STEARNS, R. E. C.

1869. *Rambles in Florida* (American Naturalist, vol. 3, pp. 281–8, 349–60, 397–405, 455–70, Salem, Mass.).

STIRLING, M. W.

1935. *Smithsonian Archeological Projects Conducted Under the Federal Employment Relief Act in 1933–34* (Smithsonian Institution, Annual Report for 1934, pp. 371–400, Washington).

1936. *Florida Cultural Affiliations in Relation to Adjacent Areas* (in "Essays in Anthropology in Honor of Alfred Louis Kroeber," pp. 351–7, Berkeley).

STOREY, C. E.

1941. *Carolina Copper Cones* (Hobbies, vol. 46, pp. 106–7, Chicago).

STORK, WILLIAM

1767. *An Account of East-Florida, with a Journal, kept by John Bartram* ... (2nd edition, London, others in 1769, 1774).

SWANTON, JOHN R.

1922. *Early History of the Creek Indians and their Neighbors* (Bureau of American Ethnology, Bulletin no. 73, Washington).

1929. *The Tawasa Language* (American Anthropologist, n.s., vol. 31, pp. 435–53, Menasha).

1939. *Final Report of the United States De Soto Expedition Commission* (House Document no. 71, 76th Congress, 1st Session, Washington).

1946. *The Indians of the Southeastern United States* (Bureau of American Ethnology, Bulletin no. 137, Washington).

SWEETT, ZELIA WILSON, AND J. C. MARSDEN

1925. *New Smyrna, Florida, its History and Antiquities* (New Smyrna).

THOMAS, CYRUS

1891. *Florida* (in "Catalogue of Prehistoric Works East of the Rocky Mountains," Bureau of American Ethnology, Bulletin no. 12, pp. 28–44, Washington).

1894. *Report on the Mound Explorations of the Bureau of Ethnology* (Bureau of American Ethnology, Annual Report no. 12, Washington).

THORNWAITE, C. W.

1931. *The Climates of North America according to a New Classification* (Geographical Review, vol. 21, pp. 633–55, New York).

U.S.C.G.S.

1940a. *St. Johns River, Racy Pt. to Crescent Lake* (U. S. Coast and Geodetic Survey, Chart no. 686, Washington).

1940b. *St. Johns River, Dunns Creek to Lake Dexter* (U. S. Coast and Geodetic Survey, Chart no. 687, Washington).

1940c. *St. Johns River, Lake Dexter to Lake Harney* (U. S. Coast and Geodetic Survey, Chart no. 688, Washington).

1941. *St. Johns River, Jacksonville to Racy Pt.* (U. S. Coast and Geodetic Survey, Chart no. 685, Washington).

n.d. *St. Johns River, Fernandina to Jacksonville* (U. S. Coast and Geodetic Survey, Chart no. 577, Washington).

VARGAS UGARTE, RUBÉN

1935. *The first Jesuit Mission in Florida* (United States Catholic Historical Society, Historical Records and Studies, vol. 25, pp. 59–148, New York).

1940. *Los mártires de la Florida, 1566–1572* (Lima).

WARING, A. J., JR. (EDITOR)

1948. *Brief of Symposium on the "Southern Cult"* (American Antiquity, vol. 14, pp. 151–6, Menasha).

WARING, A. J., JR., AND PRESTON HOLDER

1945. *A Prehistoric Ceremonial Complex in the Southeastern United States* (American Anthropologist, n.s., vol. 47, pp. 1–34, Menasha).

WATKINS, LOIS

MSa. *An Archeological Site Survey along the Oklawaha River from Cedar Landing to Gores Landing* (manuscript, University of Florida Anthropology Laboratory, Gainesville).

MSb. *Stratigraphy at Kauffman Island, Florida* (manuscript, University of Florida Anthropology Laboratory, Gainesville).

WATSON, J. R.

1926. *Florida* (in "Naturalists Guide to the Americas," Victor E. Shelford, editor, pp. 427–40, Baltimore).

WEBB, C. H.

1948. *Evidences of Pre-Pottery Cultures in Louisiana* (American Antiquity vol. 13, pp. 227–32, Menasha).

WEBB, C. H., AND MONROE DODD, JR.

1939. *Further Excavations of the Gahagan Mound; Connections with a Florida Culture* (Texas Archeological and Paleontological Society, Bulletin, vol. 11, pp. 92–126, Abilene).

WEBB, DE WITT

1894. *The Shell Heaps of the East Coast of Florida* (United States National Museum, Proceedings, vol. 16, pp. 695–8, Washington).

WEBB, WILLIAM S., AND DAVID L. DEJARNETTE

1942. *An Archeological Survey of Pickwick Basin, in the Adjacent Portions of the States of Alabama, Mississippi, and Tennessee* (Bureau of American Ethnology, Bulletin no. 129, Washington).

WENHOLD, LUCY C.

1936. *A 17th Century Letter of Gabriel Diaz Vara Calderon, Bishop of Cuba, Describing the Indians and Indian Missions of Florida* (Smithsonian Miscellaneous Collections, vol. 95, no. 16, Washington).

WILLEY, GORDON R.

1945. *The Weeden Island Culture: a Preliminary Definition* (American Antiquity, vol. 10, pp. 225–54, Menasha).

1949a. *Excavations in Southeast Florida* (Yale University Publications in Anthropology, no. 42, New Haven).

1949b. *Archaeology of the Florida Gulf Coast* (Smithsonian Miscellaneous Collections, vol. 113, Washington).

MS. *Kasita Report* (manuscript, Ocmulgee National Monument, Macon, Georgia).

WILLEY, GORDON R., AND R. B. WOODBURY

1942. *A Chronological Outline for the Northwest Florida Coast* (American Antiquity, no. 7, pp. 232–54, Menasha).

WILLIAMS, JOHN LEE

1837. *Natural and Civil History of Florida* (New York).

WINTER, W. J.

1940. *Report of the Committee on Archaeology* (Florida Historical Quarterly, vol. 19, pp. 166–9, Tallahassee).

WISSLER, CLARK
   1938.   *The American Indian* (New York).
WYMAN, JEFFRIES
   1867.   [*Florida Shell Mounds*] (Boston Society of Natural History, Proceedings, vol. 11, pp. 158–9, Boston).
   1868a. *An Account of the Fresh-Water Shell-Heaps of the St. Johns River, East Florida* (American Naturalist, vol. 2, pp. 393–403, 449–63, Salem, Mass.).
   1868b. *Explorations* (Peabody Museum, Annual Report, vol. 1, pp. 11–18, Boston).
   1870.   *From Explorations in Florida* (Peabody Museum, Annual Report, vol. 3, pp. 8–9, Boston).
   1872.   *Exploration in Florida* (Peabody Museum, Annual Report, vol. 5, pp. 22–5, Boston).
   1874a. *Human Remains in the Shell Heaps of the St. Johns River, East Florida, Cannibalism* (American Naturalist, vol. 7, pp. 403–14, Salem, Mass.).
   1874b. *Human Remains in the Shell Heaps of the St. Johns River, East Florida, Cannibalism* (Peabody Museum, Annual Report, vol. 7, pp. 26–37, Boston).
   1875.   *Fresh-Water Shell Mounds of the St. Johns River, Florida* (Peabody Academy of Science, Memoirs, no. 4, Salem, Mass.).
ZUBILLAGA, FELIX
   1941.   *La Florida: la misión jesuítica (1566–1572) y la colonización española* (Bibliotheca Instituti Historici S.I., vol. 1, Rome).
   1946.   *Monumental Antiquae Floridae (1566–1572)* (Rome).

PLATES

EXPLANATION OF PLATES*

PLATE 1. *Potsherds, Orange and St. Johns Ia Periods.*

A, Stallings Punctated, Ponte Vedra Beach. B, Orange Plain, textile-impressed, near De Leon Springs. C, Orange Plain, rim lug, Enterprise. D, Orange Plain, textile-impressed, near De Leon Springs. E, Orange Plain, rim lug, Enterprise. F, Chalky ware, linear check-stamped, Tick Island Mound. G, Chalky ware, cord-marked, Tick Island Mound. H–J, Chalky ware, simple-stamped, Tick Island Mound.

(A, U.C.A.L. uncataloged; B, U.S.N.M. 317037; C, U.S.N.M. 31938c; D, U.S.N.M. 317037; E, U.S.N.M. 31938; F–J, H.P.M. uncataloged.)

PLATE 2. *Potsherds, Various Periods.*

A, Little Manatee Shell Stamped, Ponte Vedra Beach. B, St. Johns Plain, boat-shaped vessel, rim lug, "Halifax Inlet," Rock House Mound? C, Unclassified Incised Chalky Ware, Tick Island Mound. D, St. Johns Punctated, Ocala National Forest, Kauffman Island? E, St. Johns Plain, overlapping coils, Tick Island Mound. F, Cord-marked gritty ware, Fitzpatrick Mound.

(A, U.S.N.M. 379171; B, H.P.M. 78-48-10/15376; C, H.P.M. uncataloged; D, U.S.N.M. 378402; E, H.P.M. uncataloged; F, U.S.N.M.)

PLATE 3. *Pottery Vessels, St. Johns I Period.*

A, St. Johns Plain, Racey Point. B, Deptford Linear Check Stamped, Silver Springs Mound. C, St. Johns Red on Buff, Volusia Mounds. D, Oklawaha Plain, Lake Harris, Lake County. E, St. Johns Plain, St. Johns Landing Mound 1. F, St. Johns Plain, solid bird effigy, Tick Island Mound. G, St. Johns Plain, Racey Point. H, St. Johns Plain, Racey Point. I, Weeden Island Plain, Monroe Mound.

(A, M.A.I. 17/3602; B, M.A.I. 18/359; C, M.A.I. 17/3927; D, M.A.I. 17/4501; E, M.A.I. 17/3874; F, M.A.I. 17/2203; G, M.A.I. 17/3598; H, M.A.I. 17/3600; I, M.A.I. 17/3491.)

PLATE 4. *Pottery vessels, St. Johns II Period.*

A, St. Johns Plain, miniature vessel, Grant mound. B, St. Johns Plain, miniature vessel. C, Unclassified incised and punctated chalky ware, miniature vessel, Grant Mound. D, St. Johns Plain, miniature vessel, Grant Mound. E, Little Manatee Shell Stamped (variant), Mt. Royal. F, Unclassified incised chalky ware, flanged orifice, Dunns Creek Mound. G, Little Manatee Shell Stamped, Grant Mound. H, Little Manatee Shell Stamped (variant), Mt. Royal. I, Weeden Island Incised, Grant Mound. J, St. Johns Plain, Mt. Royal. K, St. Johns Plain, Mt. Royal.

(A, M.A.I. 18/298; B, M.A.I. 18/295; C, M.A.I. 18/301; D, M.A.I. 18/303; E, M.A.I. 17/3560; F, M.A.I. 17/3392; G, M.A.I. 17/3996; H, M.A.I. 17/3561; I, M.A.I. 18/302; J, M.A.I. 17/3907; K, M.A.I. 17/3559.)

* The scale varies in each plate.

PLATE 5. *Pottery Vessels and Potsherds, Various Periods.*

A, Unclassified cord-marked gritty ware, Mandarin Point. B, Unclassified plain gritty ware, mound near Arlington. C, Deptford Linear Check Stamped, Spaldings Lower Store. D, St. Johns Check Stamped, Cooks Ferry Midden. E, St. Johns Plain, flanged tube, Mt. Royal. F, Safety Harbor Incised, Beauclerc. G, San Marcos Stamped, Anastasia Island. H, St. Johns Red on Buff, Volusia Mounds. I, St. Johns Plain, tetrapod base, Hawkinsville Midden.

(A, M.A.I. 17/3823; B, U.S.N.M.; C, U.F.A.L.; D, F.S.M. 62882; E, M.A.I. 17/3565; F, F.S.M. 82485; G, U.S.N.M. 148933; H, U.S.N.M. 149554; I, U.S.N.M. 149552.)

PLATE 6. *Various Tools, Shell Cup, and Ceremonial Hoe.*

A, Busycon gouge, Marion County. B, Busycon gouge, Lake Monroe Outlet Midden. C, Busycon gouge, Lake Monroe Outlet Midden. D, Busycon gouge, Lake Monroe. E, Stone celt, Tick Island Mound. F, Stone celt (variant), Tick Island Mound. G, Stone celt, Tick Island Mound. H, Stone celt, Grant Mound. I, Ceremonial hoe, mound in pine woods near Duval's. J, Stone celt-hammer, Tick Island Mound. K, Stone celt, Julington Creek Mound. L, Stone celt, Shields Mound. M, Busycon cup, "Site 3," Huntoon Island. N, Stone blade or scraper, midden one-half mile north of Nashua. O, Stone celt, Grant Mound. P, Stone celt, Grant Mound. Q, Flint celt, Volusia Mounds.

(A, F.S.M.; B, F.S.M. 75033; C, F.S.M. 75031; D, F.S.M. 18091; E, M.A.I. 17/2171; F, M.A.I. 17/2171; G, M.A.I. 17/2171; H, M.A.I. 17/1218; I, M.A.I. 17/1117; J, M.A.I. 17/2170; K, M.A.I. 17/2267; L, M.A.I. 17/2337; M, U.S.N.M. 378412; N, U.F.A.L.; O, M.A.I. 17/1813; P, M.A.I. 17/1813; Q, M.A.I. 17/2198.)

PLATE 7. *Chipped Stone Points, Various Periods.*

A, Southeast shore, Lake Kerr. B, C, Vicinity of Silver Glen Springs. D, Thursby Mound. E, Vicinity of Silver Glen Springs. F, Eaton Creek, 1.25 miles above Scrub Lake. G, Spaldings Lower Store. H, Vicinity of Silver Glen Springs. I, Thursby Mound. J–M, Mt. Taylor. N, Ginns Grove. O, P, Vicinity of Silver Glen Springs. Q, Southeast shore, Lake Kerr. R, S, Watson's Landing (obverse and reverse). T–V, Tick Island. W, Vicinity of Silver Glen Springs. X, Silver Glen Springs. Y, Thursby Mound. Z, Vicinity of Silver Glen Springs. AA, Racey Point. BB, Southeast shore, Lake Kerr.

(A, U.S.N.M. 378388; B, C, U.S.N.M. 378347; D, M.A.I. 17/777; E, U.S.N.M. 378413; F, U.S.N.M. 378379; G, U.F.A.L.; H, U.S.N.M. 378347; I, M.A.I. 17/777; J–M, M.A.I. 17/1557; N, M.A.I. 17/1837; O, P, U.S.N.M. 378347; Q, U.S.N.M. 378388; R, S, H.P.M. 67-1/2898; T–V, M.A.I. 17/2177; W, U.S.N.M. 378409; X, U.S.N.M. 378340; Y, M.A.I. 17/777; Z, U.S.N.M. 378409; AA, M.A.I. 17/2264; BB, U.S.N.M. 378388.)

PLATE 8. *Ornaments and Textile Fragment.*

A–C, Circular Busycon gorgets, Midden 2, Salt Springs Run. D, Bannerstone wing pendant, Thornhill Lake Mound 1. E, Unclassified stone object, Harris Mound. F, Textile fragment, Mt. Royal. G, Bannerstone wing pendant, Thornhill Lake Mound 1. H, Shell disk, Dillards

Grove. I, Bone pendant, Kauffman Island. J, Shell tube, Mt. Taylor. K, Incised shell object, Dillard's Grove. L, Bone awl, Shields Mound. M, Peg-topped bone pin, Grant Mound. N, Simple bone pin, Grant Mound. O, Expanded-head bone pin, Grant Mound. P, Expanded-head bone pin, Grant Mound. Q, Peg-topped bone pin, Shields Mound. R, Peg-topped bone pin, Shields Mound. S, Bone pin fragment, engraved, Ginns Grove. T, Two-holed stone gorget, Shields Mound.

(A–C, U.S.N.M. 378319; D, M.A.I. 17/2186; E, M.A.I. 17/1839; F, M.A.I. 17/3041; G, M.A.I. 17/2185; H, M.A.I. 17/501; I, U.S.N.M. 378394; J, M.A.I. 17/355; K, M.A.I. 17/509; L, M.A.I. 17/518; M, M.A.I. 17/621; N, M.A.I. 17/622; O, M.A.I. 17/622; P, M.A.I. 17/622; Q, M.A.I. 17/514; R, M.A.I. 17/517; S, M.A.I. 17/2314; T, M.A.I. 17/1261.)

PLATE 9. *Prehistoric Copper Objects.*

A, B, Long-nosed god maskettes, Grant Mound. C, Copper-covered mammal jaw, Tick Island Mound. D, Hollow copper bead, Grant Mound. E, Copper point, Monroe Mound. F, Copper disk, Grant Mound. G, Copper crescent, northernmost mound, Murphy Island. H, Copper-covered stone ear plug, Grant Mound. I, Copper-covered stone ear plug, Mt. Royal. J, Copper disk, Mt. Royal. K, Conjoined copper tubes, northernmost mound, Murphy Island. L, Copper ear spool half, Monroe Mound. M, Copper plate, Grant Mound. N, Copper plate, Grant Mound. O, Copper plate, Grant Mound. P, Copper-covered bi-conical wooden ear plug, Grant Mound. Q, Copper plate, Grant Mound. R, Copper plate, Grant Mound. S, Copper plate, Grant Mound. T, Copper plate, Grant Mound. U, Copper plate, Shields Mound.

(A, B, M.A.I. 17/197; C, M.A.I. 17/2979; D, M.A.I. 17/3018; E, M.A.I. 17/3033; F, M.A.I. 17/178; G, M.A.I. 17/68; H, M.A.I. 17/1221; I, M.A.I. 17/130; J, M.A.I. 17/3043; K, M.A.I. 17/65; L, M.A.I. 17/3032; M, M.A.I.; N, M.A.I. 17/3017; O, M.A.I. 17/118; P, M.A.I. 17/213; Q, M.A.I. 17/175; R, M.A.I. 17/174; S, M.A.I. 17/119; T, M.A.I. 17/172; U, M.A.I. 17/113.)

PLATE 10. *Pendant, Chisel, and Spatulate Celts.*

A, Perforated rectangular stone pendant, Shields Mound. B, Spatulate celt, six miles south of Fernandina. C, Spatulate celt, Mt. Royal. D, Stone chisel, Shields Mound. E, Spatulate celt, Mt. Royal. F, Spatulate celt, Shields Mound. G, Spatulate celt, Shields Mound. H, Spatulate celt, Mt. Royal.

(A, M.A.I. 17/2320; B, M.A.I. 6/506; C, M.A.I. 17/2104; D, M.A.I. 17/1252; E, M.A.I. 17/2106; F, M.A.I. 17/1253; G, M.A.I. 17/1254; H, M.A.I. 17/2105.)

PLATE 11. *Pipes and Bannerstones.*

A, Clay pipe, Grant Mound. B, Stone pipe, Grant Mound. C, Clay pipe, Grant Mound. D, Clay pipe, Grant Mound. E, Stone pipe, Anastasia Island. F, Bannerstone, Type 3, Thornhill Lake Mound 1. G, Bannerstone, Type 3, Thornhill Lake Mound 1. H, Bannerstone, Type 3, Thornhill Lake Mound 1. I, Bannerstone, Type 2, Shields Mound. J, Bannerstone, Type 2, Thornhill Lake Mound 2. K, Bannerstone, Type 5, Thornhill Lake Mound 1. L, Bannerstone, Type 4, Shields Mound. M, Bannerstone, Type 2, Thornhill Lake Mound 2. N, Bannerstone, Type 2, Thornhill Lake Mound 2.

(A, M.A.I. 17/2317; B, M.A.I. 17/3192; C, M.A.I. 17/2317; D, M.A.I. 17/2315; E, M.A.I. 5/2967; F, M.A.I. 17/2182; G, M.A.I. 17/2184; H, M.A.I. 17/2123; I, M.A.I. 17/1258; J, M.A.I. 17/2178; K, M.A.I. 17/2181; L, M.A.I. 17/2335; M, M.A.I. 17/2179; N, M.A.I. 17/2180.)

PLATE 12. *Miscellaneous Ornaments and Seminole Potsherds, St. Johns IIc and Seminole Periods.*

A, Copper disk, Spruce Creek Mound. B, Copper disk, Spruce Creek Mound. C, Copper disk, Peoria Mound. D, Gold disk, Cooks Ferry Mound. E, Silver disk, Spruce Creek Mound. F, Silver earring, Bayard Point Mound. G, Silver brooch, Spaldings Lower Store. H, Copper tinkler, Spaldings Lower Store. I, Copper disk, Spruce Creek Mound. J, Fine paste, mica-tempered pottery, Spaldings Lower Store. K, Incised pottery, related to Ocmulgee Fields Incised, Spaldings Lower Store. L–P, Stokes Brushed, Spaldings Lower Store.

(A, U.S.N.M. 10999; B, U.S.N.M. 11000; C, M.A.I. 17/95; D, H.P.M. 49554; E, U.S.N.M. 11001; F, M.A.I. 17/3000; G, H, U.F.A.L.; I, U.S.N.M. 11001; J–P, U.F.A.L.)

POTSHERDS, ORANGE AND ST. JOHNS IA PERIODS

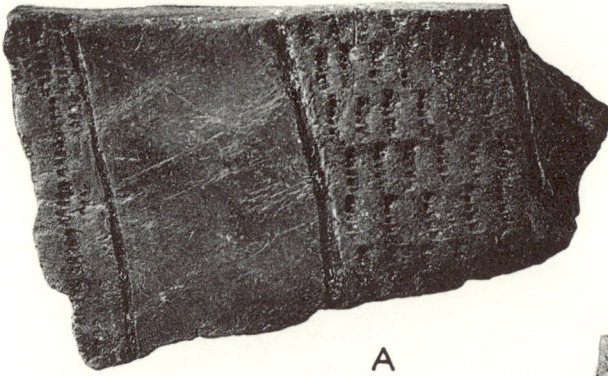

A

B

D

C

E

F

POTSHERDS, VARIOUS PERIODS

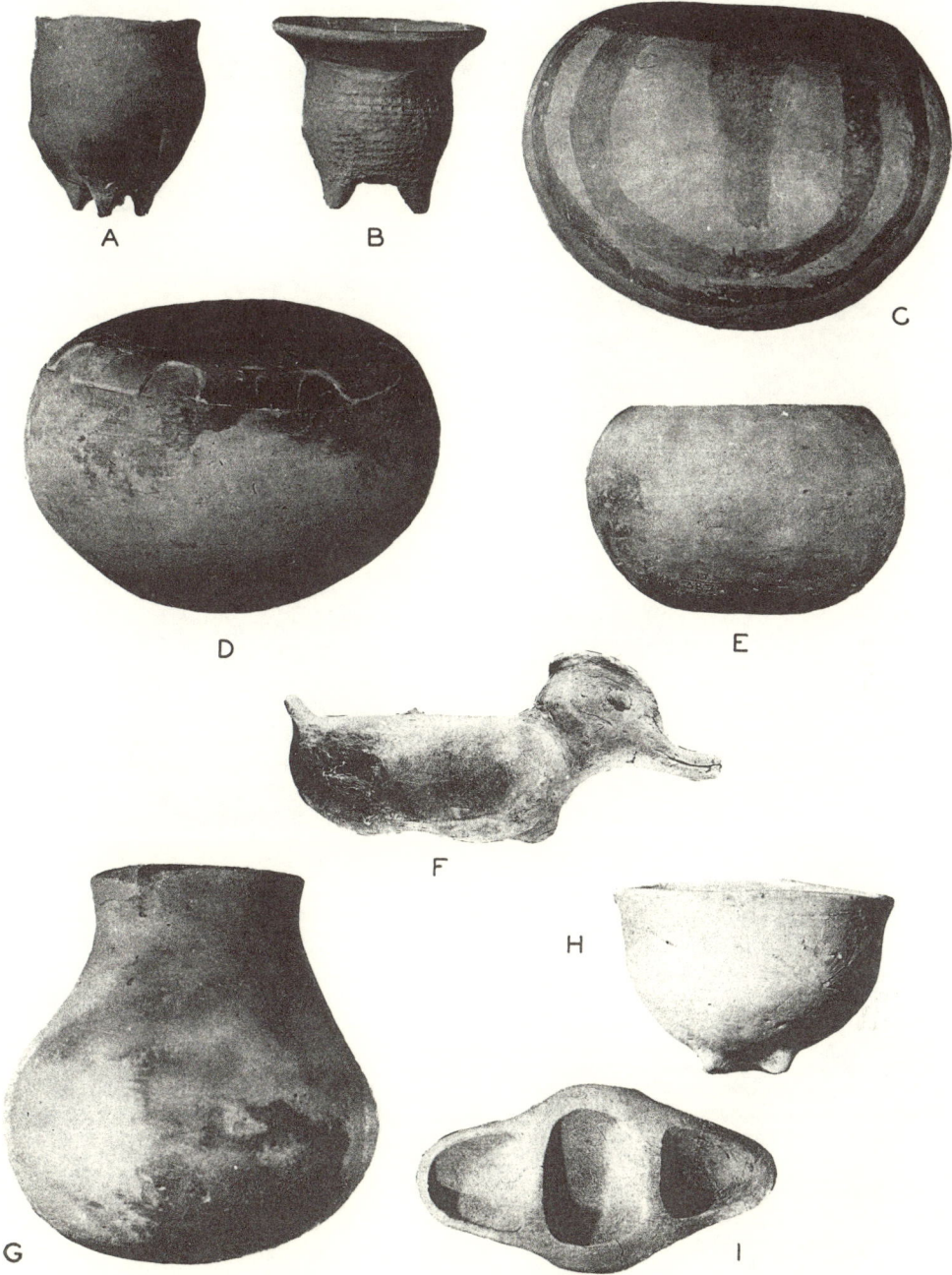

POTTERY VESSELS, St. JOHNS I PERIOD

A   B   C   D

E   F

G   H

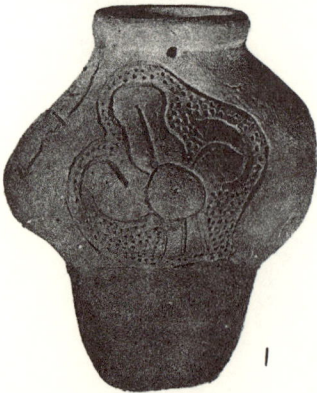

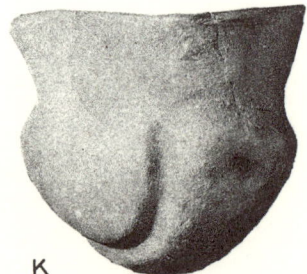

I   J   K

POTTERY VESSELS, ST. JOHNS II PERIOD

A

B

C

D

E

F

G

H

I

POTTERY VESSELS AND POTSHERDS, VARIOUS PERIODS

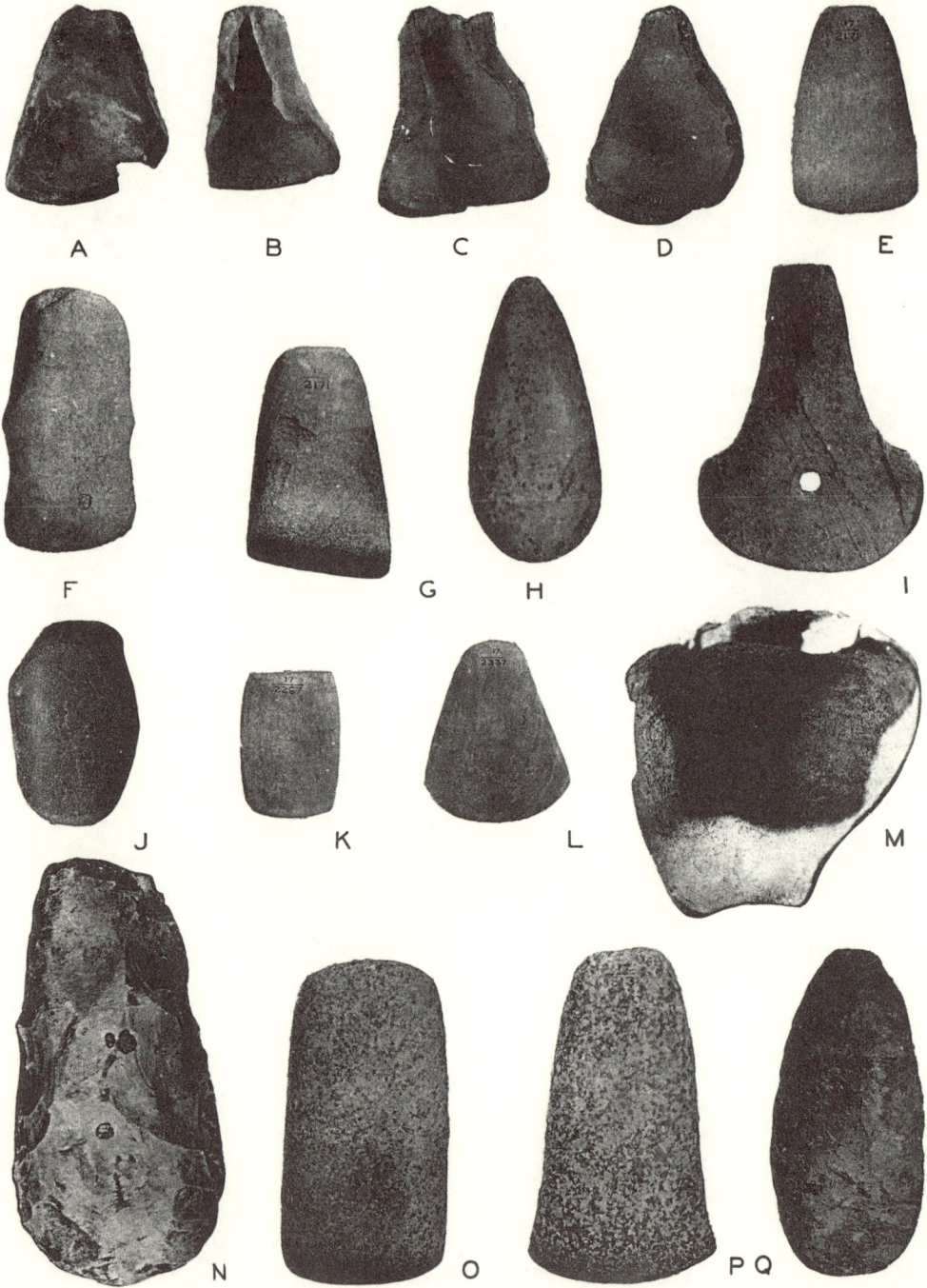

A   B   C   D   E

F   G   H   I

J   K   L   M

N   O   P Q

Various Tools, Shell Cup, and Ceremonial Hoe

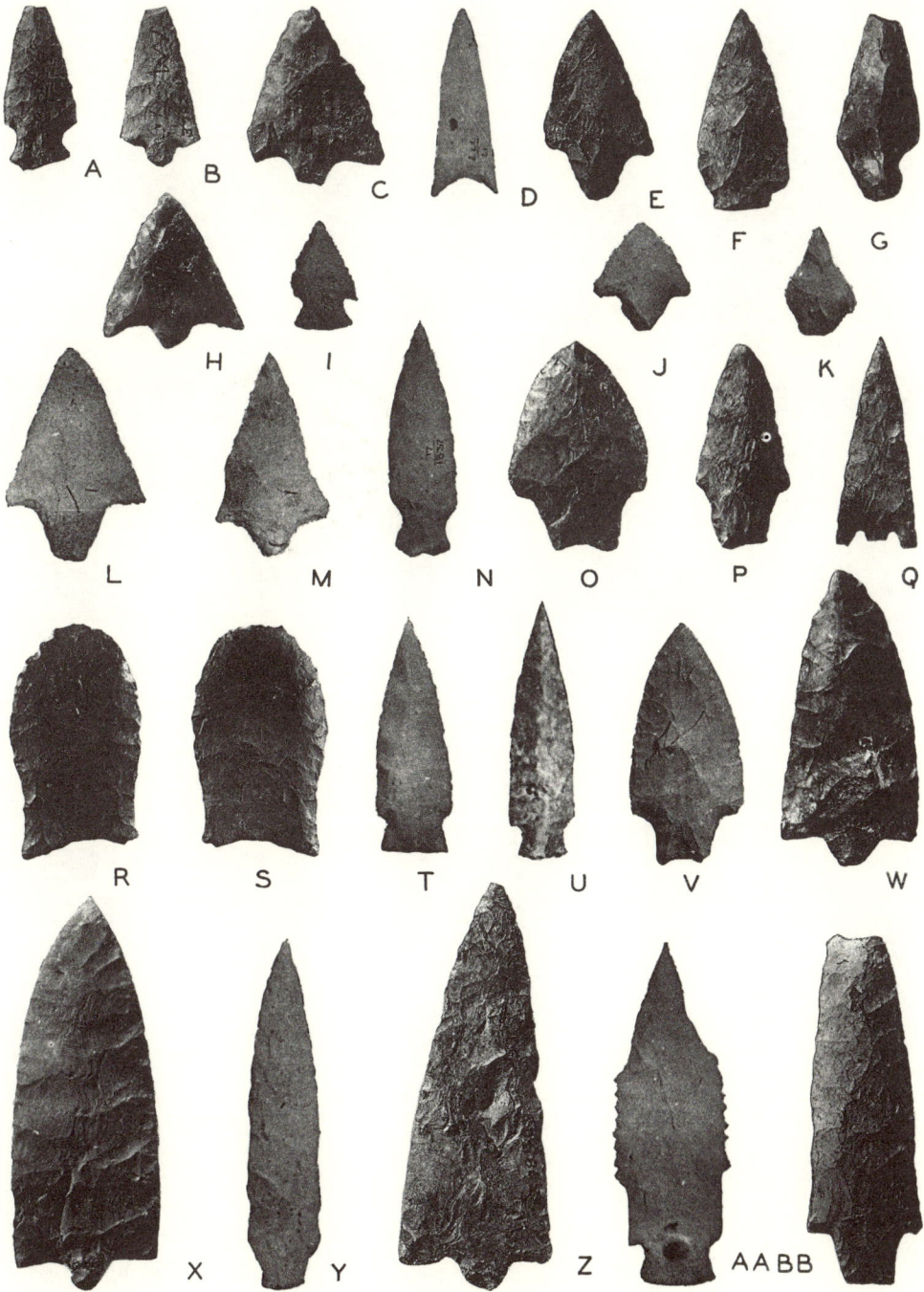

CHIPPED STONE POINTS, VARIOUS PERIODS

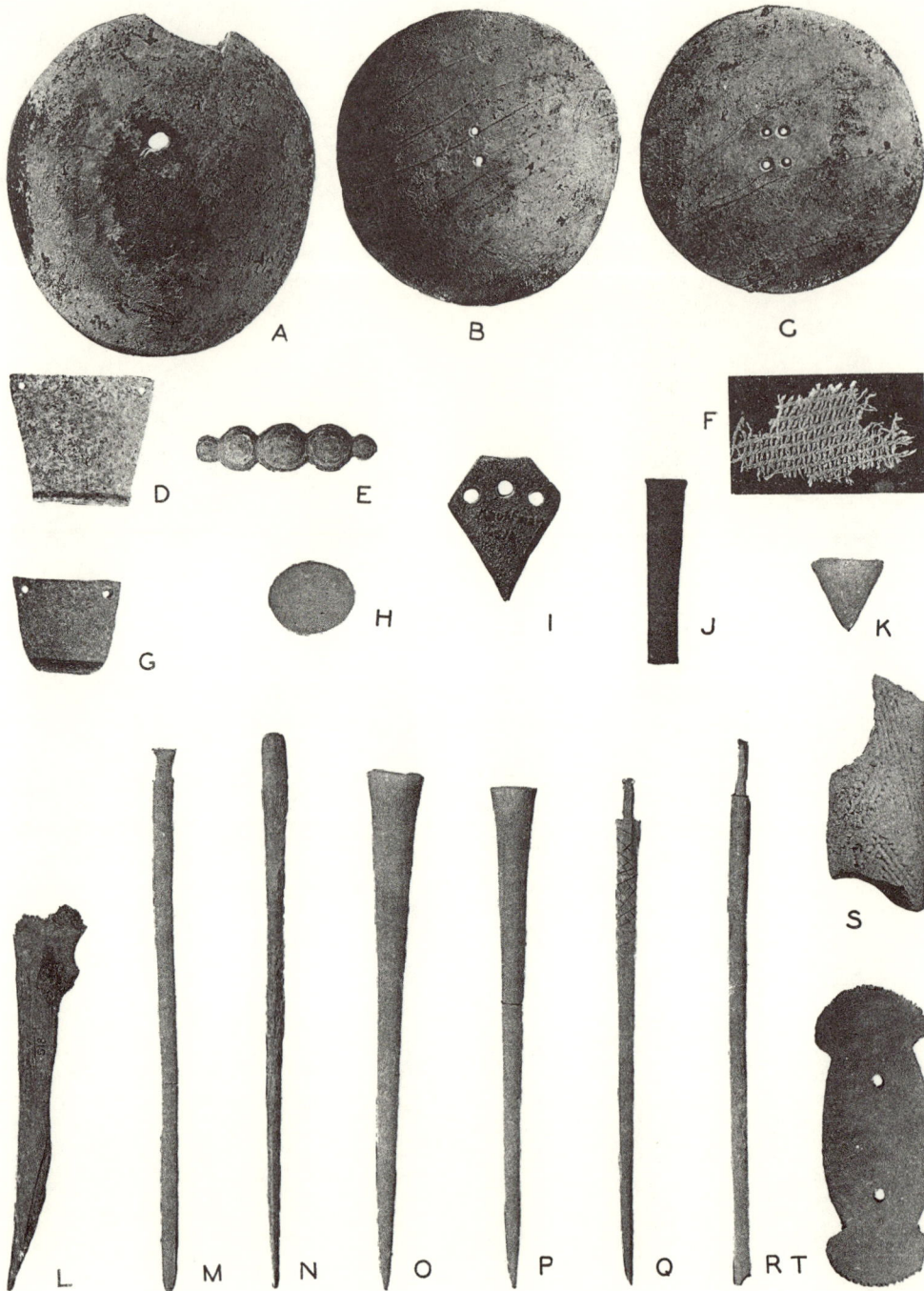

ORNAMENTS AND TEXTILE FRAGMENT

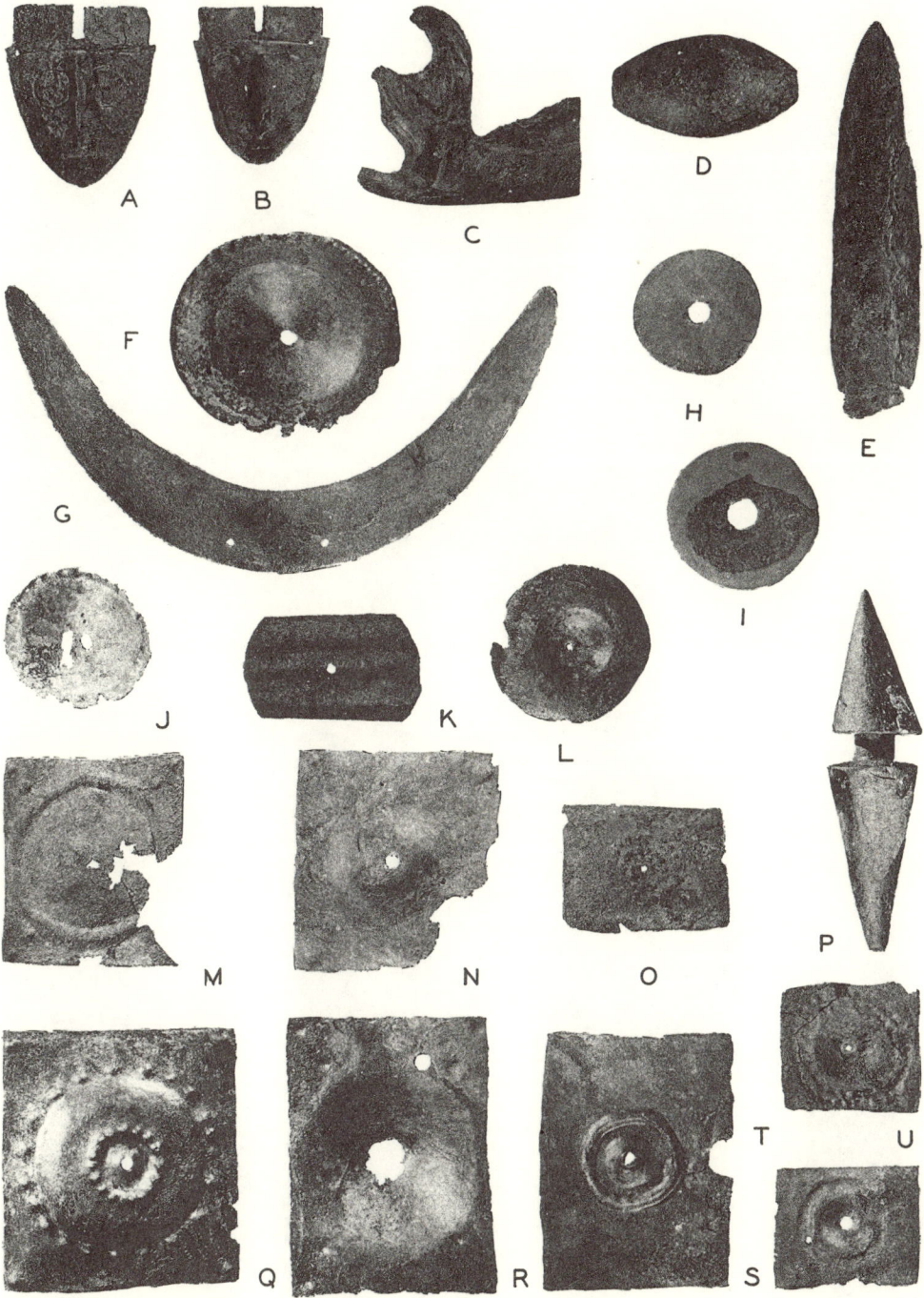

PREHISTORIC COPPER ORNAMENTS

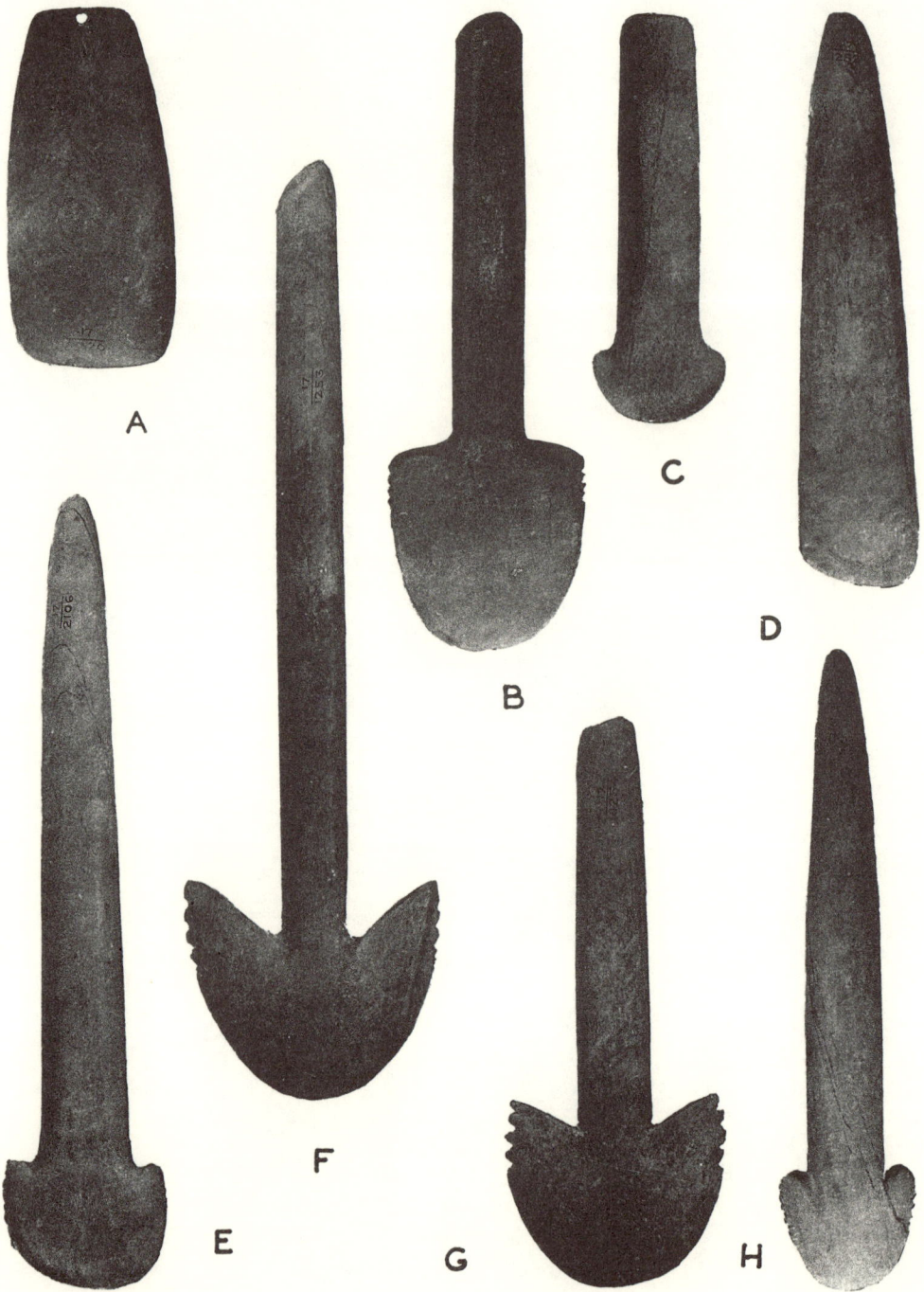

PENDANT, CHISEL, AND SPATULATE CELTS

A

B

C

D

E

F

G

H

I

J

L

K

M

N

Pipes and Bannerstones

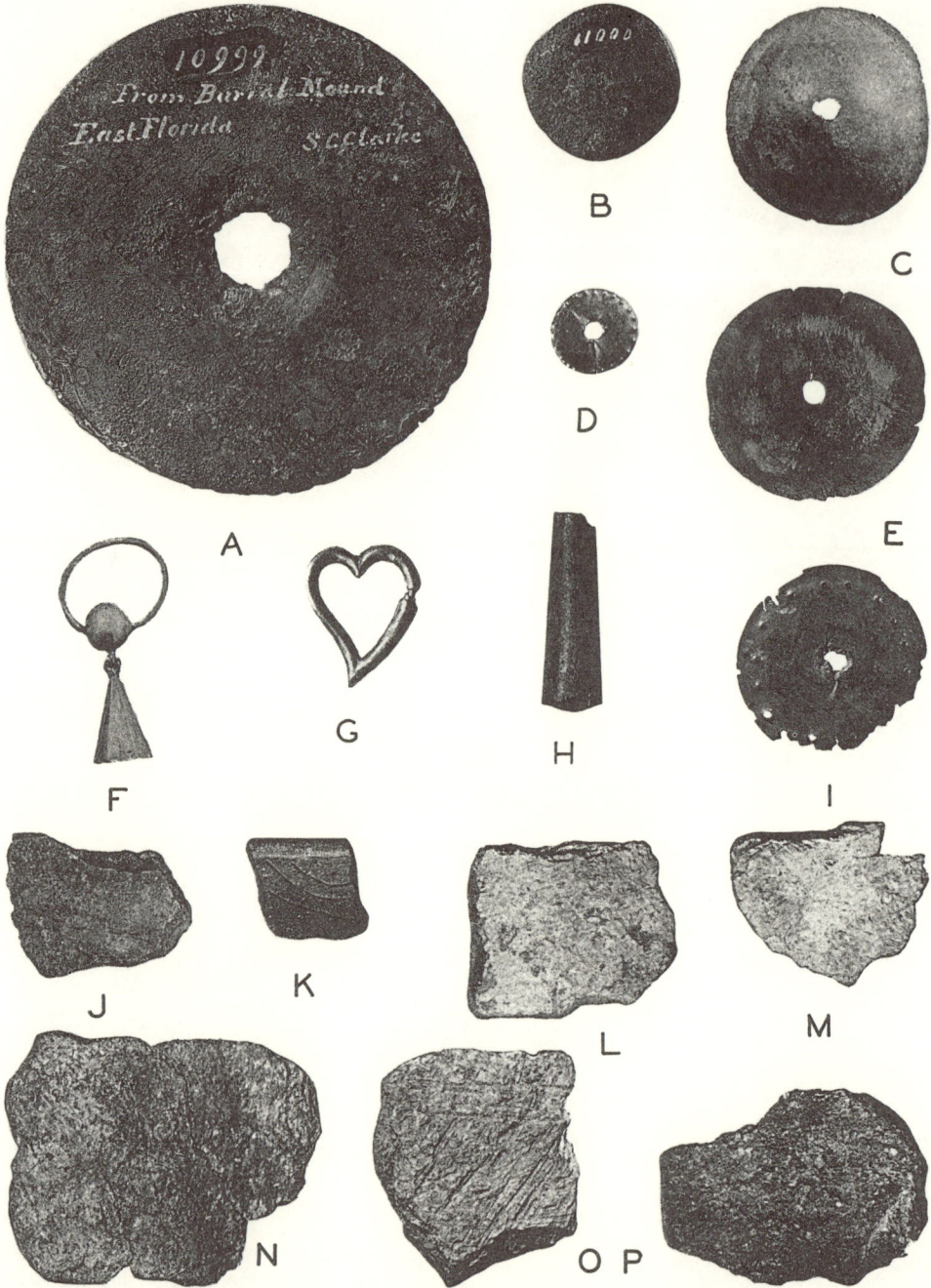

MISCELLANEOUS ORNAMENTS AND SEMINOLE POTSHERDS, ST. JOHNS IIc AND SEMINOLE PERIODS